THE ARISTOCRATS

THE
ARISTOCRATS

*A Portrait of Britain's nobility
and their way of life today*

Roy Perrott

WEIDENFELD AND NICOLSON
5 WINSLEY STREET LONDON W1

297 76179
C. Tinling & Co Ltd
Liverpool, London & Prescot

for Hella Adler

*You should study the peerage, Gerald . . . It is
the best thing in fiction the English have ever done.*

Oscar Wilde

CONTENTS

A[*]

TABLES

PREFACE

This book is meant to be a portrait of the British aristocracy as it is now, in the late nineteen-sixties. While I have tried to give the picture some perspective by relating it to the past, my primary aim has been to keep the contemporary scene in view, in attempting to discover how and on what terms this ancient elite, the heirs and inheritors of the old 'ruling class', keeps going in modern Britain.

It has, of course, greatly changed. For the portraitist the difficulty is that it is not, so to speak, a sitter that keeps very still. The hereditary nobility, the newer peerage, and the landed gentry who may be regarded as forming the 'aristocracy' now cover a wide range of occupations and activities. As younger members come up to the front it is constantly shifting its position slightly. Public views of it are also mixed. Some see the idea of a titled elite as an irrational hangover from the imperial past, a focal point for national snobbery; most people accept them as men of some consequence without always knowing quite why.

The idea of an aristocracy exists in a shadowy area of national consciousness, and this, for me, represents much of its interest. As a group they seem to represent an idea of the past – good and bad – which is one of the more stubborn features of the island personality. Life in Britain since the war has often given the impression that the more the country speeds up its surface vibrations – the more it becomes *avant-garde*, swinging, ostensibly meritocratic – the more it remains stolidly unchanging underneath. Scott Fitzgerald's phrase might apply here too: 'So we beat on, boats against the current, borne back ceaselessly into the past.' The aristocracy is not only very much a thing in itself: it is a sort of signpost to this area of native mood and attitude.

Since I set out with the reporter's habitual handicap-advantage of a wide ignorance of the subject I am especially indebted to those members of the nobility and other experts in the field who gave me information, opinions, and guidance. The book is largely based on conversations I have had with some sixty peers in town and country and with a number of landed gentry. Some are quoted by name in the text and their views reported at some length, particularly where – as in Chapter 3 – they seemed to illustrate some aspect of noble life most clearly to me. Others not named also gave me invaluable help. I should like to thank all these ladies and gentlemen, particularly those who allowed me freedom to set down my impressions of them in an informal way.

I am grateful to a number of experts in various fields. They include: Sir Iain Moncreiffe of that Ilk, Bt, Albany Herald, for a number of favours and much helpful advice; Professor C. D. Darlington, of Oxford University, for his authoritative guidance on heredity; Dr Mary Douglas, of the social anthropology department of University College, London, for some kind primary instruction on foreign elites; Dr C. B. Otley, of the University of Sheffield, for advice on the structure of the British army officer corps; Mr Peter Townend, editor of *Burke's Peerage*; Mr Quentin Crewe, Mr Anthony Howard, Mr Andrew Roth, Mr Ivan Yates, and a number of other newspaper colleagues for helping to fill in gaps. The Hon. David Astor, Editor of *The Observer*, gave me much-valued encouragement. I owe a special debt to Juliet Roeber for her diligent statistical research. Part of Chapter 13 originally appeared in *Nova* magazine in another form and I thank its editor and publishers for permission to use it here. Except where I am quoting informants directly, the views expressed and conclusions reached are my own.

Roy Perrott

PART ONE

I

LOOKING FOR A UNICORN

Anyone setting out to reconnoitre the British aristocracy in the late 1960s is bound to start off with a little cloud of uncertainty hanging in his mind. He is in the position of a hunter who, from the mixed reports of the scouting parties, can only hazard a guess at the nature of the animal he is pursuing.

Some sightings seem to describe a kind of unicorn, a creature of more myth than substance. Others claim to have glimpsed a real and living animal, skilled in adjusting to a wide variety of background colourings, still carrying weight in its domain despite its deceptively retiring habits. Peers themselves are among those who suggest that the aristocracy no longer exists in reality in the sense of an elite with a personality, a significance, and an identity of its own. One lord I consulted early on, whose family had been in the forefront of affairs since Tudor times, briskly dismissed the idea that he any longer formed part of a group with special prestige or notable distinguishing marks. 'A thing of the past,' he said. 'We have long since become merged with the general community . . .'

This sort of bold claim to absolute ordinariness, of at last being comfortably on shoulder-rubbing terms with the common man, had become fairly familiar over the last few decades; and it was an intriguing one in its contrast with the aristocracy's once equally bold assumption of absolute prestige, in politics and society, which had lasted for 850 years from the Conquest to at least the early 1900s. The gossip columns currently lent support to this theory of the indistinguishable common peer with occasional pictures of him doing emphatically commonplace things: a marquess peddling vacuum cleaners, a young earl selling socks in a department store, this or that peer driving a tractor, mowing the lawn, or simply riding a bicycle with ordinary clips round the trouser turn-ups. As percentage evidence of the activities of the peerage as a whole it hardly counted. But it was perhaps significant that, after thirty or forty years of this kind of news item, some of the daily papers still regarded it as unusual enough to deserve the space. The implication was that people did not expect the nobility to do such things, that in the public mind it was still a class apart, no more emancipated than were women a century ago, whatever the peers thought of it themselves.

If it was indeed an elite in the 1960s then this apparent desire *not* to be regarded as in any way exceptional was probably unique for any sometime ruling class anywhere.

Yet the peer who had insisted that it was 'a thing of the past' was possibly right on the balance of probabilities. For about a century the aristocracy had been the falling leaves of the British political establishment. Its decline had been signalled so confidently and so often since the second half of the nineteenth century that it had become commonly assumed in more recent times that the undertaker, showing a decent discretion, must have quietly and finally removed the body. A fine old institution which had shown the state some service had at last passed away.

It was true that numerous figures robed in scarlet and ermine attended such ritual gatherings as coronations and parliamentary openings and at these times were given primacy of place over the politicians who ostensibly ran the country. But the continuance of this pattern was generally attributed to the inability of the British to abolish anything; and the appearance of these robed personages in the seats of honour was said to be no more meaningful in modern terms than would be a regularised haunting by ancestral family ghosts.

And yet . . . had news of the death been exaggerated? Looking around, one could still find signs that the obituaries had been premature. The House of Lords was still there, to all appearances fully carrying out the duties of a Second Chamber or Senate; and its membership now contained a good many of those trade unionists and other Labourites who in radical youth had threatened to remove this alleged temple of privilege brick by brick.

The reference books on the British peerage were still easily the biggest and heaviest in the honour-giving world. *Burke's Peerage* listed some 1,093 nobles of various degrees; it also listed 4,500 people who, by reason of pedigree or other qualities, could be counted as Landed Gentry; and another 1,400 or so had the hereditary title of baronet. It was true that the Labour government in 1965 had announced that it would award no more hereditary peerages, only ones for life. But since it was over sixty years since the Labour Party had inaugurated itself as a political body, with this hereditary nexus as one of its animating targets, it might almost be said that there was an air of reluctant self-denial about even this step. Nor was there any sign that the Conservative Party would perform the same sacrifice when it came to power again. And neither party, it appeared, had any intention of abolishing the nearly nine hundred hereditary peerages currently existing.

It was such a well-rooted institution that even if no new hereditary peerages were created ever again the disappearance of the nobility would be a melodrama of tragi-comic slowness. At the present rate of peerages becoming extinct (by reason of the holder dying without an heir) most of the ranks of the nobility are numerous enough to last well into an age when men will be getting less durable honours for exploring Mars or running a profitable atom plant on the Moon. Even the smallest group, like the thirty-one dukes, could most of them expect to see a descendant still holding on to the title beyond the year 2000; and the more numerous marquesses, earls, viscounts and barons would go several centuries beyond that. So the Labour Party's gesture against the aristocracy, after all the inflammatory talk of the early days, was in fact an extremely conservative one.

There was other evidence that I was not entirely pursuing a phantom. No less an observer than Miss Nancy Mitford, herself the daughter of a baron, had recently written: 'The English aristocracy may seem to be on the verge of decadence, but it is the only real aristocracy left in the world today. It has real political power through the House of Lords and a real social position through the Queen.'[1]

'On the verge of decadence . . . ,' Miss Mitford writes. Since Disraeli himself and other nineteenth-century worthies had referred to the aristocracy in almost precisely the same terms it appeared that the verge was now about a century wide. Could British ingenuity have engineered an endless slope with no sudden precipice at the end of it? It was possible: we were highly proficient at sliding continuity. But at least Miss Mitford insisted that there was something solid to discover.

In the overseas democracies, too, it was generally accepted that England still possessed such an elite; and particularly in those, like the United States, whose constitutions expressly prohibited a titled system, there appeared to be a certain envy at Britain's unashamed ability to get the best of both worlds. She, with the Mother of Parliaments, had always been a leading exponent of democratic purity; yet pains had been taken to ensure that she could always go into the woods to relish the forbidden fruit of an honorific system. It had taken many generations of struggle to establish the House of Commons as spokesman for more than a tiny section of the community. Yet by the middle of the twentieth century Britain still retained a system which allowed peers to take part in the law-making process by right of birth alone, irrespective of talent. This was one of several things about it which tended to puzzle foreigners.

Sceptics who pointed out the many paradoxes in the system hardly disturbed native equanimity. The British had grown to accept a large element of the irrational in the working of their institutions – while, paradoxically, being proud of their reputation as a rational, disciplined, and pragmatic people. In this respect the aristocracy, such as it was, still shared some of the glittering cobweb of mystery which faintly clung around the Monarchy. Both were institutions which tended to exasperate diehard rationalists. In *The Crown and the Establishment*, Mr Kingsley Martin complained of the veil of obscurity which concealed the workings of the Monarchy and, for one thing, made it impossible to calculate

[1] N. Mitford, ed., *Noblesse Oblige*, London, 1956.

its cost to the country. 'Everything is done to decrease the element of rational understanding and increase the element of worship.'

The attitude of the public at large to the aristocracy was hardly worshipful; though when in full regalia, as at coronations, they could command a certain awe, a feeling accentuated among the watching crowds by the mysterious variety of the coronets worn by the mighty, or the curiosities of the order of precedence which put some boyish-looking duke streets ahead of some sage and venerable baron. Some thought that this glamour alone was a worthy contribution to society. Others awarded them more regard as cheerfully unpaid public servants. But they were too remote from most people for anyone to be quite sure about it.

Since there was only one peer to approximately 54,000 untitled people in Britain the chances of a commoner meeting one face to face, let along making acquaintance with him, were not high. People's feelings about the nobility were based on uncertain assumptions and were rather mixed and hard to analyse. There was perhaps a distant respect for the tribal elders, coupled with a pernickety refusal to take them quite seriously as real people. It was vaguely supposed that they still had some close personal connection with the Queen; and that they performed some useful role in society otherwise, in a country which thought of itself as purposeful and hard-headed, they would not be there. That was the illogical logic of it.

Still, the reasons for the survival of the aristocracy (whatever form it now took) through the age of democracy, had some puzzling aspects. Even to have been 'on the verge' of collapse for a century and still to be in the running argued the dogged stamina of a marathon-runner. So far as could be seen, the future also looked clear of obstacles.

Several reasons were usually given for the remarkable staying-power of this, one of history's most durable elites. Most often it was attributed to the adaptability and lack of exclusiveness of the group itself. This was partly true. The British nobility, unlike that of France and some other countries, had never been an entirely separate caste with a fixed demarcation line between itself and the people at large. The peculiar continental theory of noble 'blue blood' was never more than faintly held in Britain.

From the sixteenth century onwards, with the mutual magnetic attraction of wealth for rank, marriages of untitled heiresses into the peerage became increasingly common. Daughters of merchants, bankers, industrialists, American beef-barons and others who had made good thus set the seal on their parents' endeavours to gain the summit of the social as well as the economic ladder; and the bridegroom concerned retrieved or improved his noble fortunes. In these circles, at least, the felicity of arranged marriages had come to seem more natural than that of marriages founded on sexual attraction.

Among other reasons given for the ability of the peerage to keep going, whatever the political climate, was the English law of primogeniture. Only the elder son inherited a title (and not, as in France and Germany, each individual in the family), a fact which helped to maintain its rarity value and esteem. The estate was inherited all in one piece, and not split up among the family as elsewhere; and this concentration, it was said, had kept the nobility prominently in the swim to the present day. 'The rule of primogeniture,' Miss Mitford wrote, 'has kept together the huge fortunes of English lords . . .'

There had also been a moderately fluid interchange between classes, increasingly from the nineteenth century on, as self-made men struggled to the top and acquired their titles. At the same time the untitled younger sons of the nobility continued to leave the ancestral home to earn their own livings in the law, the Army, in business, and so on.

These movements had certainly demonstrated that the aristocracy was by no means a separate clique. But the actual strength of their links with the wider community seemed to me open to a shadow of doubt. The idea that dukes' and dustmen's daughters would find an immediate bond of romantic or other interest would be held by few people (oddly enough, perhaps only by the peers themselves: I had often heard that the nobility believed itself to have a sympathetic special relationship with the working classes and that it was the only group in Britain free of snobbery; but this was another point I had not yet explored).

However, it was still relatively uncommon for titled suitors to reach down even as far as the middle classes to find a wife. In the 1960s roughly a fifth of the lords were marrying the daughters of other lords. Of the remainder most were choosing wives who were either related to the peerage or who came from landed gentry or upper class families, that is those in the top five or ten per cent of the population in economic or social status. There had clearly been enough marriages with commoners to blur the frontier line; but did it go very far beyond that?

Again, it was commonly assumed that all lords were rich and that there were 'huge fortunes' still among them, as Miss Mitford had put it. This might be true. But if so, it left me unable to place the ones who groaned so much to the Press about their impoverishment by estate duties or the burden of maintaining a stately home; or the ones who were reputed to be very glad of the four guineas a day expenses allowed for attending the House of Lords; or the many who appeared to have no country estates left and, in some cases, gave signs of working much the same hours in a job as the rest of the population.

Richer or poorer, it seemed to me that the reasons commonly given for the longevity of this elite were not wholly convincing, because of one important omission. They assumed, wrongly I suspected, that the people at large had played no part in this preservation; that the coroneted ranks had come marching down the decades regardless of the wishes of the wider public. Could the voters be so absent-minded about such a prominent part of the constitution?

Democracy is one of the slower forms of government. Even so, the feeling of the electorate over several generations does give shade to the kind of society it wants to live in. Over the past fifty years a host of enactments, from votes-for-women onwards, responding to an undercurrent of progressive feeling, had kept society reasonably well adjusted to the twentieth century.

By the early 1900s the radical-Liberal element in the electorate was a strong one and by 1924 the Socialists, even more zealous denouncers of hereditary privilege and of class inequalities, had become powerful enough to take power for the first time. Yet the only significant statutory measure dealing with the Lords had been to ensure that they could not unduly delay any measure approved by the Commons. The radicals went on handing out hereditary titles. By 1966, when a Labour member of Parliament, the waggish Mr Emrys Hughes, had the temerity to move a private Bill for the abolition of the peerage only a handful of members turned up to listen, and that largely for the entertainment, and the idea quietly evaporated.

The implication was that to lose the descendants of the old ruling class would be an act of such absurdity to the general public as not to be contemplated. So the peerage's continued existence seemed to rest on something stronger than mere tolerance. And there was other evidence of this.

The Whitehall machinery which sorts out which persons shall be recommended to the Queen for the conferment of a title is characteristically obscure, the secrets of its methods ostensibly guarded as closely as the Crown Jewels. Names of willing candidates for a peerage, recommended by political parties and other bodies, by influential friends, and sometimes rather indiscreetly by the would-be peer himself, come flowing in during the year. The names are sifted by a small, distinguished committee whose members presumably have at the back of their minds a vague notion of the attributes which the ideal peer should have. This list, I am sure, could no more be reduced to writing than any other part of the English constitution. Though it *is* a committee, and is *called* a committee, it seldom if ever actually meets and its members appear to communicate their views to each other by telepathy.

If it were true that the nobility had been shrugged off by the British public as a purely decorative thing of no real account one might fairly expect the desire to join its ranks to be slight. In fact, I am assured by a good source, the applications for a peerage normally amount to ten times the number that the Honours Lists can sensibly contain in any one year. These days a more serious attempt is made to whittle down the applicants to a short list of those whose abilities look credible enough to fit them for the debating and legislative work of the House of Lords. This sifting reduces the original contenders by seventy per cent; and the short list has to be cut by another twenty per cent before it goes to the Queen.

So the drive for Honour, though it had become more covert than it had been in times past, remained persistent. Like the House of Commons's lightly amused attitude to the idea of abolition, it suggested that the British were more dependent on this institution, or some idea of what it represented, than was commonly admitted. It therefore seemed that the ultimate reason for the nobility's confident survival was because it derived its support and momentum from below, and from far enough down the social scale for a Labour government to be wary of changing its fundamentals.

Britain evidently felt a deep-rooted need for an honorific system while other European countries had in practice shed theirs. It seemed worth asking why. Did this elite stand for something of value, a sense of history perhaps, which we should be the poorer for leaving behind? Rather characteristically, the point was never debated: it would have seemed like arguing about the nature of limestone, something which had grown as an accretion of time. In constitutional matters the British relied upon a combination of habit and instinct. Rightly so, they felt, looking at the succession of unstable governments produced by the logical, renovating French. We played the Cartesian doctrine in reverse: we did not think; therefore it was. And this had undoubtedly helped to give us stability.

As with the Monarchy, an aura of mystery still hung around the aristocracy. What it was really like, what it did, how it fitted into society could only be mistily seen through the veil. Public attitudes towards it, whether critical or approving, were based on assumptions which might not, I supposed, square with reality.

Where Kingsley Martin was slightly off the mark, I thought, was in presuming the process of camouflage to be a deliberate one. On the contrary, it seemed to me, its very essence was that it was unconscious, literally thoughtless. These institutions had emerged out of the historical twilight, having been given their curious shape by innumerable personalities, pressures and sheer accidents. It was this element which gave the aristocracy the many self-contradictions and obscurities which provided its remarkable protective colouring. It was true that in many small ways, people outside and remote from the peerage seemed to conspire to keep the mystery intact.

There was no easy way of telling, for instance, how far the aristocracy was still distinguishable from the rest of the community and how far it was truly merged.

When, for instance, the twice-yearly Honours Lists came out the list of new recruits to the nobility was always embellished with a fine comet-trail of Orders and Companionships for midwives, inspectors of fire brigades, political party agents, station-masters and others who had evidently done their jobs without overt complaint. The shape of the list suggested that all the recipients had merely been given greater or lesser helpings of a similar substance called Honour. It ignored the important distinction between the new hereditary peers, whose male descendants were being awarded a voice in the country's law-making process for ever, and those numerous others who were merely being given a medal to wear. Another facet of the Honours List process also had its interest. On the long-awaited announcement day, the sound of high-pressure steam being raised could often be heard by the careful listener emanating from the offices of the down-to-earth, left-wing popular press; and the old nobility might well tremble as that revolutionary editorial hit the streets . . . only to find, more often than not, that it was once again merely agitating for a knighthood for the current genius of the football scene (*only* a knighthood: note the sense of propriety). This was urged with a sense of great daring, as though even these fierce radicals of the Press could not themselves quite see any natural link between a leading sportsman and a feudal dignity which was originally concerned with raising troops for the King. But I was aware that all the British, myself included, foreigners too no doubt, were afflicted with this kind of mental type-casting. In our different ways, we knew what a knight and a lord *ought* to look like. But we could be wrong.

This preliminary casting-about for a line that might lead to the reality had only revealed the complexity of the trail. And once the animal was discovered, what then? The explorer could measure the skin, take note of the colouring, the habitat and other things of scientific interest. I wondered whether this was enough. One difference between the aristocracy and other social groups was that it was believed by many still to possess an aura of sorts, faded as it might be. Like the Monarchy, it was understood to have some special essence which was either part of its own nature or which had been projected on to it by people's minds. This was clearly the unicorn which had been reported; and I did not know whether one could glimpse this fleeting shape long enough and clearly enough to be able to describe it.

So in the end I was left with all the contradictions, and I had by now realised that even these fell into a pattern of sorts. The mixture of the descriptions could only mean that it was an animal of many guises, each in some way true to itself. The hunter's eye picked out the shape he expected to see or wanted to see; and then the wily creature had only to shift its stance a little to show that it was a quadruped of quite a different order.

Before setting out it was necessary to find some working definition of what people meant by 'aristocracy', an admittedly old-fashioned term which I adopted for its convenience in embracing a fair variety of types of status. Some would say that it should refer only to the grander, land-owning noblemen. But to have confined it to these would have meant ignoring the working peers; the untitled gentry whose landed position was often greater than that of many of the peerage; and the Life Peers who were active in the House of Lords. Since the whole interest of the group lay in its modern complexity I decided to cast my net fairly wide. Thus I reckoned up this possible elite as comprising 944 hereditary peers and peeresses, 116 Life Peers, most of the 1,250 baronets and about a thousand landed gentry who could be estimated to have some degree of local position and estate – about 3,000 all told.

Because of the doubts and contradictions about the aristocracy which I have mentioned I could find few preconceptions to arm myself with at the start. When Gulliver set foot in Brobdingnag his ignorance of the inhabitants was his only credential; and I set out in much the same state of mind.

2

ARISTOCRACY . . . THE TANGLED UNDERGROWTH

The enquiring Gulliver will not have been long on the road before he realises that his most elementary expectations – such as, for instance, that the framework of the aristocracy might bear some relationship to the human reality behind it – are largely unfounded.

The various degress of noble rank (duke, marquess, earl, viscount, baron) now offer scarcely any consistent advance guide to what the holder will be like, whether in wealth, style of living, prestige, zest for public life, deference to some assumed aristocratic code, or anything else about him.

Until well into the nineteenth century these degrees did broadly reflect some sort of social scale. Dukes and duchesses were invariably grander than the rest of the peerage. It was accepted that they were the leaders of society and that their influence on the political scene should be more than a formal one. Few others could rival them in the size of their estates, their wealth, their houses, their style. Seasonal migrants who worked to a strict social time-table, they moved across the country, from London mansion to country castle, with their retinues of servants and their mountains of monogrammed luggage.

In the north, guns and grouse, ghillies and gamekeepers; in the south, the glittering political soirées, balls and dinners, and private boxes for royal occasions. They lived life at an altitude where it had to be extremely complicated to seem real. Those armies of servants can hardly have been there to make life simpler. No, they were there to show that they were needed. The laws of circular

14

self-generation in human affairs were devised in ducal households long before certain overmanned units in the Second World War caught on to the idea.

What has always fixed the position of the dukes in my mind is not their political sway, their special access to royalty, or the grandeur of their establishments. It is their special relationship with the Railway Age. As the iron network spread, an amazed public began to get used to the speed and to travel ever greater distances. As the century wore on architects wrestled over their drawing-boards for a style that would represent the nobility of steam traction. They found it in the old feudal home; and stations went up with turrets, pinnacles, and defensive embrasures, and the entrances to tunnels were garnished with battlements.

The feeling that something was monumentally Important – like steam locomotion – automatically involved associations with nobility. That was the odd thing about it: it came so naturally. What sort of man was then equal to the challenge of this era? Why, a duke of course. The dukes were the ones who hired not merely trivial seats or simple carriages but whole trains. They were the ones who built themselves personal Halts and Stations, for whom expresses made special stops at this or that wayside place in sight of the Castle. Level-crossing keepers instinctively found their proper role in the scheme of things, indifferently holding up either trains or motor traffic, depending upon which mode of transport His Grace was using. Forelocks were touched; signal levers were pulled; the world could move on again.

The dukes were clearly key figures in any enquiry into the existence of an aristocracy since they had traditionally played the most gilded role, proportionately had the most land and wealth, the most lordly way of life. The various rankings originally had some fairly exact relation to social reality. In earlier times an earl commanded an extensive county territory and, around him, was a little satellite system of barons who, in turn, had dependent knights. The style of life of each of them carefully matched his place on the scale. To have rank necessarily meant having the right amount of wealth to support it. The warrior leader who was ennobled was given land or Court offices that would ensure him the right sort of income and prestige. A duke was expected to be more rich and powerful than an earl who, by and large, was assumed to need more resources for stylish living than a baron.

The idea that the abstraction of Honour and a title needed the reality of affluence to back it up continued into fairly recent times. In the nineteenth century this essential combination of the two things was given a certain twist towards the material side, when the brewers, bankers, newspaper tycoons, and ironmasters were ennobled merely because they were rich, at least rich enough to contribute to political party funds. But as late as 1918 when the war leader, Field Marshal Haig, was given an earldom he was awarded £100,000, though his family was already socially well-established not only as rising whisky-distillers, but as having been Scots border lairds since the thirteenth century.

Despite the very mixed character of the peerage by the twentieth century the attempt was still made to slot newly created peers into their appropriate grade. Apart from the royal family itself no personage had apparently been held grand or powerful enough to deserve a dukedome since 1899, the year when the last one was awarded. It is believed that Sir Winston Churchill was offered one but that he declined.

There has long been a custom that retiring Prime Ministers automatically rate an earldom, though several, like Gladstone, have refused it. Mr Harold Macmillan, the most sophisticated Tory Prime Minister since Disraeli, evidently declined his title ('Sounds like a Lord Mayor of Birmingham,' he is understood to have remarked in a ruminative way, after rolling the title on his tongue).

Mr Clement Attlee, a Prime Minister noted for his lack of personal vanity even within the Labour Party, accepted his earldom. Even with a veteran radical like this, the system throws up around him the same luxuriant foliage of the hereditary and honorific system. The armorial bearings he acquired strangely combine a witty motto of the class struggle, *Labor vincit omnia* (Labour conquers all), surmounted by rampant lions on a shield and a plumed, knightly helmet. Lord Attlee's son and heir automatically acquired the courtesy title of Viscount Prestwood; his daughters took the courtesy title of 'Lady ——'; and his son's children got the courtesy prefix, 'Hon.'.

The Tory declines elevation; the Socialist accepts it. Even if Lord Attlee's main motive was to lend his party the benefit of his continuing voice in the Upper House, traditional attitudes to the peerage do go surprisingly into reverse gear on these occasions. If this happens often enough, can there be any comprehensible pattern left? This raises the question whether possession of a title alone is enough to qualify for membership of the 'aristocracy' – meaning a body possessing the influence, attitudes and social position traditionally associated with it. Miss Mitford appears to think that it does. 'A Lord does not have to be born to his position ... but though he may not be a U-speaker he becomes an aristocrat as soon as he receives his title. The Queen turns him from Socialist leader, or middle-class businessman, into a nobleman, and his outlook from now on will be the outlook of an aristocrat.'[1]

This view seemed to me to award excessively magical powers to the Fount of Honour: a case of 'drink me and grow tall' as in *Alice in Wonderland*. For one thing, it was a theory which did not sufficiently reckon with the fact that not all newly-ennobled peers *wanted* to be regarded as aristocrats, even if one credited them with a due share of concealed vainglory.

More accurately, perhaps, receipt of a title resulted in some cases in a kind of split-mindedness in which there was neither the absolute confidence of elite behaviour nor, on the other hand, the absolutely plain aspect of Common Man. A minor but typical example was the way in which this or that trade union leader or left-wing intellectual would hasten off to collect his Letters Patent of ennoblement as Baron Drawbridge of Moat, a little flushed with celebration, only to urge his colleagues on return, 'Please go on calling me Bert . . .'

Some did not even have these doubts about it, and would have been genuinely surprised at Miss Mitford's theory that they had been transformed. I recollected having once visited an elderly peer, Lord Lawson, who had seen service in a Labour government. It is true that, like any landed aristocrat, he still clung to the same

[1] N. Mitford, ed., *Noblesse Oblige*, London, 1956.

locality and residence where he had been brought up. But in this case it was a tiny, red-brick terraced house in a dilapidated village in the middle of a coalfield. Old colliery spoil-heaps, not lawns, marked the view from the parlour window. Her Ladyship, his wife, had just done the weekly wash and this hung on the drying rack over our heads as he reminisced in the back kitchen. He was one of that small but impressive breed of self-educated working men who grew up in the early years of the century. He was working down the pit at the age of fourteen; and picked up a potent mixture of Shelley, Dickens, Tom Paine, Blatchford, Shakespeare and the Bible in his private reading between shifts.

He stayed on in this grimy area because, for no obvious reason to a stranger, he was much attached to it and he got on well with his neighbours. The only significant family trophy he possessed was the old coal-pick which he had once used underground. Polished up to a silvery brightness, like some other nobleman's escutcheon, it hung between two curtain-hooks on the parlour wall. At one point in his reminiscences he took down this implement and, kneeling on the hearthrug, demonstrated for me the short-jabbing swing that was needed in the low coal-seams of the district. In terms of character I am sure he belonged to some sort of elite; but this was one he had made himself and he was still its only member as far as one could see.

Acquiring a peerage means fundamentally no more than that the holder has been elevated to a precise legal status. Whether he also possesses the much more complex traditional things which make him a member of an aristocratic elite are quite another matter.

As a peer he is differentiated from the common populace by a few remaining privileges, one of them important, the others more theoretical. So long as he goes through the ritual of 'claiming his seat' he becomes a member of the House of Lords. He has a right of audience with the sovereign, while others have to wait for a summons to the royal presence; but this right has not been exercised for a long while and it would be remarkable if it ever were again.

Thirdly, a peer is exempt from jury service, a duty to which all other householders are liable. Fourthly, he is exempt from arrest on matters involving civil (as distinct from criminal) law while Parliament is in session.

A peer's right to be tried by the House of Lords on criminal matters instead of in the ordinary courts was abolished in 1948. Before that, it was invoked as recently as 1936 by Lord de Clifford when he faced a charge of manslaughter.

Those are the only concise and real differences still left. Of course, if one searches around in the dust at the bottom of the archives one can produce one or two curiosities which no one has yet had the thought to abolish. A peer may apparently still wear his hat, or coronet, in a law court, a right which was last claimed in 1902 by the then Lord Egmont when he was charged with being drunk in Piccadilly. Two peers, Lord Kingsale and Lord Forester, have the right to keep their heads covered in the Queen's presence because of some custom which has got lost in the mists. It is unlikely to be a much exercised privilege. The Duke of Atholl has the unique privilege of being allowed his own private army, and the pikes and musketry are still in being up there at that ivory-coloured castle in the Highlands, should the trumpet sound.

A peerage is thus a narrowly-defined status which embraces the widest variety of conditions of men, from the rich duke at one end of the scale to the ex-miner baron at the other. Is there some more precisely recognisable label to elite status than this plainly erratic one of a title?

Some authorities suggest – they firmly insist on it in Scotland – that possession of an authentic coat of arms is the really sure guide to nobility; indeed that it has rather more validity than a title.

'In England the custom has arisen of practically restricting the use of the word "nobleman" to members of the peerage and baronetage, and those who by courtesy bear titles in virtue of their immediate connection with noble houses; it should, however, always be borne in mind that, strictly speaking, every one bearing duly authorised arms is equally entitled to be styled "noble", be he Peer, Baronet, Knight, or Gentleman.' (*Debrett's Peerage*, 1965 edn.)

B

Coats of arms were in their origins literally 'coats'. Marked with various heraldic emblems – lions, hearts, chevrons, stripes, heads of eagles, bulls or boars, and so on – they were worn over a leader's armour in battle to make him conspicuous to his followers. Eventually transferred from coats to shields, these armorial bearings became the mark of someone whose style of life and standing in society marked him out as a 'gentleman'. The task of deciding which individuals had enough wealth and position to deserve the right to bear a coat of arms was, from Tudor times, carried out by the royal Heralds. On their tours or 'visitations' of the country they checked pedigrees and other signs of gentlemanly merit and disallowed the arms of those aspirants who were merely getting above their station. Now and again they had to insist on some truly eminent local worthy accepting a coat of arms which he was reluctant to have because he begrudged the fee.

This heraldic strictness about what constitutes 'nobility', and the ancient pedigree of many coats of arms, suggest that the authorities like Debrett may be right in saying that Arms are the veritable hallmark of exclusive elite status.

But here again there is a discrepancy between scholarly theory and the facts of noble life out in the field. The College of Arms in London, a magnificently gilt-edged institution which is watched over by the Earl Marshal of England (the Duke of Norfolk) and which ultimately derives its authority from the Queen, is still the body which has control over the granting of Arms.

Hopefully, the enquirer goes along to see the Heralds, feeling rather confident that there must be some time-honoured definition of what constitutes noble or gentlemanly status and entitlement to Arms. It will naturally be written – one supposes on the way – in Norman-French script on a scroll of vellum and be regarded with biblical weight in these matters. But regrettably there is no such definitive thing. A 'gentleman' these days – in the College's view – is taken broadly to be anyone who can show some symptoms of being an educated, professional-level, middle-class person – such as having a university degree, being a member of the Bar, a chartered accountant, or in some other recognisably respectable occupation. For the fee of £150 some scholarly member of the

College will devise the applicant a suitable coat of arms which will draw upon and symbolise his family's associations with the past, if any; and which is unlikely to miss the chance of some heavy pictorial pun on his name (Lord Snow's arms, for instance, are: Azure, semy of Snow crystals proper; and a Crest containing 'a telescope fesswise between two pens in saltire proper, on either side a Siamese Cat proper').

So, in reality, the potential qualifiers for this armorial definition of the elite embraces a large part of the working population, several hundreds of thousands at least. The fact that the College has only a quiet and steady flow of applicants instead of being swamped can only mean that most people have not heard of it, that they are seeking prestige in other ways, or that like some predecessors they begrudge the £150.

Virtually the only important difference of the peerage, taken literally as an institution, is its special role as the Upper House of Parliament. That is its literal, or written-down, aspect. But beyond this, reaching out into society generally, has always been its function as an 'aristocracy', an altogether looser and more complex thing. This is the side that is concerned with influence and leadership, either directly or by example, the sort of barely detectable colouring that an elite gives to its society. If the peerage is the body, the 'aristocracy' can be defined as the spirit – the less visible element which has indisputably in times past had much effect on national ideals and attitudes, on the way the country sees itself and the way it is regarded from abroad.

It is an element which has *unconsciously* been present in the widest range of social and political matters: in the regulation of social stability and movement; the shaping of foreign policy, the formation of English attitudes to certain professions, to the ideals of education, attitudes to the countryside; the social categorising of various sports and pastimes; the code of manners which comes to be regarded as 'good form'; the design of middle-class clothes, and much besides.

From the breadth and depth of this influence in the past arises, of course, the interest in knowing to what degree it still exists. One of the first and fundamental puzzles which needs to be solved is how far the machinery which generated these effects continues in being – how far, that is, the present-day peerage can be said to be 'aristocratic'. Even an observer of Evelyn Waugh's calibre had to guess at this.

'The relationship between aristocracy and nobility is certainly baffling. I don't suppose you could find any two people in complete agreement about it. My own estimate would be that about half the nobility are aristocrats . . .'[1]

What would be regarded as a typical aristocrat in contemporary terms? To attempt a short answer would be to beg all the questions. Evelyn Waugh appears to be using the word 'aristocrat' to signify someone with a certain grandeur of style, the sort of personage who was last clearly visible to the public at large three or four decades ago. It is a fair surmise that the modern aristocrat, if he is there at all, should bear some resemblance to his predecessors; that his values and attitudes should to some extent reflect theirs.

It should not be forgotten, however, that the characteristics of the aristocracy have changed, on the surface at least, from one period to another. In the four centuries after the Conquest the hallmarks of elite membership were military prowess, aggressiveness, a strong sense of interlocking cousinly relationships among the baronage; and there was an unashamedly predatory attitude in building up land and possessions. In more centralised Tudor times the idea of the elite as settled, landed 'gentlemen', with a rather more cultivated and mannered sense of values, became developed. Ownership of an estate was accompanied by an assumption of local responsibility and authority, a paternalist outlook, and some sense of public service. Shrewdness replaced violence in building up possessions. The greater barons might hover round the Court looking for lucrative offices and generally politicking; but they too managed to combine this with the role of landed gentlemen.

The eighteenth century saw the aristocracy into its Golden Age, more than a little intoxicated with its prodigious wealth, social glitter, and oligarchic political power. They meant to be astonishing, to themselves as much as to posterity; and if one looks

[1] *Noblesse Oblige*, p. 68.

at the vast palaces which were thrown up, regardless of expense, the follies, the great parks and gardens, the collections of pictures and statuary, one can see how well they succeeded. It was a time when some of the minor nobility and gentry, marrying the heiresses of the rising merchant class, were consolidating their fortunes; and others were drinking or gambling themselves into debt.

After the celebration, the uneasy sobriety of the Victorian period; painful and reluctant adjustments to the radical challenge and the rise of the middle classes; a heavier emphasis placed on the notion of aristocratic duty and service as the century wore on – at the very time that these things were coming to seem less vital at the centre of affairs.

The brief, gay flurry of the turn of the century and the Edwardian era: champagne, a repetition of fast women and slow horses, a growing number of actress marriages in the nobility, a rather self-conscious attempt to shake off the uncongenial and un-aristocratic moral code which the middle classes had very nearly inveigled them into observing. Then the lights went out over Europe; the sacrifices among the younger aristocracy and gentry were heavy.

By the end of the Second World War it would have been a fair surmise that the elite had drawn its last breath, that its spirit had fled. Ordinary servicemen came out of it bristling with impatience about something. Significantly, one of the first casualties of this new mood was Sir Winston Churchill. Confidently expecting to lead the country into the peace, he was ejected by a landslide vote. It was an unprecedented case of electoral 'disloyalty' under the circumstances.

The swing to the Left may have been largely a matter of elementary political feeling. But it was also, in a way not so plainly manifested before, a clear rejection of the 'natural' leader, the man born to rule, a most talented son of the old ruling class. If there were landmarks in the latter-day passing of the elite, this was surely one of them.

Over the last thirty years the aristocracy had made its greatest adjustment to change, one that would once have been thought impossible. It had become self-effacing. Only occasionally did

some diehard nobleman step out on to the political stage – like
Lord Salisbury over Rhodesia – to remind people of former influence. Generally, it had become hard to see the connection between
the retiring twentieth-century aristocracy and those aggressive
predecessors who had built up the great estates. As Evelyn Waugh
had mentioned, there was much uncertainty about what characteristics an aristocracy could now be expected to have. The only
measure one could apply to the present, to see what sort of an
institution it had now become, was an assembly of its strongest
personality traits from the past.

First and foremost was an absolutely confident assumption of
leadership, locally and nationally, in all things and at all times.
This confidence was derived partly from education and breeding,
the conviction of being 'born to rule', and partly from their
wealth. A century ago several lords had incomes of around
£200,000 a year, a sum hard to imagine today, and at a time when
income tax was trifling. By the middle of the nineteenth century
there were a number of new industrial fortunes which could match
theirs. But there was a distinct gap between the new-rich and the
old. The nobility owned the great estates. Certainly into the
1870s, probably for longer, ninety per cent of the aristocracy had a
landed background, and the great house, the servants, the local
position and prestige which went with it. Possession of the land
gave them the fine odour of antiquity and a sense of immovable
timelessness. Whatever his rating in the purlieus of central government, back at home on his estate the aristocrat was a formidable
figure.

In the nineteenth century the core of the landed aristocracy con-
sisted of some 300 landed families, ranging from grandees like the
Dukes of Northumberland, Bedford, Devonshire and Bridgewater down to the greater squires. Those at the top, like the
Devonshires, who owned 200,000 acres of land scattered over fourteen counties, were truly regal both in their little kingdoms and in
London society.

Unlike the French aristocracy who only reluctantly dragged
themselves away from Court the British nobility and gentry were
attached, even addicted to, life on their estates. One could certainly

paint too sentimental a picture of the dutiful concern of many squires and major landlords. But, by and large, they accepted their local responsibilities. They supervised the law; they and their sons supplied the officers for the Army; they ran the local Hunt, and the Big House was the natural centre of whatever social life there was.

Their stake in the land, their concern to preserve their station up on the plateau, bred their extremely conservative political attitudes. Property was the paramount thing; and their political influence was to some extent related to the size of their estates.

The aristocracy remained primarily a landed one at least until 1920 when sales of land led to the break-up of the great remaining estates all over the country. But the landed interest continued to set the tone since, even if he had no land left, it was country pursuits and leisure, local power and local duties, which had done most to nurture the conception of the lord and the gentleman. Their consensus of feeling on this was the chief thing which, until perhaps 1920, gave the aristocracy its sense of corporate identity.

'The landed aristocrats had much in common . . . their upbringing, way of life, family setting, occupations, avocations, social outlook and political beliefs were all shaped by a readily identifiable mould. They formed a loosely-knit club whose unwritten rules ensured that all members were gentlemen, and it was they above all who formed the standards of gentlemanly conduct . . .'[1]

The strength of the class lay in the absence of any niggling self-doubts about its values. Corporately, there was a strong sense of patriotism, a deep loyalty to the idea of Church and Monarchy and a conviction that the gentlemanly class was the country's greatest stabilising influence. However one interpreted it, it was a reasonable claim in many ways. Honour and duty meant something real to them in an almost knightly, romantic sense. There was a deep regard for the idea of England (tending to mean exclusively landed England) and for the Empire which was the beneficiary of the values and the ideals of service which had been bred out in the shires.

The other side of the coin was that a most extreme degree of

[1] F. M. L. Thompson, *English Landed Society in the Nineteenth Century*, London, 1963.

self-interest also lay veiled under this dedicated outlook; and much of the apparatus of their code of manners had been devised to conceal the reality that money was involved to a high degree in their lives and thoughts. The gentleman's income came from sources made more honorific, not less, by being inherited; and it was always an assumption that it passed from source to owner invisibly, like air.

Unutterably confident on their estates, gallant in the military field, there was also a streak of fear in their make-up. The things that disturbed them were anything that concerned the dark, industrial urban areas. From afar, they perceived – in the phrase coined by Thorstein Veblen, the American sociologist – 'the dishonour attaching to productive employment'.

By the 1920s the great landed domains were falling apart. The foundations of a life which had meant privilege, status, and seclusion, and cast this special group into the role of leadership, appeared to be cracking. Nearly fifty years later it was worth seeing was what was left of such an historic structure.

3

LANDSCAPES WITH FIGURES

A damp October twilight was falling on Derbyshire as I approached Kedleston Hall, the residence of Viscount Scarsdale. The low rounded hills had already receded behind a light haze of rain. The narrow country road wound between dripping hedge-rows and over an occasional stone bridge below which a stream rushed in spate.

Lord Scarsdale was the present head of the Curzons, an originally Norman family which had come to England in the wake of the Conqueror. This in itself gave it a certain rarity within the peerage. There was a persistent myth that the British nobility was still largely Norman in its affiliations. This belief appeared to be based on the notion that the invading military elite which had introduced the feudal system to Britain must somehow have retained a majority holding in what was left of it.

It might also be a hangover from the keen desire of the nine-teenth-century ruling class and aspiring social climbers to have a pedigree which put them indubitably on the winning side at Hastings. It was a strange pretension anyway in a country of such hybrid origins, and the more severe genealogists of the time occupied themselves in felling bogus family trees and lopping off the fanciful Gallic prefix which this or that Jean de Bull had tried to award himself.

In fact, the admixture of Norman blood had not been especially concentrated in the nobility since the fifteenth century. Now-adays only about twenty of the present 900-odd hereditary peers could claim certain Norman descent through the male line.

For me, a more impressive fact about the Curzons was that they had kept their family headquarters in this corner of Derbyshire without interruption for 850 years. In a relatively small, socially mobile country it was certainly a feat of sorts, and I wondered how they had managed it. Part of the reason was that much of the English countryside containing the great estates had managed to hold its frontiers against the town, despite constant pressure. Behind me, only a few miles to the south, the sky over the city of Derby was putting on its sultry evening glow, silhouetting tall chimneys. What, barely fifty years ago, had been mainly a market town had swollen into a place that milled steel, made aero engines, Rolls Royce cars, locomotives, cloth, paper, ironmongery and all sorts. But out here, not far away from it, England was still an empty-seeming country where the sheepwalks followed an un-changing line across the uplands and, like them, most things were allied in a conspiracy against change.

Through a fine curtain of rain the tall iron gates leading to Kedleston Hall appeared. Gusts of wind shook the flanking avenue of beeches along the drive. Groupings of trees set here and there across the rolling parkland made darker shadows in the dusk. The drive traversed an ornamental three-arched bridge and there was the silvery glint of a waterfall below it. On the wide lawns beyond it, scores, maybe hundreds, of large and mysterious bird-shapes huddled silent and motionless. Suddenly, as we swished past, this massive squadron of Grey Canadian Geese took off in unison, filling the air with beating wingshapes and the sighing noise of fast propulsion. I had heard that Lord Scarsdale was keen on decorative fauna.

The great outline of the house loomed behind them, like a sombre cliff, or the freeboard of a majestic liner hove-to in mid-ocean. High overhead, along its summit, three stone goddesses stood out against the sky. A line of marble columns rushed up towards them, sounding echoes of Imperial Rome. Behind the rain-spattered, leaded window ahead a face appeared. A door opened into the cliff.

The young, dark-suited butler had no Jeevesian airs about him. He led the way along a broad, gently-curving corridor across whose tapestried walls wraith-like figures floated among stylised trees, hunting the boar. There were passing glimpses of big and elegant formal apartments. Classical landscapes, portrait heads, the disarrayed limbs of nymphs glowed briefly from the gold-framed canvases on their walls. There were brightly burnished suits of armour, evidently kept up to a state of war readiness.

At the end of this march through a grander age, the owner of the splendour appeared: Lord Scarsdale, otherwise Sir Richard Nathaniel Curzon, Bt, a figure of medium height, wearing well-worn tweed jacket and corduroys, an outfit which I later came to recognise as the characteristic uniform of the landed nobility. A fit-looking man of sixty-nine, grey hair brushed straight back, with forceful nose and brow, it did not seem too fanciful to detect traces of Norman warrior origin in his face or to sense that he would still look absolutely right in chain-mail and casque.

In the small, modestly-furnished sitting-room which he and his wife use, Lord Scarsdale poured tea from a big china pot and took up a question of mine about family resemblances. 'Yes,' he said, 'it's an underground stream and it does keep coming back century after century in the most extraordinary way. We descend from the Coursons who held lands near Calvados before the Conquest. They still exist in Brittany as people of some rank. Well, not long ago a woman member of the Courson family came to visit us and we were quite astonished at the resemblance to my own daughter, face, voice, everything, though there hadn't been an intermarriage between us and the French side since the eleventh century. There's a stone carving of one of the medieval Curzons in our church and a lot of us look very much like him too.'

The first of the family to settle here was a Richard de Curcun who in 1135 held four knights' fees on this spot. This was a feudal grant of land, amounting to about a thousand acres, in return for raising a certain number of troops for the King's service. Thirty men were drafted from the estate to fight at Agincourt. This land still forms the kernel of the estate and the present Hall is the fifth house the family has built on the same site.

The estate has had the usual ups and downs. Having been built up to a peak of around 14,000 acres in the early 1900s it has been reduced by death duties to its present 6,000 acres, but it is still one of the largest in the county even at this size. The big jump in the value of land over the last couple of decades has easily overtaken the decline in the value of money. 'When I succeeded to the title in 1925 the land was worth £40 an acre. Now it's worth £330 an acre as farmland and if you're selling for building it might raise between £5,000 and £10,000, there's such a demand for it. So you can see the whole estate is worth an incredible amount.'

At Kedleston, it means that the old feudal centre of the estate plus the later additions are now together worth upwards of £2,500,000. Landowners like Lord Scarsdale who can stand back and watch this growth of capital value like to make the point that it has its drawbacks, and that they are millionaires 'only in theory'. Since the estate is regarded as a family trust to be passed on to the heir they are unlikely ever to realise much of this fortune by selling. The sad fact of the family wealth – or this tends to be the lugubrious way they put it – is only brought home to them when the heir has to pay death duties calculated on the same high valuation.

But brighter prospects occasionally gleam out of these imagined shadows, particularly where an estate has land near a town (the Kedleston acres stretch to the fringe of Derby) and even a small nibble of it sold for building can fetch a big price. 'But with land everything depends on the government of the day,' Lord Scarsdale went on, telling me an anecdote to illustrate the pitfalls of a landowner's life. 'When the Labour government was in a while ago I had to sell seven acres to the local council to build a school on and they paid me the absurdly low price of £100 an acre. When the Tories got in we saw fair play for a change and the council paid us £38,000 for another seven acres.'

Most of the estate is rented out to twenty-two tenant farmers and the gross income from these rents might average £40,000 a year. But most of the income had to be ploughed back in maintenance and improvements. 'We've been putting electricity and water into every tenant's cottage and that can be pretty costly. Yes, it's taken a while to get around to it but there it is.' He also owns three villages in the locality: Kedleston itself, Quarndon and Weston Underwood, which have a combined population of about

2,500. I asked him whether any trace of a 'lordly' relationship still existed in the old feudal sense, between himself and the people living within his domain.

He couldn't think of any particular instance of it. 'I just seem to go round inspecting my tenants' roofs and gutters. We throw a tenants' party every three years, by the way. Now and again one's asked to open a fête or make a speech. Of course, I read the lesson in church on a Sunday – if you can call that a lordly duty. The Curzons have had the right to appoint the vicar at Kedleston ever since Norman times. It can be very irksome finding the right man for the job. One usually consults the Bishop about it – if one gets on with him, that is.'

Lord Scarsdale said he had been out most of the day helping his three woodmen to plant trees. This was the sort of thing he had been doing every working day for the last forty years. 'We put in some oak, beech and chestnut. With a waxing moon and the leaves falling it's just the right time to plant. In a couple of centuries,' he added – rather confidently I thought, considering the time-span – 'a good hardwood could be worth £250.'

I wondered how he could think that far ahead. Was timber going to be a useful material in AD 2100? But he did not catch the drift of my question. 'You've got to think of the future owner,' he went on, 'That's what the aristocracy is all about, or should be. You know, we've still got oaks in the park that must have been planted by the Curzons in Tudor times.'

I asked him how he thought the family itself had survived so well. It was mostly a matter, he thought, of not having been too greedy or ambitious, especially in those centuries where climbing high carried risks as well as rewards. The Curzons had been plain but prosperous country gentry for much of their span, occupying posts as members of Parliament or High Sheriffs for the locality, and seldom overreaching themselves as a good many families did. 'King John fined us for joining in the Barons' Wars against him, but we kept our heads. We were on the wrong side in the Wars of the Roses but we got away with it. Then we were on Cromwell's side in the Civil War – Sir John Curzon was in charge of seizing Royalist property – but somehow we got back into favour at the

Restoration. The last time we were under temptation to go the wrong way was in the Jacobite rising of 1745. The Highlanders who had marched south came to Kedleston asking for help. Sir Nathaniel had the presence of mind to stay in bed. The Scotsmen stole two horses and departed. So on the whole history was rather kind to us.'

Lord Scarsdale led the way out to show me some of the state apartments, normally only open in the summer months when the general public pay their half-crowns and file respectfully through. Oil heaters glowed dimly in the middle of vast rooms. In the Marble Hall the air was chilly. Here the architect Robert Adam best expressed the idea of the grandeur which his employer, Sir Nathaniel (he who stayed in bed) evidently thought was his due. The twenty huge alabaster columns which line the walls give it its monumentally dignified air; the arabesques of the ceiling design and the neat classical alcoves add a softer effect. It was a splendid place but of no conceivable practical use now except, say, to receive guests in at some exceptionally grand state ball.

Lord Scarsdale stooped to turn up a heater. 'Got to keep out the damp, you know.' I wondered whether people expected him to keep up a style of life to match the house these days? 'Oh, I hardly think so. We couldn't afford it anyway. Uncle George (George Nathaniel Curzon, the empire-minded statesman who was Viceroy of India in 1898–1905, Kedleston's most famous son) used to live at the rate of £50,000 a year. Incredible! He married Mary Leiter, an American heiress. My wife and I just stick to a few rooms in this wing and we rent three flats to people on the other side of the house. I used to keep four hunters but now that it costs a thousand a year just to keep one I've given them up. Entertaining's costly too. We tried to give a ball in the saloon once but with this modern swing stuff the floor began to collapse.'

We passed a pedigree chart of the Curzons, set into a wall. It was about ten feet high and elaborate with heraldic devices. 'There, you see, I'm absolutely directly descended from Robert de Curcun in the male line.' Lord Scarsdale was clearly proud of the length of his lineage. But what it mainly supplied, it seemed to me, was not so much any special personality traits; it was rather a source of more family anecdotes than most people would have access to.

We moved towards the door, switching off chandelier lights behind us, restoring the great rooms to their own dark and empty existence. 'A branch of the Curzons went to America in the early eighteenth century so we often get visitors, mostly from Baltimore and New York, claiming descent from us. The name is spelt "Curson" over there. Do all these spellings confuse you? They ran a shipping company in Baltimore during the American Civil War. Only the female line exists there now. The last of the male Curzons there was killed in a duel in New York City in 1786 . . .'

Outside, lights twinkled briefly from somewhere across the gently rolling sea of the Park. Yes: people without neighbours. That might be one definition of the landed lords.

Anthony Powell once observed that a prime characteristic of the nobility was their melancholy. Not in the present case, perhaps: Lord Scarsdale evidently had enough buoyancy to carry the isolation and the centuries behind him. But later and elsewhere I saw what Powell meant. A craving for space and privacy was one of the hallmarks of the traditional peerage. Or, even if they did not desire it themselves, some ancestral view of life expressed in stone still required them to live like lighthouse-keepers.

This way of life was often accompanied, I found, by an un-admitted nervousness and puzzlement about the vulgarising world beyond the walls. With few people close enough to distract them with pressure and demands, they had been cast in the role of con-templatives who seldom had the inner resources to find it satis-fying. This was what the melancholia was all about, I thought.

Along the drive, the perfectly symmetrical waterfall still tinkled below the beautiful ornamental bridge. The bird-shapes stretched wings again and soared away into the dark.

The Laundry Game

Lord Redesdale was on the telephone when I arrived. 'Hello, Clem Redesdale here . . .' he was saying. Then followed a con-versation about laundry machinery of mystifying technicality.

He is the 5th Baron Redesdale, Clement Napier Bertram Mitford; aged 35; succeeded uncle in 1963; educated Eton; married with five daughters; cousin of Nancy Mitford.

He lived in a quite handsome, but not opulent, Regency house in a side-street near one of London's parks. This first-floor room is used as an office from which he runs his dry-cleaning and laundry business (trade-named 'Redeclean' after his title) and other enterprises. His secretary typed a letter among the piles of paper and documents on the table beside him.

'Sorry to keep you . . .' he said. He was young-looking, energetic, plainly a good mixer. No, he said, the family didn't have much land left to speak of: only a thousand acres and a cottage up north. The Redesdale estates up to about fifty years ago covered nearly 30,000 acres of Northumberland and the family seat was a castle. Now nearly all of it had gone to pay estate duties. The Army now used the land as an artillery range.

The family had been well-landed gentry in the north until, in the late seventeenth century, they also became London merchants. The head of the family at that time, John Mitford, had been Speaker of the House of Commons and Lord Chancellor of Ireland. He was made a Baron in 1802 and a later Mitford had risen to an earldom by 1877. But both titles had become extinct in the absence of male heirs, and a successor only regained the barony in 1902.

Lord Redesdale said he didn't much regret not being a landed peer, he enjoyed business so much. I said that some people supposed there were still some inhibitions among the peerage about going into business. Not so many decades ago, I suggested, heads would have been shaken about a lord of landed descent who owned a chain of dry-cleaning shops; not only owned, but shamelessly enjoyed taking a big hand in running them.

'I don't think there's any of that feeling left now. A peer can do whatever he wants . . .' He was recalled to the phone for another talk about laundry or some such subject. 'Sorry, where were we . . .?' he resumed. He told me how, without an estate, he had had to make his own career. He did his Army service in Malaya with a tough Scots regiment and quite liked that. Then he worked in advertising for ten years, doing everything from the hard slog of selling space to handling an account. Then he pulled out and went into business on his own. From ownership of a few dry-cleaning shops he had expanded into supplying boilers and laundry equipment and most other parts of the show.

Did a title help him or had it got in the way? Other lords I had seen had affirmed that it was always one or the other. People were never neutral about it. 'Well, I didn't *try* to make the title help me. But in the early days it just happened to do so quite a bit, making business contacts and so on. After that it helped in an oblique way, I suppose, because the business-men you're dealing or bargaining with always seem to expect a lord to be a complete mug in any technical field. By that time, though, I knew quite a lot about laundry engineering so I was really one up on them.'

He didn't think there was anything you could call an aristocracy left. 'It should mean people with power, and we haven't got any.' But what about the House of Lords? Yes, he said, he occasionally spoke there from the Liberal benches, but only when a subject cropped up that he knew something about. Dry-cleaning for instance.

He was plainly not one of the remote lighthouse-keepers. Lady Redesdale brought us in two cups of coffee on a tray. Then the phone rang again. 'Yes, Lord Redesdale here . . .'

'. . . A peculiar country'

'I don't see how you can possibly justify the hereditary principle,' said Viscount Norwich, another of the younger peers, who inherited his own title in 1954. 'I can't see any reason why I should have the right to speak in the House of Lords. I think it's a useful institution to have, though, because we can give an airing to things the House of Commons won't touch, either because it's too busy, too timid, or too regimented by the need to toe the Party line. But there's a lot of old-fashioned deadwood still in the Lords. We could do with a lot more younger chaps to replace them. Perhaps they could appoint some as temporary peers . . .'

Lord Norwich is the son of the late Duff Cooper (first holder of the title) and Lady Diana Cooper. He is 38; was educated at Eton and Oxford; spent several years in the Diplomatic Service before resigning to become a full-time historical writer. He is married with two children and lives in a middle-sized Regency house in north London.

When I called, he was busy correcting proofs of a book he'd just written about the Normans in Sicily. Lord Norwich is one of the completely landless peers. 'We've got nothing except the front garden and even that's only on lease like the house.'

I asked him whether inheriting the title had got in the way of his evident ambition to be a serious professional, whether it had changed his life much? 'Well the thought of being a lord wasn't a particularly exciting or remarkable prospect. My whole life had been spent in that world. Half my friends had been lords . . .'

But had people's attitudes to him changed when he eventually acquired the title? 'Oh, yes, to a quite incredible degree. I've never stopped being surprised about it. It's extraordinary that these attitudes are still there when you think that the House of Lords is full of trade unionists and life peers. Yet the mystique of the title on its own – even when you don't have a landed estate like me – still seems to pull people up in their tracks. Take an example . . . I had a small part in a television programme the other day, appearing with a chap who's originally working-class but has made himself one of the best jazz critics in the country. I once asked him whether his family weren't proud of the way he'd got to the top. No, he said, they were more impressed that he'd been on the telly with a lord. Odd, isn't it?'

'Having a title means you can usually get a better table in a restaurant. They daren't tuck you away in any old corner, it seems. But you're expected to leave a much bigger tip than some untitled diner who's probably got twice as much money as I have. This annoying assumption that a title means wealth still goes on. I thought everyone knew the aristocracy wasn't rich any more. We all live in flats and so on. Abroad, of course, you run into even higher expectations of what a lord should be like. When I was doing a spell at the British embassy in Beirut our ambassador there was a plain "Mister" and I, a viscount, was just one of his staff. Local people found it most puzzling.'

I wondered whether younger, working peers like himself still felt any sense of *noblesse oblige*, a feeling that they were required to perform some public service as a way of justifying their rank (or shedding the guilt of it, as social Freudians might have it). Lord Norwich thought that ninety per cent of the nobility, old and new, did try to do some public work. 'My cousin, the Duke of Rutland, is on dozens ¦of committees, just never stops doing unpaid work.'

'The moment I succeeded to the title twelve years ago I was absolutely overwhelmed with requests to become chairman, patron or president of this or that charity or organisation. They never even bothered to ask whether I had any qualifications for the job. Extraordinary, isn't it? They all said, "It won't take up much of your time . . ." But soon I was spending every morning of the week on this sort of unpaid work, never getting any of my own writing done, missing publishers' deadlines. Now and again I tried to suggest a friend for the job who I knew was genuinely interested in a certain area of charity work and much cleverer than me at it. But the charity secretaries always turned down the idea simply because he hadn't got a title. We're a peculiar country in some ways . . .'

The Landed Gentleman

The landed gentry, or what used to be called the squirearchy, is a particularly British group. Nothing quite like it exists elsewhere in the world. Its members have no constitutional title or privileges. The duties they take on are, broadly speaking, only the ones they give themselves.

Many gentry families have shown remarkable tenacity in holding on to their land from medieval times to the present day. What they have also notably had, and still have, is a subtle sense of their place in the class system. The greater landowners among them especially are clearly part of the aristocracy and, in any meaningful measuring table, would be given precedence over a good many of the newer peers. They have often had the closest association with the peerage either through similar schooling, Army service in one of the smarter regiments, a mutual liking for the hunting field, inter-marriage or other affinities.

Yet their style of living is commonly only fractionally more stylish than that of the comfortably-off yeoman class from which they arose and can be detected only in such subtleties as possessing a few family portraits from an earlier century, though now almost opaque under their patina of varnish; or in boasting a decent lawn in front of the house as well as the few thousand acres behind; or in having a more discriminating drinks tray on the sideboard.

They have often managed to preserve almost precisely the same social position down the centuries, slightly elevated yet un-assuming, unofficial pro-consuls of their locality yet quite un-known in London or even beyond the county boundary, and possibly without a title in the family for all its long and notable existence. Managing to avoid ennoblement, when a shade more ambition might well have got them there, almost seems to have been a stoic family tradition in some cases. It apparently suited them. While the more assertive members of the nobility were hovering round the Court, acquiring offices and honours, making or losing fortunes and prestige, running through all the highs and lows of the elite's musical register, it was often the even wood-wind note of the gentry which emerged most steadily at the end of it. Naturally, they thought themselves morally superior to those more show-off lords.

What cachet the gentry have within the aristocracy is usually intensely localised and it is charged with romantic undertones when, as in a few cases, the family has a territorial surname derived from the land it first settled on. The gentlemen who have an ancient and customary right to call themselves, say, Plowden of Plowden (Mr W. F. G. Plowden), Craufurd of Craufurdland (Mr J. P. Houison-Craufurd), Medlicott of Medlicott (Mr E. S. D. Medlicott), Fulford of Fulford (Lieut.-Col. F. E. A. Fulford), or Craster of Craster (Sir John Craster – 'Telegrams: Craster, Craster', says Sir John's notepaper) – these names, all associated with the same place from the twelfth century or earlier, have a discreet glamour denied to the more drum-rolling titles of the peerage.

On my way to visit Fulford of Fulford it occurred to me that if any such personage as a 'Squire' still existed, he would surely be one. The Fulford land in Devonshire is mentioned in Domesday Book and has certainly been occupied by the family since the time of Richard Lion-Heart, possibly earlier.

I stopped in the little village of Dunsford which is near the estate and asked the most elderly inhabitant available if he could tell me where the squire lived. The hesitation was fractional. 'Oh, you mean Squire Fulford? Up the lane to the left, go two mile, and there's the gates.' In fact, the term is hardly ever used any more, even in out-of-the-way places like this, except perhaps to humour innocent strangers. But the place of the Fulfords as leaders of the local community has always been strong and, in some respects, survives.

The small, square Norman church which stands on a knoll in the village centre still has its big box-pew (it would seat about twenty if needed) for the Fulfords. A small door in it allows Colonel Fulford easy access to the lectern so that he can read the lessons to the congregation on Sundays. The display of *memento mori* around the pew present the church-going Fulfords with unwavering intimations of mortality. There is no escaping them whichever way the eye roves during the sermon.

In front of them, a monument in the style of a four-poster bed commemorates Sir Thomas Fulford and his wife, who lived in Tudor times. Recumbent, hands clasped in prayer, the kneeling figures of their seven children overhead, the armoured knight and his lady lie under their canopy. The coloured coats of arms along the side display those which, through marriages down the centuries, particularly with other West Country families, the Fulfords impale on their own: Fitzurse, Courtenay, Mourton, St Aubyn, Challons, St George, Cantaloupe, Belston, Bozam.

The inscription on this and other slabs and memorials around demonstrate what a struggle to survive it must have been in times past even for a tenacious family like this. Of the seven children of a nineteenth-century Fulford, six died before they were thirty and a similar story is repeated on other tablets. There is nothing especially grand about this corner of the church, so fully occupied with family remembrances. The big family prayer-book, the full names of several generations of Fulfords scrawled in faded ink in the front, is left casually on the front seat. The general effect is a strange mixture of great modesty and total assumption. The leading place was never given by anyone. It was simply occupied by custom, as it is still. The sense of stoic continuity is strong too, not least in the family's ability to sit among these sombre anecdotes of the grave once a week.

The lane, red with mud, went in a switchback up and down steep-sided combes, past tangled woods. In the distance, across a vivid green stretch of meadowland, the house appeared – Great Fulford, a high, square, white, and handsome frontage with fifteenth-century lineaments, its windows set like eyes, not so much for letting light in, more for an occasional opportunity to look out.

Over a low gateway was set the Fulford crest, a bear's head flanked by two Saracens and, on an undulating scroll below, the family motto: *Bear Up*. In the small courtyard beyond Colonel Fulford appeared, a man of about seventy, of slight build and a gently ruminative manner, wearing cuffless corduroys and an old tweed jacket. I was struck with his facial resemblance to the effigy of his Tudor ancestor. 'Did you notice the family vault under the pew? On a Sunday, we sit on the bones of our ancestors,' he said with a slight smile. 'There must be thirty or forty heads of the family down there.'

I asked him about the role of squire. He was amused that a parishioner regarded him as such. 'I don't think anyone under sixty would have known what you meant. I think there is some squirearchy left, though. I don't throw my weight about, I just do jobs. I'm chairman of the local Conservatives, the British Legion and the church council. Since we appoint the church living we appoint the vicar. And we often have a village children's party or a church fête in the hall downstairs.'

The estate of 5,000 acres at Great Fulford which was noted in Domesday Book, was granted to the first incumbent, de Folfert, for military service. It has diminished relatively little, to 3,500 acres. The house still stands at the centre of the Domesday land. The Fulfords farm none of it themselves, but rent it out to eighteen tenant farmers. 'A lot of our tenants like the Sewards and the Dickers have been here for a great many generations.'

Col. Fulford was a regular soldier until his retirement and served in both World Wars, in India, Egypt, Palestine, Greece and Crete. 'Yes, the family's always had a military tradition which we like to carry on . . . By the way, you must see our Crusader.' In the bare, medieval-style hall of the house there is a contemporary carving of Sir Baldwin Fulford, wearing turban and fiercely curling moustachios, flanked by two Saracens. He was Sheriff of Devon about 1400 and the records show him to have been a doughty warrior – *a great soldier and a traveller of so undaunted resolution, that for the honour and liberty of a royal lady, in a castle besieged by the Infidels, he fought a combat with a Saracen, for bulk and bigness an unequal match, whom yet he vanquished and rescued the lady.'*

On the wide, oak staircase outside are the portraits of a seventeenth-century ancestor and his wife, both with untroubled faces, though they withstood a siege during the Civil War. Peering through a window, we could make out a hump in the ground beyond the duck-pond where the Cromwellian besiegers had tried to mask their cannon with an earthwork. Almost inevitably, none of the later Fulfords had concerned themselves with trying to level it. 'That time we declared for the King. But we were pretty flexible in our allegiances, I suppose, and that may have helped us keep going. We supported the Monmouth rebellion. Then switched back to James II. The family's had its ups and downs, but we stuck it out . . .'

A Left-wing Peer

The 15th Earl of Huntingdon is one of those peers who, to the outsider, appear to be a splendid contradiction in terms. He is a hereditary peer who is also a Socialist. Twelve members of the House of Lords are in this apparently double-dyed position. In his case the contradiction seems greater since his family lineage is one of some pedigree and has held its earldom from the time of Henry VIII.

When I met him at his London flat – in one of the most discreet and least revolutionary blocks in the West End – I asked him whether his combination of roles caused any difficulties. 'Well, in a way. Americans are always extremely puzzled by the fact that I'm a left-winger. In the House of Lords, while they're tremendously polite about it there, some of the right-wing chaps feel I've let the side down. They feel it isn't done for a hereditary peer to be a radical in politics. With the trade unionist lords, the Socialist outlook is tolerated of course. With people like me it's apparently different . . .'

Lord Huntingdon, otherwise Francis John Clarence Westenra Plantagenet Hastings, is sixty-six and was educated at Eton and Christ Church, Oxford. He is tall, moustached and amiably relaxed in manner. He is a professional mural painter and has had commissions from such bodies as Birmingham University. His wife is Margaret Lane, the writer.

I asked him how his political views had developed. Basically, it seemed that they were encouraged to lean leftwards by a nonconforming temperament and the fact that his family had been virtually landless for long enough for him to feel able to break away from the traditional conservatism of the landed classes.

The family were already powerful landowners and holders of royal offices in Plantagenet times though they did not escape one beheading by Richard III. Up to the late eighteenth century they held rich estates in Leicestershire with a castle – now a ruin; but thereafter they lived on a smaller estate in Ireland.

'My father was a Master of Foxhounds. I found I didn't agree with my parents and, though I was the heir to the Irish estate, I shot off to Australia, sheep-farming, and worked on a copra plantation in the South Seas.' Lord Huntingdon went out to the kitchen, returned with a tray of tea, and poured.

'Then I took to painting and studied with Diego Rivera in Mexico and the States. Rivera (a Communist) had an effect on my political outlook . . . that, and being in the States during the

Depression. I worked with a medical aid team on the Republican side during the Spanish Civil War. So when I succeeded in 1939 I was well and truly a Socialist.'

How did Labour people react to a hereditary peer in their midst? 'I'd say that acceptance in politics with my views, from my own side as well as the other, is probably more difficult than anything else. One should not get out of category, it seems, or there's prejudice. Yet I'm really a professional man now, like any other. We have no land left, just this flat and a house in the country. That's another disadvantage of a peerage – people take you for a dilettante whatever your skill, unless maybe you're in one of the recognised professions.'

'The reason may be that the nobility got stuck with the Amateur Tradition – we were founder-members, so to speak – because up to recent times there were so many things and jobs a lord wasn't allowed to do. Now I think the time may be coming at long last when a peer can be judged purely on his professional merits, and I'll be delighted to see it.'

Lord Huntingdon seemed to have no very radical views about his ancestors. 'Only the first earl was interested in politics, so we never got our fingers burned. The third earl in Elizabeth's time had to look out, though, because he might have come in line for the Throne, and everyone like that was suspect. I suppose we survived because we were mostly shrewd, opportunist people.'

I asked whether his non-conformity might be a hereditary trait. 'Could be something in that. One of my ancestors, Selina, Countess of Huntingdon, was a disciple of John Wesley and Wycliffe and wanted to reform the upper classes. She founded a religious sect called the Countess of Huntingdon's Connexion, rather Methodist and Revivalist in tone. It still has about two hundred members and is probably the richest church per head in the country.'

I wondered what a Socialist saw as valuable in the existence of an aristocracy. 'One good thing is essentially its probity. It's harder for you to disappear, abscond you know, if you have a title – and possessions. Old ladies trust a Board of Directors if there's a peer there. Despite all their faults – and there were certainly many in the past – it has always been invaluable to have a class you could rely on to administer justice fairly in remote parts of the Empire. They did it because they were bred to a code. But I think the class is dying out pretty quickly and the so-called aristocracy is very uncertain of its function now.'

But didn't the logic of his political views suggest renouncing his title? Maybe standing for the House of Commons? 'Oh no, the House of Lords is a very valuable chamber and underrated because people have wrong conceptions of it. You can't justify it on pure democratic principles, perhaps, but in practice it works remarkably well. I go down and speak regularly when foreign affairs or social matters, hospitals and so on, come up.'

'You know, the main danger these days is of the government of the day getting too much power. The trend is always towards it getting too much control of the House of Commons through the party machine. In the Lords, though, a lot of minority views get an airing. An odd thing to say, I know, but the House of Lords is one of the last bulwarks of democracy . . .'

Morning at Wilton

'If I went to a race-meeting and looked around a bit,' said the Earl of Pembroke, 'I suppose I shouldn't have much difficulty in recognising thirty or forty people who were my cousins . . .' I was talking to him about family connections, and had asked to what degree the nobility was aware of its kinship these days. Where a family has intermarried within the peerage a good deal, as much of the older nobility have, a network of blood relationships is built up which can come to be one of the most significant aspects of an elite. A number of the English peers whom I had met up to this point had been surprisingly vague (considering the cachet which outsiders suppose attaches to the idea of pedigree) about exactly whom they were related to.

Lord Pembroke was one of the exceptions. 'Yes, I'd say that my awareness of family connections is enormously wide. Necessarily so, because my great-great-grandmother was the old Duchess of Abercorn and had fifteen children. Then my grandmother was one of thirteen children. She was a Lambton, the Earl of Durham's family. So when she died, aged ninety-four, in 1906, she had two hundred descendants, and their children must have made it into a thousand by now.'

Were these kinships purely a matter of theory, a sort of invisible cousinage? 'No, not really. I keep track of most of them and see a lot of them. I could make a very long list if there were any point. Alec Douglas-Home's mother and my father are first cousins, for instance. The Duke of Buccleuch is a cousin. I try to tell my children about these family relationships because I find them interesting. But they tend to throw up their hands and say, "Oh, not again!"'

Lord Pembroke, a tallish, spare, country-suited figure, talked to me in his sitting-room at Wilton House, which has been the home of the Herbert family since the time of Henry VIII. It lies on the outskirts of the small and ancient borough of Wilton (or one might say that the borough lies on the outskirts of the House), which is just south of the vast chalk hump of Salisbury Plain. Here the country takes on the aspect of a slow, pale-green sea-swell, where broad and shallow valleys rise gently into wooded ridges and then slowly dip again.

Many fanciers agree that Wilton is one of the finest houses in England still left in private hands. It is sturdy, compact and elegant. Several generations of the family added new bits to it or took away old ones, the common habit with stately homes, but without in this case affecting the harmony of its main design, which was by Inigo Jones.

It carries a distinct air of continuity about it. Its fine rooms, in a decor of crimson, white and gold, are certainly opulent, but in a restrained way, as though their occupants could afford to keep some of their lordly importance in reserve. Its great central apartment, known as the 'Double Cube' room because of its dimensions, still richly equipped with several large Van Dyck canvases, is understandably reckoned to be one of the finest rooms in Europe. The Wilton picture collection contains 247 canvases with, besides the Van Dycks, some fine early Dutch, Flemish, Italian and French works.

As a whole, Wilton is a handsome setting for any family playing a part as a cultural focus, as the Herberts did in times past. John Donne, Edmund Spenser, and Ben Jonson were among the visitors here; Philip Sidney wrote his *Arcadia* in the garden; it appears to have been the scene of one first performance of a Shakespeare play; and in the eighteenth century it was a meeting place for the political luminaries of the time. In the last war, much of the planing for D-day took place in the Double Cube room when Wilton was a military headquarters.

Through the window there was a view of lawns stretching down to the little River Nadder, delicately spanned by a five-arch Palladian bridge. A pair of seagulls, driven far inland by stormy weather, settled sedately upon it.

What was it like, I asked, spending a childhood in a place like Wilton – was it mystifying, overpowering, or enchanting? 'It was nothing remarkable, oddly enough, simply because one grew up to accept it as normal. I vividly remember the fact that we had fifty-two gardeners, and they were mostly just shapes to me because they were always bent over weeding or something like that . . .'

Like virtually all other owners of Great Houses, the family keep in domestic use only a fraction of the total space – a sitting-room, dining-room, the library, and the bedrooms. Lady Pembroke runs this with a staff of five: butler, footman, cook, two house-maids – and some daily cleaners.

Lord Pembroke speaks of his forebears with a certain detachment. 'The first of our line, a Welshman, seems to have got into a scrap in Cardiff in the early sixteenth century and fought and killed a man. He hastened off to France but came back and made good, which was possible in those times if you were both lucky and aggressive.'

The family fortune was built up in these earliest years to a level that assured a high degree of durability. The Herberts impressed the early Tudors with their loyalty and soldiering ability and were given commanding positions in the Army and in the body that attempted to keep the peace on the Welsh borders. The first Earl was one of the leading noblemen of his time and married a sister of Henry VIII's last wife, Catherine Parr. It is recorded that he once rode to one of his castles led by a retinue of three hundred mounted men dressed in his livery.

The present and 16th Earl of Pembroke (who is also 13th Earl of Montgomery) is a direct descendant of the first one. He is Sidney Charles Herbert, aged sixty-one, has one son and one daughter; was educated at Eton and Oxford; has been a trustee of two national picture galleries; and lists as his recreations, shooting, fishing and racing. He has edited and published two volumes of eighteenth-century letters and diaries.

He has also been Lord Lieutenant of Wiltshire for fourteen years and is an alderman of the County Council. 'The Lord Lieutenant's job was originally to raise armed militia in time of trouble as local representative of the monarch,' said Lord Pembroke. 'That side of it these days only means doing a certain amount of work for the Territorial Army.'

'One of my main duties now is to preside over the advisory committee of magistrates, seeing that the courts operate efficiently and as the Lord Chancellor wants them to, and recommending the names of people one thinks would make good magistrates. And being a magistrate is not as popular a job as it once was, by the way. As for public duties generally, one has to pick and choose County functions. After all, one can't open or inspect everything and I think Pop stars are more of a draw these days, don't you?'

As a landowner, Lord Pembroke is still in the 'territorial magnate' class – relatively speaking, that is, in these times of reduced holdings. The Wilton estate runs to 16,000 acres and includes several valleys and tracts of woodland. It is about a quarter of the size it was at its peak fifty years ago. The value of agricultural land here has shot up in the last twenty years from £30 to £200 an acre. Sold for building development (that is, the small part of the estate which is near residential areas) it might fetch up to £1,000 an acre.

So, on paper at least, the land itself has a capital value of upwards of £3,500,000. 'But we sell only very reluctantly,' said Lord Pembroke. 'When the councils do need some for houses, we try to persuade them to buy the bits that will spoil the looks of the country least.'

Much of the estate still comprises the lands of the former Abbey at Wilton (the house is built on the site of it) which were given to the Herberts by Henry VIII after the Dissolution. 'We still have the deeds going back to the year 1100, and the interesting thing is that you often find the same yeomen families going on here for century after century. Some of those families, like the Combes, the Thatchers and the Swantons, must have been here just about as long as we have and we still have them as tenants. We try to keep the tradition going if we can by re-letting the farm to a son when the father gives up.'

'So the answer to your earlier question about why the aristocracy has lasted so well is simply that its local roots are so strong. I think that the German nobility have much the same attitude to their people, a responsible one, while the French aristocracy seem out of touch and the Spanish and the Italian never seemed to care much.'

I asked Lord Pembroke how far he thought these individual and local roots grew into some collective plant: how far they produced a titled fraternity with a common influence and outlook. 'Oh, there isn't really a club in that sense – except maybe at the House of Lords. Outside that I don't really see any stick-together business.'

Even the aristocracy's local attachments might be easier to understand – I suggested – if titles had any logic in their geography. People unversed in the devious ways of the system might well presume that an Earl of Pembroke and Montgomery must have land or influence in those counties. 'Oddly enough, I've never even *been* to either place,' Lord Pembroke said, and laughed. 'Anyway, the Welsh estates which were in Glamorgan and Monmouth were disposed of in the seventeenth century. We do get American visitors who make the same point about the title. We also had one who said, "I must be related to you, my name's Montgomery." I had to break the sad news to her that Montgomery is the name the family always gave to its illegitimate offspring.'

Ancient and Modern

Most peers usually claim, or so I found, that 'Nowadays, we're free to do just about anything' – meaning that the old taboos which kept them out of certain kinds of work have gone for good. But it is worth pointing out that while there may well be a theoretical freedom there has been no great rush to take advantage of it in some areas.

If one discounts the life peers, all created within the last ten years, then the ranks of the peerage show a relative absence of scientists, engineers, industrial technologists and members of similar professions which, in their primitive origins, depended on a knowledge of techniques and a use of the hands. What lingering inhibitions remain in this score exist most commonly among the sons of the older landed peerage and gentry. This gives a special interest to that small group of peers who effectively knit together some of these supposedly conflicting strands. They hail from a family of some lineage; they have inherited an ancient stake in the land; and they have also been successful in a technical area which landed gentlemen have formerly regarded as outside their experience, if not beyond the pale.

To find out how this combination worked in practice I went out to see the 6th Earl of Verulam, otherwise Sir John Grimston, Bt. He is managing director of the Delta Group, a combine of seventy companies which covers all kinds of manufactures in the non-ferrous metals field. He is also a landowner. Before he succeeded to the title in 1960 he was Conservative member of Parliament for St Albans. He is 55; was educated at Oundle and Oxford; and has one son and four daughters.

The big metal-rolling mills where he has his headquarters is out on the tattered industrial edge of north London. The straight concrete road leads out through a sprawl of housing estates where the workers live, past a muddle of factories designed in what I think Osbert Lancaster called the Transfusion, or Early Bloody style, and twists back over a level-crossing. And there ahead are the tall, dark chimneys of the mill and its expanse of black sheds.

At the factory security office by the main gates they were checking in a lorry-load of what looked like copper scrap metal. I said to one of the uniformed security men, 'Lord Verulam is expecting me'. He turned to a colleague and said, 'Charlie, gen'leman to see Mr Grimston'. An interesting point, I thought, if peers in industry found it helpful or more 'realistic' to shed their titles during the working day. 'Oh, yes,' said the second gateman when I asked about it, 'we always call him Mr Grimston. You'll find him a most approachable man.' He wrote me out a pass to go through the works. 'To see . . .' he wrote, and his pen hovered momentarily, '. . . Lord Verulam.'

On the top floor of the office block was the managing director's office. The strip on the door said 'Lord Verulam'. I crossed the wide room and greeted him with a cautious mumble. The protocol of titles, in local usages, is sometimes hard to grasp.

Lord Verulam, a tall, greying, dark-suited figure, who looked as though he had had a hard professional day, smiled slightly and resumed his seat behind the large, bare desk. His office was spacious but absolutely devoid of any photographs, pictures or the other visual distractions which most senior executives like to have about them during working hours.

Pale spring sunshine streamed in through the windows. There was a rhythmic clanking from the sheds below. The view was industrial, unlovely, and precisely the sort that an aristocracy was instinctively supposed to avoid. Even the leaves on the nearer trees of Epping Forest, its fringes visible a couple of hundred yards away, were plainly more sooty than green.

I asked Lord Verulam how he had found his way into heavy industry, since it wasn't commonly regarded as a natural ambition of the peerage. 'My father was somewhat ahead of his time. He was very anxious to keep our estate at Gorhambury (near St Albans) intact at a time when many of them were breaking up. He realised he could only do it with outside resources. So he trained as an engineer and eventually became an industrialist in a very big way.'

'I decided to follow the same line so I took an engineering degree at Oxford, then worked in a German company for a while before starting here.'

At their peak period the Verulam estates were very extensive, possibly 30,000 acres. The acreage owned is now 2,200 at Gorhambury and 3,000 in Norfolk. Together, they might be valued at around £1,250,000 as agricultural land. The family also owns two farms in Rhodesia.

The telephone on Lord Verulam's desk, the only object there, burbled slightly but the secretary was taking the call. Lord Verulam was evidently a bit sceptical about the more glamorous or irrational aspects of the peerage; and the spartan look of his decor seemed to me an attempt to remove any suspicion of frills from his surroundings. At the same time he clearly liked the idea of a family tradition. A highly qualified technocrat, he also apparently had a strong regard for the notion of a rooted family locality, as much as any prototype squire.

The family had come over about the time of the Conquest, he said, and a junior branch of it had settled in East Anglia. By the fifteenth century the family was prominent enough to produce a son who became the King's ambassador to the Court of Burgundy (his portrait is the oldest one known of any Englishman). Another ancestor, Sir Edward Grimston, captured by the French armies, escaped from prison in Calais in 1558 by filing out the window bars and lowering himself down his knotted bed-sheets – conceivably another 'first' for this now rather conventional form of getaway.

The family moved to Gorhambury in 1660. Harbottle Grimston was Speaker of the Restoration Parliament. He married a niece of Francis Bacon, who also lived at Gorhambury (the ruin of his house is still there) and had the title of Lord Verulam.

I asked how difficult it was to combine a major industrial job with running a big estate. Didn't the fact of moving out into the modern business world necessarily mean making a break with the landed tradition? 'Oh, not really. My agent looks after the day-to-day running of the farms and the tenants' side of things, but I naturally take a close interest and come in on all the important decisions. Keeping Gorhambury going well is my major interest in life. I get my main income from my work here but I put a large part of it back into the estate. Gorhambury could be self-

c

sustaining now but I want to go on improving it. After all, it's
been in the family for three hundred years.'

Did he find that he was expected to play any local role, beyond
the one of being a major landlord? 'Well, we have seven church
livings to fill, for instance. I think it's a very important job to
find the right vicar and we always take great trouble over it. It's
not all that difficult though. The main thing is to get it properly
organised . . .'

A Scottish Dukedom

A keen desire for space around them is one of the persistent
characteristics of the landed aristocracy. Up in the Scottish
Highlands this appetite is satisfied to excess. The land itself may be
worth only a few pounds an acre and will be populated as much
by sheep as by people. But, by way of compensation, the greater
estates generate a special, lordly atmosphere, the romance of
size.

They are empty-seeming kingdoms which roll on for mile
after mile, taking in heather-clad moorland, pristine woods or
new plantations, a river and a loch or two and, almost as a
reluctant afterthought, turning aside to embrace a craggy hill or
a quite useless stretch of tussocky peat bog.

Out in the wilder places the baronial castles frown down on a
scene that has little changed for generations. The big landlord's
difficulty here is not the one that occasionally occurs in the south,
of the urban sprawl pressing up to his gates and ruining the view.
Here the tide is receding. Places which were built on the confident
assumption that they would always have enough retainers and
servants to run the place and fill out their character now find that
most of the potential recruits have gone off to jobs in the city.
Even if they had stayed, the lord would probably claim that he
couldn't afford them anyway.

There was a time, around the seventeenth century, when a
Duke of Argyll could instantly summon up an armed force of
five thousand clansmen, such was his territorial influence. Nowadays, the Duke and Duchess are largely preoccupied with the

challenge of remoteness and absence of help. 'It's hard to find capable people on every level,' said the Duchess, 'and we're all overworked.' Thirty years ago there were sixteen maids and six manservants to look after the Argylls at Inverary Castle, which has eighty-four rooms. Now the Duchess runs the establishment herself with the assistance of a temporary butler, a cook, and a daily char. 'We've no chauffeur; we both drive ourselves to pare the expenses down to a minimum. I join in wherever I'm needed, and that's all the time – in the kitchen, helping keep up the gardens, selling tickets on the public opening days. No, we don't do much entertaining, we're neither of us very keen on the social whirl. We go to town very seldom. One aspect of the remoteness is that we run up a quite enormous phone bill just ordering groceries and so on ...' But the Duchess (who is American by birth) evidently likes the place.

Inverary Castle is a relatively domesticated, eighteenth-century structure in Gothic revival style whose most distinctive feature is its four pointed 'pepper-pot' towers which rise in a story-book way above the surrounding pine and birch woods. It stands at the head of Loch Fyne, a narrow and fiord-like tongue of sea which extends some fifty miles into the west coast from the Atlantic. In its hey-day, a few decades ago, some six hundred herring boats managed to prosper on the fishing of the Loch approaches. They have disappeared like the shoals. On this misty, autumn day only one small drifter puttered across the water, helping the scene to compose itself into an opalescent and vaguely romantic water-colour.

The Duke was in the library, putting in another session at the job of sorting out the Argyll family archives, which fill many chests. His predecessors have added to them, but never really looked at them. He broke off to tell me something about the estate, whose 96,000 acres ramble away into the wooded hills behind the Castle.

Ian Douglas Campbell is the 11th Duke of Argyll. He is sixty-four; was educated at a school in Massachusetts (his mother was American) and at Oxford; and until he succeeded to the title in 1949 spent much of his life abroad. He was a captain in the Argyll

and Sutherland Highlanders in the last war and had a lengthy
spell as a prisoner of war.

A lean, active, high-complexioned man, he was wearing cuffless corduroys, an off-the-peg worsted jacket and a tieless woollen
shirt, his invariable working-day outfit. He led the way to the study
through the pleasant, white-and-gold panelled state-rooms;
across a lofty hall on whose walls hung a glinting display of
muskets used by the Argyll militia at the time of the 1745 rebellion, pikes, halberds and shields.

Coming out of a door marked 'Private' we came upon a group
of the visiting public on tour. There was just a momentary twinge
of disbelief in the public's eyes as the Duke passed by, doubtless
registering a suspicion that he was not wearing properly ducal
regalia.

The estate was in a badly run-down condition when he took
over twenty years ago, the Duke said, and he had to raise £500,000
to pay death duties. Now they were getting near the end of the
struggle to get the estate in good financial shape again, clearing
woods, planting new timber (the main source of revenue), and
draining waterlogged land. 'No, I had no agricultural training.
I've had to learn it all by ear. But I'm a countryman at heart
and that helps.'

The home-farm part of the estate carries 120 cattle and 5,000
black-face sheep. The rest is let off to ten major tenant-farmers
and a large number of small crofters. The general running of the
estate is in the hands of the Duke's agent, a personage who in
Scotland is grandly known as the Chamberlain.

It is disappointing not to find him wearing cocked hat and
gold braid. Peers below the rank of duke in Scotland call their
land-agents 'factors' though they do precisely the same job as
chamberlains.

The Duke's domain also reaches out westward to the sea. He
owns the off-shore islands of Tiree, Iona and part of Mull. With
the Duchess, he was shortly due to embark on an inspection trip to
Iona. He knew most of the island's 250 inhabitants personally, he
said. He chiefly wanted to persuade them to keep the island a
little tidier. One of the Duke's hereditary, honorific titles is

'Admiral of the Western Coast and Isles'. But he is an admiral without a boat; so they would have to travel on the ordinary MacBrayne's passenger steamer.

The Campbells are traditionally supposed to have settled on this rugged part of the coast in the eleventh century and, by skill in aggrandisement, loyalty to the reigning Scottish monarchs, and carefully arranged marriages with influential families built themselves up to a powerful position. They gave their backing to Robert Bruce and after the battle of Bannockburn were given all the lands which had belonged to the Earl of Atholl. Holding a succession of court offices, they were earls by 1457, marquesses by 1610, and dukes by 1701. The many titles which the present Duke has inherited (virtually unused now, of course) indicate the steady march to fortune. He is Marquis of Lorne and Kintyre (the title used by his heir), Earl Campbell and Cowall, Viscount of Lochow and Glenisla . . . and several more.

The family history has generally mixed the military and the political. There was, for instance, Archibald the Grim, 7th Earl of Argyll, who was employed by the Crown to suppress disorder in the Western Highlands and was rewarded with land. Policing functions of this sort did not endear the Campbells to their neighbours. The eighteenth-century Dukes were soldiers of Field Marshal rank. The 9th Duke was a politician in Gladstone's cabinets and later Governor-General of Canada.

Other honorific titles have attached themselves along the line so that the Duke is also hereditary master of the Royal Household in Scotland, Keeper of the Great Seal of Scotland, hereditary keeper of the royal castles of Dunoon, Dunstaffnage, Tarbert and Carrick, and hereditary Sheriff of Argyllshire.

There is a fine drum-roll about them, but inevitably they offer neither pay nor duties to the holder any more. 'The Secretary of State has got the Great Seal. Being Sheriff means that if and when the Queen happens to visit Argyllshire I greet Her Majesty with a rose and a handful of snow taken from the top of Cruachan – that's the hill that gives its name to our war-cry. On the last visit we couldn't manage the snow, I'm afraid.'

The Duke is also Chief of the Clan Campbell, yet another position that in practice passes on down the family with the dukedom. Neither does this involve any special duties or ceremonies. But since far-flung Scotsmen have a persistent sentimental attachment to the clan idea it does mean that Campbells from the Dominions, the United States and elsewhere drop in from time to time to shake the Chief's hand and gaze for a while at the rough and romantic territory in which their forebears were raised and did their feuding. Clansmen are also great letter-writers and a good many requests arrive from overseas at this, the Campbell head-quarters, asking for help in clarifying someone's pedigree and so on. Clan lineage being the much-entangled vine that it is, with everybody related to everybody so to speak – the Duke himself inevitably being a cousin of some degree to Mr Campbell, the grocer down the road – it is hard to separate out some nicely precise idea of origin for the enquirer. But the Duke does his best to help.

I asked him how he saw his position in relation to the people of the district and the township (Inverary, population 1,000, is half-a-mile down the road). How much of a 'chief' element was there in this? The Duke gave the impression that, so far as it existed, it was a matter of great informality. 'I suppose I've been to the town less than three times in the last six months. One or two of them drop in for a chat about something now and again and, of course, I'm delighted to see them. I've got no time for council work myself but since I'm a big landowner here the councillors consult me a fair amount on what we can do on Highland development and encouraging local industries. They know I make an occasional trip to the House of Lords to talk on those subjects and they like to give me points I can raise. Yes, I suppose you could say I'm a useful go-between with London in that sense. But that's about the size of it . . .'

There was an interruption as one of the staff brought in one of the stately-home visitors who had asked to see the Duke, saying that he was an old acquaintance. He was a burly but immaculately turned-out Scotsman from London (apparently) wearing a superbly well-cut biscuit-coloured kilt set off with matching jacket, leather sporran and *skean dhu* stuck into the top of the sock

in the traditional manner. The contrast with the more relaxed
wear of the Chief of Clan Campbell was hard to ignore. The Duke
poured a large and hospitable single-malt whisky for the visitor
who, hugging one dark and hairy knee on the settle, prompted a
fitful conversation about Great Houses. When he took his leave
half-an-hour later the Duke frowned and said, 'Interesting man
. . . but I just cannot think where I've met him at all before . . . '

The Duke then told me the story of The Wreck. This is a saga
closely entwined in Argyll history. Looking for the gold has
become as hereditary a matter as the estate itself. It seems that a
Spanish ship called the *Florencia*, one of the Armada and supposedly
carrying treasure, blew up when at anchor in Tobermory Bay.
The 7th Earl of Argyll went to Spain and apparently discovered
that it had been carrying gold and silver worth around £2 million.
The 8th Earl claimed ownership of the wreck as a perquisite of the
Admiral of the Western Coast and Isles (the title has had its uses)
and was granted it by Charles I after paying the usual fee.

Some jealousy about the treasure, helped by court intrigue, is
said to have been part of the reason for the execution of the Earl in
the reign of Charles II. Undaunted, the 9th Earl rigged up a diving
bell and recovered some gold coins, a cannon with a design said to
be by Benvenuto Cellini, and other relics. The present Duke has
organised skin-diving expeditions in recent years and a few
objects have been recovered, though the wreck has evidently
drifted. He keeps up a correspondence with leading diving technologists, hoping to find some machine that will reliably locate it. He
thinks hopes are good, and the charts stay confidently spread out
on the library table.

The Duchess came in, and I asked her how people managed to
adjust themselves to a house with eighty-four rooms these days.
'It's not easy to find the right balance,' she said. 'We're fairly informal, spontaneous people but a house like this imposes standards
you can't reject. So we try to be comfortable and keep some slight
formality going like dressing for dinner and not allowing the
children to run around like campers . . .'

'In fact,' added the Duke, 'most of the rooms are in constant use
for one thing or another, and there's the practical point that unless

you keep some civilised attitude going – I mean let the Castle call
the tune to some extent – then things would become quite chaotic.
For instance, if you absent-mindedly put a book down just anywhere it simply disappears. You can spend eighteen months looking for it. Really, it's happened. The amount of time we spend just
looking for things is quite unbelievable . . .'

Just then an old friend of the Argylls arrived, an elderly but very
spry gentleman with a stick. He was warmly greeted. He apparently
shared his hosts' enthusiasm for gardens and had come up to see
how things were flourishing. The Guest quickly animated that
layer of amateur scholarship and private enthusiasms which lingers
just under the surface in many such noble households – an easy
readiness to dive into entertaining and informed conversations on
horticulture, country lore, regimental history, aspects of little-
visited places in Bengal, pewter, book collecting, ornithology.

Guest: 'There's been an invasion of Bluethroats at our place . . .'

Duke: 'Really, from Sweden . . . ? That's very unusual . . .'

Guest: 'Yes. What's the usual route?

Duke: 'Well, the white-spotted one would normally travel
down one of the Russian rivers to the Mediterranean . . . Have you
ever seen a Little Stint by the way? Lives in the tundra . . .'

Guest: 'Do they really? . . . (chortles) . . . what damn fools.'

The Duchess suggested an expedition to show their guest a new
plantation. He had already, it seemed, examined every plant in the
garden with the eye of a connoisseur and was not yet satiated. The
Duke led the way out through the state-rooms, past the pikes and
halberds, and the visiting public. 'So much for the Gainsboroughs
. . .' the powerfully-built Scotsman who was acting as guide was
saying, with a pleasant burr and strong arm extended upwards . . .
'and over the mirror, ladies and gentlemen, we have a well-known
painting by Richmond, called *The Dancing Females* . . .'

The Duke led the way in his estate car. The Duchess followed in
her car which is an ordinary but very chic-looking 1952 Mercedes
Benz which she used to have when she lived in Paris, with the
Argyll coat of arms now enamelled on its doors. By the time we
reached the plantation the Duke and his friend were deep among
the trees. The mist had now lifted and the high hill that commands

the end of the Loch, an old stone watch-tower on its summit, came into view through the coppery autumn leaves.

The Duke, with some pride, showed us a wider area of young birch which he had personally cleared. 'It was a devil of a tangle before.'

'Ian, where on earth's that *Abies Delavayi* you planted?' Not pausing for an answer, the Guest set off to track it down himself among the daunting wall of foliage ahead, to me an undifferentiated blur of evergreen. Murmurs of appreciation trickled back through the trees: '... jolly well, now that really is doing *jolly* well.' Another swoop through the undergrowth to the right, the flight of the quick and zestful humming-bird. 'And the *Nothofagus Obliqua* ... doing magnificently, quite magnificently ... !' The latter was a kind of South American beech, raised by the Duke from seeds procured from Chile. The tradition of aristocrats as garden-developers clearly lived on in this quarter.

At dinner that evening – the touch of self-disciplined formality that had been mentioned as desirable in castle life – the Duchess wore an ankle-length dress in the Campbell tartan which is in two shades of deep bluish-green, a stunning colour for a woman of fair complexion. The Duke wore Campbell tartan trews, a velvet dinner jacket in royal blue, and silver-buckled 'shoon'. The Guest, still twinkling a little from the spell in the woodlands, wore a highly personalised suit of well-cut grey flannel with wide-bottomed trousers and dark green decorative piping on seams and pockets. The Duchess was the first to identify it as Tyrolean.

Lord Colin (the Duke's younger, 21-year-old son), conservatively dinner-jacketed, acted as waiter between courses because the temporary butler (I think I have it right) was helping the temporary cook. This kind of thing, too, has become more or less traditional in some places.

Next morning, around eight o'clock, the visitor to Inverary finds that custom has one more card to play before departure. He awakes to the sound of bagpipes. Peering out, he finds a square and sturdy figure in blue serge working suit pacing slowly round the interior gallery of the castle, playing a Highland lament, a pleasantly quiet and poignant tune, for Reveille. The player is

c*

Ronnie, one of the gardeners, who used to be a pipe-major; and this style of awakening has been practised here since the eighteenth century, so far as anyone knows.

At nine o'clock, the weather-beaten face of Dolly (the elderly gamekeeper) appeared at the window of the emptying breakfast room. He had come to collect 'the young master' to go salmon-fishing. He stepped in with heavy delicacy in his wading boots and, while Lord Colin found him a cup of coffee, sorted through a tin of artificial baits. The Duke and his guest were already out on the lawns, heads bent low over the flower-beds.

Show Business

From the main gateway, the drive swoops down as straight as an arrow to the front door of Longleat House, a mile away across the Park. Most of the great houses like to hide themselves behind a screen of trees. This one holds itself out to plain view, but at a distance, so that the first glimpse looks like a small replica of the real thing – an Elizabethan miniature perfectly set in a bowl in the low Wiltshire hills.

Longleat's builder, Sir John Thynne – a very robust, tough, domineering character judging by his portrait – was one of those extraordinary dynastic founding-fathers who, though strictly amateurs at the architectural game, displayed apparently inexhaustible staying-power, passion, and judgment in seeing that they got a palace fit for the dynasty to live in, very often producing their own structural ideas off the cuff to embellish it. Sir John began the building shortly after completing a two-year prison sentence in the Tower, allegedly for trying to defraud the King. He imported a small army of stonemasons from Scotland to help – which can have been no mean feat of recruiting in Tudor times; and these incomers left such an indelible mark by their long stay that part of the nearby village is still known as 'Scotland' to the locals.

Sir John drove his builders on for twelve years. But in the end he got what he wanted, and that included the attractive flurry of turrets which crowns Longleat's upperworks, an idea which he conceived.

But most of the 230,000 paying visitors to Longleat each year do not come specifically to see the first classical house of the English Renaissance. They come to see the lions. It was near feeding-time as we arrived and a throaty roar came from the direction of the old stable-block. By the look of him, Sir John would have accepted these newcomers manfully.

The lions have now become a well-known part of the special attractions with which Sir John's descendant, the 6th Marquess of Bath, Sir Henry Frederick Thynne, Bt, hopes to bring in enough revenue to keep this ancestral home in existence. A good many other stately home owners, saddled with costly running problems, have admitted the paying public, but remain uncertain whether a gentleman should really launch his house like a three-ring circus. A small new breed of showmen-peers, scorning the inhibitions of their fellows, aim to do more or less just that.

In a way it is yet another by-blow of the glorious aristocratic Amateur Tradition. They can rule; can build great houses; can run Empires; and now they can beat Barnum and Bailey at their own game too. That eighteenth-century nobility which threw up the architectural follies would have much liked the idea of a menagerie in the grounds. Indeed, a few had them, along with negro footmen and other touches of overseas merchant-venturing glamour. The only difference is that then it was for fun. Now it's business, though Lord Bath seems to get a little of each out of it.

A tall, lean, sporting-looking figure, he was sitting in his public relations man's office, a small compartment off Longleat's hammer-beamed Great Hall, surrounded by piles of Longleat jig-saw puzzles, pots of Longleat honey, brochures, pottery, model lions. He was wearing tweed jacket, old cords, and his habitual red, white-spotted handkerchief, hung like a flamboyant ensign out of the top pocket. In the hall, just outside the door, stood the yellow, horse-drawn coach (shafts empty now, of course) in which he drove to the Coronation, to the consternation of the police, while more timid and conformist peers crept there anonymously by taxi.

'Do you know,' he said, 'we had a visitor get out of his car the other day and walk right up to a lion to take its photograph.

Wouldn't you think that people knew about lions by now?' The animals, forty of them, are kept in 92 acres of enclosed woodland during the season, surrounded by a high double-fence. Visitors pay £1 to drive through. Lord Bath said that all the takings had to be put back into the house and grounds to keep them going. 'We took £31,000 last year but most of that went on roads. Now we've got to find £80,000 to beat the death-watch beetle in the house. It costs us £1,000 a week to house and feed the lions. They eat half a bullock's head a day each.'

Lord Bath is in partnership with Jimmy Chipperfield, one of the circus family. They were toying with the idea of adding chimpanzees, maybe a hippopotamus or two to their collection.

Lord Bath, now sixty-two, made over the 10,000 acre estate nine years ago to his son and heir, Viscount Weymouth, who lives in part of Longleat. This is to take advantage of the rule that if the estate is transferred five years before death no duty is payable. The need to raise funds to pay duties in the past has already reduced the estate from the 52,000 acres it was in his father's time to its present size. He obviously finds it a wrench to have had to give up the job of managing the estate and the income from it so early. He now occupies a seven-bedroom mill-house down the road from Longleat and, he says, he has to live on his capital. All he has retained at Longleat is the house itself and the 700-acre park surrounding it; and they are self-sustaining without showing any profit.

'I believe he started life as somebody's cook, didn't he?' says Lord Bath of an early Tudor ancestor, with a glance that flickers out towards the stern portraits of the past, as though challenging them to deny this mischievous rumour. His P.R. man broke in with a query about ordering Longleat book-matches. Personally geared to buying them one at a time, I got the impression from Lord Bath's reply that he was ready to go in for them in a really prodigious way: Longleat sunk up to the turrets in book matches, this gallant Tudor vessel foundering in a sea of souvenirs . . . But I fancy he was being playfully challenging again. In conversation, he doesn't go out of his way to impress his attachment to the house on anyone, or the fact that he knows a great deal about its history.

While there may have been an element of the hot stove, or rather the turning spit in the origins, the allusion to the 'cook' seems to have been a wry gloss on the fact that the builder of Longleat was the son of Henry VIII's Clerk of the Kitchen, a position which cannot have been quite so lowly in such trencherman times. Originally a family of Poitevin adventurers who had come over to help King John fight the barons, the Thynnes' rise to fortune in the Tudor period was remarkably rapid. Like the many families of peers and gentry whose present well-landed position is traceable to having done well in that era, the Thynnes' good luck was in having an ancestor as shrewd and aggressive as Sir John functioning at a time when the dismemberment of the monastic estates was offering an attractive sort of Klondyke to the speculator. Sir John picked up some land bargains; and he and his son consolidated the position by marrying the heiress daughters of wealthy Lord Mayors of London.

After this the family history was not particularly eventful: perhaps it could afford not to be. One of the few incidents that stand out are the assassination in Pall Mall of a seventeenth-century descendant, Thomas Thynne – known as 'Tom of Ten Thousand' because of his great wealth – by the hirelings of a certain Count Königsmark. Tom had secured the hand of yet another great heiress; and the Count was the disappointed suitor. The 1st Marquess appears to have been a fairly typical eighteenth-century figure. He held a number of Court offices and, in 1765, was made Lord Lieutenant of Ireland. Because of its unpopularity with the natives, he did not take up the appointment, though he had the presence of mind to draw the salary of £16,000. He was a keen wine-bibber and gambler, and satirists listed Burgundy as one of his recreations. Outside that, county concerns seem to have largely occupied the family.

Lord Bath talked about how things had changed since his father's time. 'I can easily remember when we had forty servants in the House. We used to have eight gamekeepers, too, and now they're down to one. My father would have been quite shocked at the people who go huntin', shootin', and fishing these days. Taking part in his exclusive sports indeed! Quite shocked.'

'Most younger sons get jobs in the City these days. You know, my father wouldn't have let me touch that sort of thing with a barge-pole. Most *infra dig*, you know. It was never quite the done thing actually to *talk* about money. He respected it deeply so long as it was in big enough quantities. But never the thing to *talk* about it. When he went into his bank I remember he used to doff his hat as a mark of his deep respect for the institution. When he wrote to them it was always, "Gentlemen . . ." and, for rounding off, "Your Obedient Servant, Bath".'

'Politics? Well, I was in the House of Commons for a spell in the thirties. But on the whole the Thynnes have kept out of it. I expect that's why we're still here. There's not much else I've really time for after we've finished with the house and the lions and so on. Father used to have twelve church livings to fill. Quite a job. I've given them all away. No one's ever satified with the chap you've chosen for vicar and, anyway, it would be quite ridiculous for an out-and-out atheist like me to do the choosing, wouldn't it? . . . Now we'd better go and see how things are down at the zoo . . .'

Grand Old Family

'Before he succeeded to the title' – the Duke of Newcastle said to me – 'my father used to go and gaze at the old family residence. It was a huge, sprawling place up in Nottinghamshire called Clumber Park, with fifty-six bedrooms. It's all demolished now. Well, he used to go and look at it and come away feeling most apprehensive about getting the house and the title. Yes, I think part of the reason was financial. Places like that can cost a devil of a lot to keep up. But it was also the feeling that it was all going to be too grand and meaningless to him as a person, more burdensome than anything. He didn't like the ducal set-up at all, and I suppose I've acquired some of my sceptical attitudes from him . . .'

When I met him at his present house in Somerset, the Duke helped to crystallise for me one rather ironic and inequitable fact about the titled system: that while there are a good many people with a keen desire to become a peer, equally there are many peers whose main inner ambition is to be people. It might be instructive to have a meeting and an exchange of views between the two groups.

The more individualistic peers I had met had already described to me how the possession of a title could have its difficult aspects. A lord, particularly if he was of older stock or grander degree, seemed required to carry a kind of shadow-image around with him – an idea of what he ought to be like, projected by the past, the collective public mind, or both. The psychology of it could be insidiously confusing – or so I had been told – unless the shop-window ideal was kept at arm's length and quite separate from one's own personality. I was sceptical; but could see there might be something in it.

If it was true, then the Duke of Newcastle was one of the personalities who had managed the job of separation with apparently total success. A stocky, tweed-suited figure, he met me at the entrance of his handsome country mansion, called Shocker-wick Park, near Bath. There was the setting of any comfortable, tradition-minded, landed gentleman; but there was also the im-pression of one who had learnt to do a good many things outside the conventions of the class, of one who might well be happier doing a first-class repair job on a tractor rather than getting dressed up for a ceremonial levée. There was a very capable look about him.

Henry Edward Hugh Pelham-Clinton-Hope is the 9th Duke of Newcastle. He is sixty; was educated at Eton and Cambridge; has held the title for twenty-six years; is married, with two daughters.

I asked him what personal changes had resulted from succeeding to the title. 'Well, I was a happy and quite anonymous young man until – in April of one year it was – my father succeeded to the dukedom. This meant that I automatically acquired a courtesy title as his heir so I became the Earl of Lincoln. I believe a former Earl of Lincoln appears now and again in the Robin Hood legend. Well, within a month or two I appeared to have very suddenly shed my anonymity. I was astonished to find I was getting masses of invitations to parties and London season dances from old ducks I had never met or even heard of. Strange, don't you think?'

'I joined the Royal Air Force as a regular in 1936. I did my best

to keep the snob element out of my relationships, but a handle to
your name can certainly be a handicap. People find it hard to
accept that you have any skills at all. There's a constant assumption
that you're just a title with nothing behind it, and I must say that
some of the peerage encourage this attitude. Take an example.
During the war I went with a brass-hat on a trip far out into the
desert. I was standing there surrounded by miles of emptiness when
another flying officer rolled up in a Jeep, right out of the blue. He
introduced himself, saying "I'm Lord So-and-So. How very odd
for two peers to meet in a spot like this . . ." I was quite staggered
that the matter of titles should occur to him out there.'

The Newcastles have, in their time, been among the grandest
and most affluent families in the peerage. 'Are not the great families
of Clinton, Holles, Pelham, Cavendish, Gresham, and Harley, the
confluent streams that unite to form this illustrious line?' asked,
rhetorically (and with caustic undertone) one nineteenth-century
critic of the old nobility,[1] setting out to demonstrate the fairly
self-evident fact that there had been nothing saintly in the way the
powerful families had fought their way to the top. Working his
way through the peerage list, demolishing pretensions to virtue,
this critic took a deep breath when he reached the Newcastles,
taken aback by the sheer size of their prestige, affronted by their
success in the sixteenth century rush for monastic lands. They had
an earldom by 1572. Over the centuries the family went through
a wide range of the profitable state and household offices: Lord
High Admiral, Governor of the Tower, Lord of the Bedchamber,
Master of the Horse, Cofferer of the Household, Comptroller of
the Customs for London, Lord Warden of the Stanneries . . .

A modern historian has described how they flourished:

'In 1711 young Thomas Pelham-Holles, aged eighteen, succeeded his relative the Duke of Newcastle in estates . . . and
became the possessor of thousands of acres in a dozen counties of
England, enjoying a rent-roll of more than £30,000 a year
[£360,000 in modern money]. At twenty-one he was made
Viscount and Earl and Lord Lieutenant for two counties, a year

[1] Howard Evans, *Our Old Nobility*, London, 1879.

later Marquess and Duke, two years later Lord Chamberlain and Privy Councillor, and a year after that Knight of the Garter and so forth. He could personally influence the election of a dozen members of Parliament. Nottinghamshire and Sussex knew him as their master. The great houses that he built or adorned ... these were the necessary symbols of his territorial greatness. Like the gold plate that loaded his table and the hordes of servants that attended him on every journey, they were necessities of his social status. Vast palaces, extravagant living, profusion in every act of life were compulsive in a world that equated wealth with power.'[1]

The younger sons of the family mostly went into the Army. One became governor of New York. The Newcastles had great estates, roughly 40,000 acres all told, including 5,000 acres of Sherwood Forest, until the 1930s. Then the need to pay two lots of death duties within twelve years at a time of agricultural depression reduced it to a fraction of its former size.

It was already a remarkable story of rise and fall, but it did not end there. In 1947, leaving the remainder of the estate in the hands of trustees, the present Duke went out to farm in Rhodesia. He did well enough to be able to rebuild the English estate on his return twelve years later to its present 9,000 acres. This sort of restoration of a landed position to some semblance of lordly size is extremely rare. Once an estate has slipped, the means to win it back, possibly the energy too, are seldom there. All the new land is in the West Country, a long way from Sherwood Forest and the estates which had family associations.

This means that there is no local sentiment or tradition present now which might automatically cast him in the role of 'squire' – not even some vague modern version of the part. In this sense his position is unlike that of those other landed lords who still derive some sense of *noblesse oblige* and a paternalist outlook from long family rootedness in one spot.

Comparing him with them – at least the ones I had met – it is possible to sense the personality difference which this produces. In

[1] J. H. Plumb, *Men and Places*, London, 1963.

a subtle way, he is more free to be 'himself' and dispense with the shadow-image of the landed nobleman.

But old feudal duties do have a curious way of continuing their existence under the surface, waiting to draw the modern-minded peer back into his connections with the past. At the time of the coronation of George VI it was recollected by some delver into the archives that the lords of the manor of Worksop had always had the duty of providing the gauntlet for the monarch's right hand. The Duke does not know how this custom originated. At the time, the manor was still part of the Newcastle estate. So, deputising for his father, the Earl of Lincoln responded to the ancient summons. Wearing pilot officer's uniform, he supported the King's gauntleted hand as required in the procession up the Abbey aisle.

I asked the Duke whether he had tried to keep up the Newcastle interest in politics. 'No, I've never even bothered to claim my seat in the House of Lords. I think it should be an advisory body with really qualified people in it, each of them reasonably expert in some line or other. I don't think someone like me should just clutter up the place . . .'

As I was leaving I noticed the pictures for the first time. On the sitting-room wall were two full-length portraits by Peter Lely of Charles II and Nell Gwynn. 'It's nice to have the old family pictures around,' said the Duke.

4

ON GETTING A TITLE . . .

It's lovely to be a Lord . . . Lord Boothby

It feels so funny not being a Countess . . .
Lady Douglas-Home, (after her husband had renounced his earldom)

The voracity for these things [titles] quite surprises me. I wonder people don't begin to feel the distinction of an unadorned name . . . Sir Robert Peel, *c.* 1830

Being an aristocrat is a state of mind, and it bears repeating that possessing a title is not necessarily a vital part of it. It has always been most helpful, however, and nowadays it may be the only thing that distinguishes a lord from the commoners around him.

A title has normally functioned in two ways. It has often done no more than confirm that a person is so rich, eminent or politically influential that he is an aristocrat already in all but name. Or it can act as an honorific hoist, lifting a man from his ordinary class level to the altitude of the elite plateau or near it, in one quick movement. This hoisting motion is now much the commonest of the two: the title itself has to do most of the work. It is an important first step, as all aspirants recognise, because it lifts a man into that area of illusion, tradition and public imagery which converts him from the ordinary into the special. To define his altitude, one might say that he is now in the class which is above the struggle for status. As an institution the peerage wears an aura, so that it appears somewhat larger and more luminous than the quantity and quality of the human material which composes it. Examination of this aura from the outside shows that it is riddled with openings for disbelief, if the observer really wants to regard it objectively. Yet it has been proved time and again over the centuries, as it still is, that some of the country's most rational and hard-headed men have only to get within sight of it and their compass needles become fixed. They are suddenly ready to take the irrationalisms on trust; and this is the very mainstay of the elite framework.

For example, the monarch is the Fount of Honour who is presumed to bestow all titles. A new peerage is awarded, as it has been for the last five centuries, by royal Letters Patent. This is an illuminated scroll in which the recipient is addressed in cousinly terms by his Sovereign. The royal seal, which is a lump of sealing wax about the size of a saucer, is attached. The tubular red leather case in which each peer keeps this document has a circular bulge part of the way along it to contain the seal so that it looks like a curious musical instrument. Though the constitutional fiction is maintained that the peer has been personally picked out by the monarch, titles have effectively been the gift of the Prime Minister of the time, as part of his political patronage system, since about 1700. It would be an unthinkable breach of custom and protocol for the Queen to ennoble anyone she wanted to, and virtually out of the question for Her Majesty to so much as mention a candidate's name, except in the case of close relatives who get titles by tradition.

Her grandfather, King George v, found that he had no pull even in the case of a mere knighthood. When he once asked for an inventor of flying boats to be made a 'Sir', the Prime Minister's secretary replied that there were inventors with prior claims for one. The King rather plaintively replied: 'As I so seldom ask for a knighthood, I really think that I might be treated anyhow with some consideration occasionally.'[1]

The candidate is always sounded beforehand about whether he will accept the honour which the Prime Minister 'has it in mind' to recommend to the Queen. In a fraction of one per cent of cases it is declined. It is much rarer for the strictly private and confidential news of the refusal not to leak out; and the one who has declined

[1] Harold Nicolson, *King George V* (Constable, 1952).

thereafter wears his non-title with as much quietly inverted panache as actual recipients wear their honour. This variation must be unique for any tribal honours system. It has seldom been the case that the refuser feels unworthy. More often he feels that he has won such distinction as a commoner – as Sir Winston Churchill could legitimately do, for instance – that he hesitates to disguise himself with a dukedom or earldom. He feels, in Peel's phrase, the 'distinction of an unadorned name'. If he already has a title he can renounce it, but only on condition that he does so for his heirs as well. Since the Act of 1963 which permitted this, eight peers have renounced.[1] Some give them up; but others fight tooth and nail for them. In the courts from time to time there have been cases in which people have been ready to go to the great expense of litigation to establish the family's rights to an old title. There is now virtually never any land or money to be gained by it; it is simply the honour they want.

The reasons for recommending a title are mixed. Now, more especially with life peers, it is a way of promoting a public or intellectual figure to the muted glories of the House of Lords; or of kicking upstairs some time-expired member of the House of Commons whose very seniority there is blocking the way of new talent. There need be – as Melbourne once said of the Order of the Garter – 'no damned merit in it'. The Honours Committee which sifts the names for the Prime Minister works on mysterious lines and it is rare for any newly-ennobled Lord to step forward and admit that he helped to swing the choice in his favour.[2]

The part played by money has become a relatively slight and

---

[1] The stiff opposition in the House of Lords to allowing peers to give up their titles was a rare example of group solidarity. Lord Stansgate (now Mr Wedgwood-Benn) had to fight every inch of the way.

[2] A shining exception to all the false modesty was Lord Thomson of Fleet (formerly Mr Roy Thomson), the newspaper owner. With a fine Canadian candour he told a television interviewer (David Frost) something about it. Asked how he had set about letting people know he wanted a peerage he replied, 'Well, look, when I want something, everybody knows about it!' Pressed for more detail, Lord Thomson said, 'Well, this is very, very embarrassing, but I talked to the people that mattered.' Frost: 'And they said, "OK Roy, anything you say?" ' Lord Thomson: 'Well, they didn't just put it that way. I had to talk several times. I had to use very convincing arguments. And I had a few . . .' (David Frost show, Associated Rediffusion, 25 January 1967).

obscure one. Contributions to party funds and charity must have helped a good many candidates. But direct purchase has been taboo since the Maundy Gregory scandal of the nineteen-twenties. Lloyd George created 91 new lords between 1917 and 1923. Parliamentary enquiries revealed that a number of these had been blatantly sold to people of little merit and sometimes of dubious business backgrounds. Gregory, the son of a Southampton vicar, and a minor theatrical figure, set himself up in a Whitehall office where he acted as middleman between those who wanted titles and the managers of Liberal Party funds. It is said that he charged at least £10,000 for a knighthood, £35,000 for a hereditary baronetcy, and about three times as much for a barony, taking a commission on the deal himself. Gregory was eventually gaoled for honours touting. His biographer thinks some form of traffic in honours must have continued until about 1931 but not thereafter.[1]

Perhaps the only fault with these title bargain-sales was the old crime of being found out; and the fact that Lloyd George's nominations were too cynical even for an arbitrary system. Otherwise the protests were a shade self-righteous, historically speaking. It was not until the reign of Victoria that elevation to the peerage became associated with some idea of personal merit and moral fibre. Before this they had commonly been granted to men of all sorts of character either for money or for service to King or state. Under the Stuarts the sale of peerages and other honours had been an accepted source of income for the King and his favourites. James I, assisted by his right-hand man, the Duke of Buckingham, sold the earldoms of Warwick, Northampton and Devonshire, and the baronies of Teynham and Houghton for £10,000 each.

The number of creations of peerages tended to come in waves, depending on political expediency, the monarch's need for cash or security, and so on. In the reign of the first Elizabeth there were never more than seventy Lords. The early Stuarts doubled it. Charles II went a little wild with dukedoms to reward mistresses and natural sons. The really big expansion came towards the end of the eighteenth century with Pitt and his successors, in a gust of creations. But it is worth noting that in 1789, the year of the

---

[1] Gerald Macmillan, *Honours for Sale*, (Richards Press, 1954).

French Revolution, the French aristocracy was reckoned to consist of about 100,000 noblemen, a closed caste which was enjoying such privileges as tax exemption. The English peerage, which restricted inheritance of the title to eldest sons (and not, as the French, to all the family) numbered some 300 at that time, certainly an enormously wealthy group but with no legal privileges that marked them off as a caste. The peerage went on growing in numbers as the new men of industry got their titles – the masters of coal and iron, the brewers (known as the 'beerage' – brewers and titles have always had a strong affinity for each other), the tycoons of textiles and shipping. Between 1916 and 1945 some 280 new peerages were created, the great majority of them representing business interests.

As the new peer surveys his colleagues in the House of Lords (even there he will never see more than a minority of them all at once) what sort of conclusions can he draw about the unique and relatively exclusive group he has joined? First, it is essentially a fairly recent peerage – that is, a light-to-medium wine and not the ancient and crusted port it is sometimes imagined to be. The titles of more than half the peers have been created since 1906 and only one-fifth date back before 1800.

The pecking-order of the peerage – duke, marquess, earl, viscount, baron, in descending order – has lost a good deal of its significance due to the changes made by time and fortune since they were created. When one has some barons many times wealthier and more publicly important than some dukes then the order of precedence can look distinctly arbitrary. The senior ranks naturally get very few brand-new recruits these days. The last non-royal duke was made in 1899 and there are unlikely to be any more new ones unless the royal family keeps up the tradition of having them awarded to close relatives. The twenty-six non-royal dukes include some of the biggest landowners and moneyed men. Perhaps half could be described as millionaires in terms of capital assets or income. At the other end of the scale there is one duke who has described how he gambled away his patrimony in his early twenties and has had something of a financial struggle since.

The present twenty-nine marquesses (not 'marquis', which is the French version) are almost certain never to see a new recruit. Most were created in a short burst between 1780 and 1837; the last was made in 1934. Like the dukes they are a mixed group; but my impression – and no more than that – is that they are a specially sophisticated lot, often given to sharp touches of individuality; several could be transported back to the Regency period and feel perfectly at ease there.

Earls – 159 of them – possess the oldest title. It dates back to the Saxon *jarl*, a chieftain who had the supervision of a large tract of territory. Most earls with titles of any age have cousin-links with the royal family, and older ones have no doubts about possessing a special prestige within the peerage ('Earls are better than dukes,' said one Scots earl to me, in a way that was both casual and confident). Those earls who are not proud and venerable often seem to be at the other extreme: young and jaunty, with a foothold in the more racy professions, photography and so on. An earldom is the title traditionally offered to a retiring Prime Minister.

Viscounts, numbering 110, are mostly politicians, retired and elevated from the House of Commons. There have been thirty created since 1944. Most of all they suffer from the cloak of anonymity which a title casts upon a man who was once reasonably well known.

The barons, totalling 535, naturally contain the biggest admixture of the new industrial and business peers. But there are also a number of very old titles among them. The oldest barony is held by a woman, the 26th Baroness de Ros, a title created in 1264. She is one of the nineteen peeresses who hold a title in their own right and not merely because they are married to a lord. Some titles can only be inherited in the direct male line, that is passed on to a son. Others can be passed on to the next closest male relative. A small number of older titles can be inherited by the next in line of either sex. Between 1950 and 1965 a total of 102 peerages became extinct because there was no heir; the number of new creations just about balanced it. Unless Parliament suddenly were to abolish the hereditary principle, which is unlikely, then the peerage clearly has several centuries of life left in it, even if the rate of creation falls off.

The other hereditary group in the honours list are the baronets who are not, of course, members of the House of Lords – 'a baronet is one who has ceased to be a gentleman but not become a nobleman' is an old definition. There are now 1,480 of them. The original members of the order were well-off country gentlemen whom James I enrolled for a fee of about £1,000 to help to pay for the troops in Ulster, and later to finance the settlement of Nova Scotia. There were so few takers at that price that he had to reduce it and enlarge the numbers. It has always been prone to muddles of succession and false claims (a baronetage book of the 1880s has a thick appendix dealing with these, simply headed 'Chaos').

In trying to describe the character of the aristocracy one has to take account of two different viewpoints – the inside and the outside one. What most of the public see is simply an undifferentiated group in which all lords are simply lords. The popular view is probably that all members of the nobility, save for a handful of eccentrics, are immensely rich, live in stately homes, do not need to work and, at home, that the lord and his wife dine each night (as Hollywood has always affirmed) among a glittering dinner party of at least fifty people; or, if alone, that they take opposite ends of a very long table so that conversation is impossible and even sighting difficult.[1]

As a portrait it is, needless to say, seriously over-simplified. But the view of noblemen themselves tends to go to the other extreme. Not one whom I met saw himself as belonging to any cohesive group or sub-group of the aristocracy. 'No, we don't hang together if that's what you mean,' was a typical reply; or 'Put us

[1] Such is the power of Hollywood myth-making that the remoteness-at-table image had also stuck in my mind. I am glad to confirm that on only one mealtime occasion at a noble house – seated in the middle of the long leg or touch-line stretch of the table – was a Wimbledon movement of the neck required to talk to host and hostess at the same time. Most tables are adjusted to a fairly intimate size. However close the places, one rule always observed is the upper-class custom that each must have its own salt and pepper containers. I mention this small point only because such an odd amount of upper-class superstition seems directed against the communal, middle-class cruet. It is one of the most distinct frontier-posts between the classes.

down as individuals who happen to have a handle to their names' or even 'There are at least two lords in the county I haven't once met!'

No one likes to be thought of simply as one of a clique and peers naturally insist on their individuality. It is true that their community-spirit as lords is very slight. The activities of the House of Lords have offered evidence enough that concerted political action on any matter is not easy to arrange. However, the outsider can see categories which peers are not always aware of themselves. The main dividing line is between those who are major landowners (about one-third of the total, I estimate) and those who are landless, and engaged in business or the professions. The importance of this is that land-ownership on the lordly scale breeds an outlook which is more attached to tradition and the 'aristocratic' values. It is clearly different from that of the peer who is working in an advertising agency.

The group has been described – Mr J. B. Priestley's phrase, I think – as 'a plutocracy disguised as an aristocracy'. Like most descriptions applied to the nobility as a whole this is almost, but not quite, true. The first point – which may be no objection at all – is that it has *always* been largely a disguised plutocracy, at least since about the sixteenth century when the search for titled respectability, as a way of 'disinfecting' wealth, developed its enduring pattern. If, by 'plutocracy', one means possessors of business fortunes made in the last century or so – which is about the minimum period required for the disinfecting process to be really convincing – then this might embrace about forty per cent of the peerage, but not much more. It does not take account of the landowners and the couple of hundred peers who are in the salary-earning professions. It is true that wealth has become more important as a hallmark of aristocracy as other attributes, like pedigree and political influence have fallen into abeyance. There are a good many peers whose financial situation is neither better nor worse than that of the professional classes. There are also more rich men outside the peerage than there are in it. But Mr Priestley is right in implying that there is quite enough wealth within the peerage to give it a materialist reality as a class elite. It has recently been estimated that about half the private wealth in Britain is owned by two per cent of the population. If land is included, then I would estimate that at least two-thirds of the titled nobility would come within this two per cent.

The differences between English, Scots and Irish peers are rather a matter of temperament and tradition. The Scottish Lords are important because of their more sophisticated awareness of noble status and their unashamed pride in it. If those few English peers who secretly hanker to be commoners ever came out into the open in significant numbers there would always be their claymore-swinging cousins from across the Border to tell them to straighten up their coronets and behave like lords. It all makes for continuity. The special characteristics of the Irish peerage, if any, are elusive. 'Eccentricity,' suggested one (English) peer; but I hardly think it is fair and it is, anyway, statistically unprovable.

In religion it is a highly conformist group. There are no figures on the subject, but it is likely that ninety per cent of the English peerage are adherents of the Church of England, mostly of a Low persuasion. The number of Nonconformists must be very small. Historically, the nobility has never liked the levelling doctrines of the Nonconformists and it has been usual for a Methodist family which has acquired a title or otherwise risen in the world to join the Church of England fairly speedily. It is an important part of the apparatus of becoming a gentleman. There are eighteen Jewish peers: a small group, but including men eminent in banking and business and, in Lord Rothschild, one of the peerage's few distinguished scientists. Intermarriage with Jewesses has been fairly common for aristocratic heiress-hunters in past times. The attachment is so close that it can hardly be seen as a separate group.

The Roman Catholics, numbering sixty-five in the peerage, besides some of the more eminent of the landed gentry, are more distinct. Like the Scotsmen, they have more pride in lineage, a greater awareness of cousin relationships, are more attuned to the traditional idea of aristocracy than the English peerage as a whole. In addition, the older families take a special pride in having held to the faith, despite the great tribulations that this meant. Until emancipation came in the nineteenth century they could not take up any of the accepted professions like the Army or the law; they had to go abroad to university. Lord Clifford, who was *aide* to Lord Raglan in the Crimean War and won the V.C., was one of the first Catholics to get an army commission. One or two of the Catholic country houses still have private chapels which have been in use for centuries (like the one described by Evelyn Waugh in *Brideshead Revisited*). The Catholic gentry includes some of the oldest-established families, like the Scropes, Stricklands, Tichbornes, Fitzherberts, Blundells, Sykes and Welds. It is also interesting that the influence or example of the Big House has been instrumental in keeping the religion of the neighbouring village predominantly Catholic up to the present day. This is the case at Tichborne, Hampshire, at Lulworth, Dorset, and in one or two places in Yorkshire. Like their Anglican colleagues, the Catholic peers take a fairly cool and sober attitude to their religion, with a typically English suspicion of pomp and ostentation. One peer is a monk: Lord Vaux of Harrowden is the first nobleman of this vocation to sit in the House of Lords since the sixteenth century.

These groupings – which are, of course, hardly noticeable in day-to-day affairs – help to create the internal patterns of the peerage. While it is true that lords are individuals, there are also a number of factors which serve to give the peerage some identity as a group. An important one is their common membership of the House of Lords. Then there are such things as educational background, regimental experience, family connections and heredity, clubs, the degree of selectivity in marriage, all of which give an appearance of conformity to some sections of the aristocracy, though in some areas, of course, their experience is shared by the upper class generally. But first, mention should be made of the College of Arms, which acts as a sort of regulator or whipper-in of the peerage, adviser on titles, creator of heraldic devices and other such arcane matters.

Hark, the Heralds

The College of Arms is part of the royal household though it is housed in its own seventeenth-century building in London. It is supervised by the Earl Marshal, the Duke of Norfolk, and is run by thirteen heraldic officers of quaint and colourful names. The three Kings of Arms are Garter, the senior officer, Norroy and Clarenceux. Then there are six Heralds: Richmond Herald, Chester Herald, and those of York, Lancaster, Somerset and Windsor. Below these are the four pursuivants or junior officers: Bluemantle, Rouge Dragon, Rouge Croix, and Portcullis.

For those unused to medievalry in modern life, it should be emphasised that these are real people who work a fairly ordinary office day. They dress up in their resplendent uniforms only on special occasions. Their salaries, fixed centuries ago, are a pittance and amount to little more than £300 between them; but they earn very sound professional incomes for private heraldic work, tracing pedigrees and suchlike. Each officer does a week of duty at a time; one might say that he is rather in the position of the officer-of-the-watch on a ship. His own personal banner is hoisted on the flagstaff outside the College so that the curious passer-by can know instantly whether it is Bluemantle or Rouge Dragon or some other officer who has command of the armorial destiny of the nation at that moment, and make his plans accordingly.

The duty officer takes all the business that comes in during his week, whether it is an American millionaire who wants his ancestors traced, or some aspiring gentleman who wants a coat of arms devised for himself. A fee will be charged for the service; in the case of a laborious search for a family pedigree it could be a hefty one. The senior officers take a share of the fee.

When a person is raised to the peerage one of his first appointments will be with Garter King of Arms who will help him decide on a title. This can require some intricate thinking and negotiation. Mr Smith may simply want to become Lord Smith so that the public may still remember roughly who he is and was. But it may be judicious not to have too many Lord Smiths. Then he will need a territorial attachment to his title to preserve the fiction – it is seldom real nowadays – that he is a man of landed estate. Lord Smith of Birmingham, say, if he is getting an earldom and has important ties with the city; or simply a village name will do if he is a baron. Heraldic tact is occasionally called for. One new lord wanted to be called after a famous medieval warrior-nobleman. The College thought this might be seen as a shade presumptuous in those districts where the warrior had heroic associations. The new man was asked at which barracks he did his army training. He revealed it; the name rang musically on the heraldic ear; he now bears that title. Either out of desperation or ingenuity, in at least one case a place-name has been invented out of the blue. Lord Douglas of Kirtleside is a highly-esteemed peer; but Kirtleside cannot be found on the map.

All hereditary peers have coats of arms, the sign of nobility or gentlemanly rank in the pure sense of the word. A new peer is encouraged to take up arms and the College will work out a coat for him, with ringing family motto, for the appropriate fee. He can certainly decline if he likes; but in that case he should be ready to endure the rather deprecating glint in the heraldic eye. The Heralds expect lords to live up to some of the pomp of the position occasionally. In the gentlemanly discipline they engender, and their strict regard for all the formalities, the Heralds help to keep the peerage away from too much backsliding into being merely titled commoners; and they are thus an important element in preserving what differences it still retains.

When the Heralds really want to impress, they can blossom in the most exotically medieval way. There is still a Court of Chivalry, which is part of the Earl Marshal's curious domain; it has proper legal jurisdiction in all matters of heraldry, the use of coats of arms, and so on. It last met in 1954 after a gap of 219 years. One is almost surprised that anyone remembered it was still there. It was a magnificent sight, enough to make the heart of any heraldic philanderer quail. There was the Lord Chief Justice in scarlet robe; Sir Bernard Marmaduke Fitzalan-Howard, Duke of Norfolk and Earl Marshal, in his splendid uniform and plumed hat; and, flanking the judge, six Officers of Arms in their scarlet tunics and gold-striped blue trousers, swords at their sides. The cause at issue was a complaint by Manchester Corporation that one of the city's theatres, the Manchester Palace of Varieties, had been improperly using the corporation's coat of arms on its drop-

curtain and on contract seals. The Court ordered the theatre to
stop doing so.

In theory, it seems that the Earl Marshal could cast offenders
against the armorial rules into the dungeons. This is unlikely and,
in any case, the Marshal is one of the least ferocious of lords. His
officers are only too ready to offer that combination of rule-book
precision and flight-of-fancy which seem necessary for the production of a proper coat of arms for the new-made gentleman or
peer, especially those who are short of an eventful family history.
Applications arrive in such numbers that you might almost suppose that jousting tourneys were still going on somewhere. In
Scotland, more coats of arms have been granted since 1930 than
in the 300 years before it. The armorial hunger, a phenomenon
noted in Tudor times, has not yet abated.

Pedigree, Heredity, Marriage

The important thing with pedigree is not so much in having it
but in knowing it. Everyone naturally has a lineage reaching
back into the distant past. But relatively few know its details
because, of course, their families have not had their heads far
enough above the crowd to leave any easily-discoverable trace in
public records. There is currently a keen appetite for having
family pedigrees traced, but to find a line that goes back more
than a few generations is still uncommon. The 20,000 families
whose pedigrees are appearing in the current three-volume
edition of *Burke's Landed Gentry* is a figure which gives an idea
of the number of people with knowledge of a family history, and
relatively few of these are of any great age.

Pedigree is no longer one of the essential attributes of the
peerage, taking it as a whole. The twenty per cent of peers whose
titles were created before 1800 will naturally have some lineage.
Most of them possess records which trace the family back one or
several centuries to the times when they were gentry or yeomen,
before they acquired the title.[1] A small number of those ennobled

---

[1] A number of titled families are traceable to late medieval times, but it is extremely
rare to find an ancestry, either in Scotland or England, that can be confidently traced

in the later nineteenth century and after have been of a gentry background with a known history. Still, the proportion of lords who can look back, say, six or seven generations, is smaller than one would expect.[1]

The fact that there has been no strict theory of preserving 'blue blood' – a perverse biological idea, anyway, like Aryanism – in the British nobility has meant frequent marriage outside the aristocratic circle. It is true that partners have not often been sought far outside the gentry or upper merchant class. But the fact that younger sons and the daughters of the peerage have covered a fairly wide range in the marriage field does mean that British genealogy, over the centuries, shows a frequent intertwining of great and humble family trees. The cousins of even the most venerable noble families are not only very numerous but, if traced far enough, show people in the lower walks of life. This certainly does not mean that the lord himself knows who all these relatives are, far less that they are often seen taking tea with him. But a few of the older peers and gentry who are keen on lineage claim to know personally at least a hundred cousins.

There was a time when this cousinage connection between the great families was highly important, especially in a political sense. The eighteenth-century Whig oligarchy were well on the way to becoming a closed social caste by keeping their marriages within the group. When Lord John Russell formed his first government (1846) his opponents alleged that it was mainly composed of his

---

before the twelfth century. One of the oldest pedigrees is that of Lord St Davids (Jestyn Reginald Austen Plantaganet Philipps) who descends through an illegitimate line of Henry VIII. The family has written records dating back to 1050; and there is a gavelkind or oral ancestry reaching back through the Dark Ages to the year AD 50. Lord St Davids can recite these twenty-two early generations of his family in an impressively bardic manner.

[1] Whether or not they have ancestry, some hereditary peers who are trying hard to fit into the professions find talk of pedigree almost an embarrassment. Similarly, to some extent, with titles. It made me wonder whether a peer of the more radical sort could go through life so pointedly ignoring his special status that he was hardly *aware* even of having a title. It seems not. This is revealed by one of the family jokes which seem common to a number of families, telling how the lord was mistaken for a commoner. One version told to me by a very commoner-minded earl goes like this: Lord X, tinkering with his car, is wearing overalls. Visiting tradesman says, 'What's 'is lordship like . . . must be crazy living in a place like this.' Lord X: 'Afraid I can't say. It's *me*.' Tradesman: 'Cor, I thought you was the blinking chauffeur.' Always produces hysteria when related at the noble family table.

cousins. From John, Earl Gower (d. 1754) were said to be descended 'all the Levesons, Gowers, Howards, Cavendishes, Grosvenors, Russells, and Harcourts who walk upon the face of the earth'.[1] There was a brief revival of the charge of 'cousin-politics' in one of Mr Harold Macmillan's administrations. There was indeed a rare opportunity to tell family stories round the Cabinet table in those years; but some ambiguous apologists suggested that the family connection was purely incidental to the fact that they were all Etonians. Nowadays, according to the peers I met, the awareness of the cousin connection is usually tenuous. Certainly the old custom by which hordes of relatives used to encamp free of charge on the stately home is now severely discouraged.

The old idea of 'breeding' as a kind of aristocratic birthright producing a superior quality of person is also a dubious one considering the mixed nature of most lineages and the fact that too narrow a field of marriage selection – as one can see in any primitive village – has a debilitating effect. Over the centuries offspring of royalty and nobility have spread far and wide. It was estimated by 1911 that the number of Edward III's descendants then living might total 80–100,000 persons. If offspring of illegitimate lines of the medieval kings is included (Henry 1 is reckoned to have begotten nineteen bastards) then the branches would stretch much wider. Nineteen settlers who were in New England before 1650 apparently had well-established descents from Edward 1. It is recorded that the Duke of Norfolk in 1783 decided to invite all the living descendants of the first Duke (killed at Bosworth in 1485) to an enormous party. When he had traced no fewer than 6,000, he abandoned the idea. To come to more recent times – a survey made in 1957 managed to trace 1,908 people in Britain who were the legitimate offspring of royalty, dukes or duchesses.[2] Conversely, Queen Elizabeth the Queen Mother is fifth in descent from a plumber's daughter.[3]

The custom of lords finding their marriage partners within the

[1] G. W. E. Russell, *Collections and Recollections*, London, 1898.
[2] *Population Studies*, London School of Economics, July 1957.
[3] Sir Anthony Wagner, *English Genealogy*, London, 1960.

D

titled nobility has gradually declined. In the eighteenth century about a quarter married the daughters of peers; now it is about seventeen per cent.[1] Among the older aristocratic families and the senior ranks it is still remarkably high, however. Of the twenty-six non-royal dukes, fifteen married noble wives; of the twenty-nine marquesses, eight married peers' daughters. The percentage also underestimates the limitations of the marriage field. The present Duke of Northumberland is related by marriage to a quarter of the dukes. Peerage marriages over the past century would still show a criss-crossing network of connections between the hereditary families or branches of them, and other links with the prominent landed gentry families. The majority of people in Britain marry their tenth cousins, or somewhere near it. Within the nobility the majority would probably be found within the range up to fifth cousin.

The reason which has persuaded lords past and present to look outside the aristocratic circle for a partner has often been money. The cash was not only attractive in its own right, and as a way of enlarging status, whatever the state of the noble bank-balance. It was sometimes the only way of staying solvent. The Lord Monson who succeeded in 1841, for example, was constantly urging his son to find an heiress whose money would rescue the family. He kept up a lively correspondence with a sister who was also scanning the scene on his behalf for the glint of a marriage chance. Lord Monson once wrote to his son: 'She [the boy's aunt] says Miss Clara Thornhill who is about just coming out promised to be a very nice girl and has £9,000 a year – that would do eh! – there are two younger daughters of £40,000 each, not bad but the first is the large prize. I should be very sorry for you to marry for money,' he adds ambiguously, 'but a nice wife with it would not be bad.' Three days later, after reproving the lad for missing a chance with another heiress, he returned to the matter of Miss Thornhill. 'I understated it . . . Miss T. has £15,000 a year.'[2]

These over-ambitious heiress marriages were often the undoing

---

[1] The figure is twelve per cent if one counts marriages to daughters of British peers alone, but seventeen per cent if one also takes in those to foreign noblewomen.
[2] Quoted F. M. L. Thompson, op. cit.

of an aristocratic family. Since the heiress possessed the family fortune it meant that there were no sons, and she was commonly the only daughter – both implying a stock of low fertility. The aristocrat got his heiress and her money; but she was not a good child-producer and his line tended to die out. Oddly enough, this fact seems not to have dawned upon the heiress-hunters though there were many examples of it which they must have known about. Possibly they knew it was a gamble, and took it. Warwick the Kingmaker built up his great fortune and power by an heiress marriage; but it seems that his line failed through infertility. A nineteenth-century geneticist, Sir Francis Galton, was perhaps the first to point out the risk involved and to show that, within a hundred years, heiress marriages had been responsible for bringing to an end the lines of four Prime Ministers – Walpole, Grenville, Rockingham and Canning.

This question of marriage and heredity is one of the most interesting aspects of an elite because it is so nicely charged with irony, the vanity of human wishes. To some degree the elite man prefers to marry the elite woman. But if he does it too consistently the line becomes etiolated. Biology does not like too rigid a regard for the class system. It is possible that this is demonstrated by one of the most celebrated of aristocratic families, the Cecils. After the famous statesmen of Elizabethan and Jacobean times, no particularly important or talented offspring were produced until, in the nineteenth century, a Cecil married a middle-class girl, Frances Gascoyne, and produced stock among which (eventually) figured a Prime Minister, a general, a bishop, a minister, a member of Parliament, and another who won a peerage in his own right.

This reaching out towards the commoners seems to have come in phases though it is hard to find any special reason for it. One was towards the end of the nineteenth century (perhaps it was connected with the English agricultural depression) when American heiresses became popular marriage partners. But, again for no particular reason that one can see (the naughty' nineties?) this was a time when actresses – presumably not notably rich – were sought as brides. Between 1884 and 1914 nineteen actresses were married by lords. In the earlier years it seems to have been a last fling, a case of stage-door desperation, by peers of a certain age. But gradually they became first marriages by younger men after the older codgers and pioneers had hoisted the flag of respectability over such unions. Lords have always tended to marry late in life – to a remarkable degree compared with the rest of the population. An analysis of noble marriages between 1550 and 1949 shows that husbands' ages ranged between 28 and 34 over the period, and wives' ages between 22 and 28.[1] Since 1800 the peerage has also had a higher proportion of non-marriage than the rest of the population. It is hard to say whether this results from inhibitions produced by a genteel upbringing, barriers of class consciousness, and so on. They are possible explanations. Especially at some periods, the aristocrats have been no slouches when it came to womanising; but, considering the equipment available, their contraceptive precautions seem to have been fairly effective. It was only the occasional peer who had an illegitimate family of any size. The first Lord Ferrers (1650–1717) was one. He had thirty bastards to add to his twenty-seven legitimate children.

How far does heredity go towards creating an aristocracy? The peers I met uniformly thought that it was a negligible quantity – the reverse, in fact, of the attitudes of the medieval nobility for whom considerations of 'blood' were important. The lords, even those of older family, made a point of saying that it was all to do with environment; that the miner's son (this seems to be a favourite example in their minds), given a stately home up-bringing from childhood, with Eton to follow, would emerge as a person indistinguishable from any member of the patrician upper crust. An interesting view; but I wondered how much it sprang from the present compulsive modesty of the nobility.

I asked Professor C. D. Darlington about it. He is Sherardian Professor of Botany at Oxford University and a leading authority on human genetics. He found the 'miner's son' theory more amusing than I had expected. He thought there was a degree of humbug in the claim and suggested that some of the more celebrated families – he named a few – would deny such an idea with their last breath. It is important to note that the point at

[1] T. H. Hollingsworth, *Demography of the British Peerage*, London School of Economics, 1964.

issue is not whether the child of working-class birth would be
'better' or 'worse' given a patrician environment, but whether he
would be reared to the same outlook as an aristocrat. The professor certainly did not think so. 'All sorts of things like moral
fibre, amenability to certain situations, are deeply inbred. These
stay the same even if you put a child in a different environment at
cradle age.' He mentioned the evidence of adoption societies who
recognise and avoid such a thing as 'overplacing' – that is, that a
child of lower-class parentage, though it may be adopted when a few
months old, does not adjust well to an upper class environment.

Professor Darlington said he did not think there had been
excessive inbreeding among the peerage, considering that the ones
who had married a title had still had a fairly wide group to choose
from. But it did occur strongly in certain lines. The trouble was,
he thought, that there was little natural selection: whatever the
vitality of the individual in the hereditary peerage he inherited a
place at the top, and it tended to make the group static in its ideas.
'The pattern is that as soon as a rising family reaches a certain
eminence it hesitates to marry beneath itself and it gets genetically
stuck, with no recharging of the batteries.' He thought that the
concentration on 'socially well-regarded Englishness' as a desirable
quality in a marriage partner had reduced the vitality of the elite.
They had, for instance, studiously avoided much contact with
rejuvenating immigrant groups and those non-conformists who
had helped to get the Industrial Revolution moving.

Another distinctive thing about the aristocracy and marriage is
its high divorce rate. The increase has been phenomenal since
1900. Roughly one-third of all dukes, marquesses and earls have
been married more than once; the rate for viscounts and barons
is about twenty-four per cent and twenty per cent respectively.
By contrast, the rate for life peers is about three per cent. One
can only hazard guesses at the reasons for it. It is certainly puzzling
considering that the life of the English nobleman – compared to
that of any Hollywood denizen – is outwardly a bedrock of
placid stability. Can it mean that the 'gentleman' is not quite as
firmly integrated as his manners pretend? The possession of money,
since marriage break-ups can be costly, may have something to do

with it; even more that aristocrats have few inhibitions about
'what the neighbours will think', a point which deters the middle
classes from divorce as well as from a number of other actions
they would like to take.

The Old School

*We are often told that they taught us nothing at Eton. It may be so, but
I think they taught it very well*—Lord Plumer's speechday address, 1919.

Whatever the part played by heredity in producing the aristocrat,
family background and education are clearly of high importance.
For 'education' one can fairly substitute Eton pure and simple,
since its links with the aristocracy outshine those of all other
public schools put together. Two-thirds of the dukes and an
average of fifty-five per cent of the other ranks of the peerage
were educated there. About half its 1,200 pupils in any year are
from families who possess coats of arms. But it is not – an important point in sizing up the nature of the elite – essentially a school
for the sons of the merely rich. According to one analysis,[1] only
one-seventh of Etonians' parents have the primary distinction of
being rich and only one in fifty is a self-made rich man without
inherited prestige of some sort. It is an expensive education,
costing £3,720 over five years; but not so much so that it cannot
be afforded by gentry who see themselves as of moderate means.
Etonian parents do not live in the main centres of population. A
county like Rutland, which many English people have never
even heard of, produces as many Etonians as all of populous
Lancashire.

So some feeling of separateness is present in the Etonian even
before he starts, and the nature of the school encourages this
without the slightest apparent effort (to *try* to make it different
from other schools would be quite ruinous to the school's conception of itself and to the gentlemen it produces, whose outlook
must essentially be *effortless*). It was founded by Henry VI. The
royal patronage encouraged aristocratic interest from the start

[1] R. Hall, 'Family background of Etonians', in *Studies in British Politics*, ed. R. Rose,
London, 1963.

and it became *their* school largely by force of habit and tradition. It has kept its differences. It has its own teaching method (the individual tutorial system), its own special clubs, its own kind of football game, its own terminology (e.g. a roll-call called 'Absence'), loyally preserved for one generation after another with a positive schoolboy relish for affectation and curious jargon. But it is fundamentally the Etonians themselves who set the aristocratic – in the broadest sense of the word – tone of the place. There are always quite enough of them with an assured future to remove all the stress of competition and to lend an atmosphere in which self-assurance, the special Etonian characteristic, can be cultivated. Etonians are generally bright but not necessarily the cleverest schoolboys around. But their self-confidence, whatever else lies behind it, gives them an especially winning way in politics and to a quite unreal degree. In the House of Commons of 1960 there were seventy old Etonians, about a tenth of the membership and one-fifth of the Tory party strength. The gentlemanly virtues are taken for granted, especially patriotism. In the First World War, of the 5,687 Etonians who served, about twenty per cent were killed, twenty-five per cent wounded, and 1,292 won either the D.S.O. or M.C. Thirteen won the Victoria Cross.

Eton offers a first-class education but in choosing it so consistently as a school it is another way in which the aristocrats indicate their desire to stick together. When they go up to university their instinct takes them most frequently to the traditionalist Oxford rather than to the more liberal, science-minded Cambridge; and at the former place aristocrats prefer Christ Church far more than any other college. (Until about 1860 titled undergraduates wore mortar-boards with gold tassels and were excused the need for taking degree examinations. This was surely a remarkable example of elite-superstition in a supposed centre of scholarly objectivity. It thus reaffirmed the tribal principle that *gentlemen do not compete*). It might be argued that this pattern in education is a matter of family habit rather than of conscious discrimination. So it possibly is. But that is the stuff that elites are made of, the thing that keeps their pulse alive.

PART TWO

5

ARISTOCRACY AND THE MONARCHY

'We're only a small country and it makes us a bit special having royalty.' So said a young shop-assistant in a recent public-opinion poll on attitudes to the monarchy.[1] The survey suggested that the great majority of people liked it because of the colour and ceremony it brought to life. It gave a glamorous form to the idea of being British. No fewer than thirty per cent of those asked thought that the Queen had been 'especially chosen by God'.

Beneath the complex of attitudes revealed the most common theme is the feeling that 'it makes us a bit special' – that the monarchy is a rather grand and venerable stage-prop which lends status and prestige to the nation, one which graciously distracts the eye from the rockiness of the national budget at any particular time, and from the ups and downs of Britain's political standing in world eyes. One sometimes wondered whether sceptical foreigners suspected that we were cheating a little by keeping this royal trump-card in our hand.

It is doubtful whether many people think of the aristocracy as God-given. But the close ceremonial association of the nobility with the Queen, their sharing of the hereditary principle, does mean that the lords are regarded with some of that mixture of curiosity and mystification – altogether as hard to grasp as a flickering light – which the British have come to project on to their monarch.

Those European countries which retain a monarchy have renounced honours lists; while those which still have an aristocratic nexus have abolished the Throne. Only Britain has both

[1] Quoted in Leonard M. Harris, *Long to Reign Over Us?* London, 1966.

in quite such a pronounced form. Its most important effect, as critics have often pointed out, is to perpetuate the idea of a hierarchical class structure. A social elite can still draw strength from its supposed association with royalty, however close or distant it is in fact.

Without a sovereign, the Fount of Honour from which the peerage springs, a titled aristocracy would be pointless, as are the Continental nobilities. For better or worse, the Queen would probably be a less mystical figurehead without supporting lords. They seem to encourage reverence by their numbers, their ability to look reasonably grand in coronets and ermine, and their seeming remoteness from the adulatory middle classes. The fact that the monarch rises above even such notables as dukes and earls also affirms his or her status in the popular view.

Lords can be seen as supporting players or, as the first Elizabeth put it to Sir Philip Sidney, they are planets who reveal the brightness of the sun. In Tudor times this satellite system was clear and true enough, when the majesty of the throne was based on a political reality. It is much more shadowy now that the monarchy consists of a network of constitutional fictions.

As the real power of the Crown has waned, so has the element of symbolic drama and solemn make-believe become the most prominent part of its function. The Queen is required to go through motions of rulership which once meant something practical – councils, consultations, signing of decrees – which nowadays do no more than give visible shape to an abstract idea. And she cannot reflect any more *real* power (as distinct from the mystic kind) upon the aristocracy than she possesses herself.

The Queen could not conceivably obstruct a Bill which had passed through both Houses of Parliament. The last time a monarch refused assent was in the reign of Anne, 250 years ago. Her Majesty's seal and signature on a statute, required before it becomes law, are necessarily automatic; though her assent is still announced to Parliament in the old Norman-French, 'La Reine le veult' – 'The Queen so wishes it'. The Queen's participation is used to confer a sense of national approval, as well as weight and solemnity, on the transactions of ordinary men.

'The use of the Queen, in a dignified capacity,' wrote Walter Bagehot, 'is incalculable.'[1] There is rather more scepticism and free-thinking about the place of a monarchy these days than there was in the age of Victoria, but there is still a good deal of truth in this. It all depends on how the monarchy is used.

Bagehot went on to suggest that monarchy was a strong government because it was the most intelligible to the people. Their imaginations were too weak to take in the complex machinery of the real government; but they could understand a single ruler on a throne, particularly if there was the background of a family behind her. 'Royalty will be strong because it appeals to diffused feeling, and Republics weak because they appeal to the understanding.'

Granted that the electorate is a rather more sophisticated and better-educated one than in Victoria's time – and even she had only tough *attitudes* to her ministers rather than any semblance of real power – this would nowadays be a weak and lazy way of justifying the monarchy. There are perhaps better ways of doing so.

Bagehot's theory would also now be misleading. The Queen reigns and occupies the throne; but obviously does not rule. If democracy is to have any active meaning then it would be a pity if that 'diffused feeling' for the single figurehead aroused confusion about the different functions of the Queen and the elected government. It may well be that something of this sort exists already and – a major part of my point – that some of this confusion is developed into the popular view of the aristocracy. In a recent public opinion poll in Britain, seventy-five per cent of those asked indicated that they still regarded the Queen as a figure of some power, in the political and governing sense, that is.

The symbolist nature of the constitution makes it easy for some confusions to arise. It still likes to display itself on the public stage in terms which, to the innocent eye, are the reverse of the truth. No wonder the foreign visitors go away puzzled.

The Queen is the Fount of Honour and bestows the new peerages as well as all other decorations. But it would be an un-

[1] Walter Bagehot, *The English Constitution*, London, 1867.

thinkable breach of custom for her to suggest who should have one. This list comes from the Prime Minister. Even in the unlikely event of the monarch objecting to a candidate for a peerage it is clear that this need not weigh decisively with a Prime Minister who felt inclined to be firm. When George v quite understandably . objected to ennobling some of the doubtful characters who had paid Lloyd George (his party's funds, that is) large sums for the honour, the latter confidently ignored the protest until the scandal had spread too far to sweep under the carpet.

The monarch has the right to dissolve Parliament. In practice this is only done at the request of the government. Almost the only occasion when the sovereign is required to exercise a personal judgment is in choosing a Prime Minister. Usually this simply means a straight acceptance of the advice of the majority political party about whom they want as leader. Difficulty arises when, as has happened more than once in the last few decades, there is a split of opinion within the party. If one faction claims to have an edge over the other then it is extremely hard for a monarch who must stay out of political controversy to resist the pressure for this or that candidate. And by 'pressure' one need only mean a show of confidence by mature politicians, a claim to speak for the party as a whole. It is thought conceivable that something of this sort happened when Lord Home was chosen to succeed Mr Macmillan in 1963. According to the pro-Home group, party soundings disclosed that he had more support than the other front-runner, Mr Butler. The Queen was invited to send for Home and within a few hours, to the chagrin of the Butler group, which claimed growing support, he was Prime Minister. The facts of the incident are still not clear. But it looks as though, by a 'gentlemanly' desire to spare the Queen involvement in a troublesome choice, her role can be exploited in a purely incidental way. On these occasions, the difference between the *symbolic* presentation of the power of the Crown and its *real* weakness in any controversial matter is well illustrated. The figurehead may be 'intelligible to the people' in Bagehot's words; but it should not be allowed to obscure the truth of the political in-fighting.

The symbolism, of course, also takes the aristocracy into a

close embrace. Almost the only occasion in the normal year when the Queen has the company of any number of her noblemen (with the possible exception of one of the smarter race meetings) is at the annual opening of Parliament.

This is a piece of formal constitutional theatre whose curiosity – at least for beginners – is that the role of the Lords and the Commons are inverted. The virtually powerless nobility are placed in the seats of honour; the all-powerful Cabinet and House of Commons are allotted, and accept, an apparently humble walking-on part. This helps to disguise the fact (one of the subtleties at the heart of the constitution) that at the critical point in the proceedings the Commoners will turn out to have written the script of the show.

Witnessing it for the first time, one is reminded of those children's fables in which we know all along that the shabby beggar is really the strong prince in disguise; while he in the shining regalia is the one who shall be made low. It is charged with that dramatic irony from which the British constitution continually draws its nourishment, its sense of balance and ancient compromises, and its power to bemuse outsiders. When the Queen arrives at the entrance to the House of Lords she is met by the Great Officers of State, splendidly garbed. Leading them are the Earl Marshal (the Duke of Norfolk) and the Marquess of Cholmondeley (who is Lord Great Chamberlain, the Queen's chief representative at Westminster).

The Queen enters the Chamber of the House in the magnificent Robe of State, which is an ermine cape with an eighteen-foot train whose weight is supported by two small Pages-of-honour. On her head is the bejewelled and sparkling Imperial State Crown. She is accompanied by her Kings of Arms, Heralds and Equerries (the Heralds would not like it to be thought that they are the sort who play long trumpets; they are scholars of heraldry) and these gilded figures help to fill out the medieval look of the panoply.

The peers stand bareheaded (coronets are only worn at coronations) on either hand, splendidly robed in scarlet. Those who do not own their own set of robes have hired them at six guineas for the day from the well-known tailors in Covent Garden.

When the Queen has taken the throne and the lords are seated the official called Black Rod goes off to summon the Commons. In a couple of minutes, the members of the Cabinet and the Opposition Front Bench are filing in wearing nothing more grand than their best suits. There is room for about fifty of them to stand at the Bar of the House, which is a small enclosure at its lower end. Some of the keener back-benchers of all parties press in behind them.

There is something deeply and sentimentally touching about the scene: it is an irony played out in deadly earnest. It has the look of a special schoolboys' outing to see a pageant. Nothing could more effectively render the idea – if that is what the constitution requires – that there is something mystical above the democratic process which is transmitted, in symbolic form, by the seated figures: the neutrality of the Crown, some notion of a traditional wisdom passed on by the tribal elders, the power of ancestry and custom.

Then comes the climactic moment of the drama. The Lord Chancellor, Head of the Judiciary, looking grandly baronial in his black and gold robes, steps forward with an embroidered cloth purse in his hand. From it, he draws the Speech, ascends the steps to the throne, and hands it to the Queen for her to read to the Parliaments. It has been prepared, of course, by the Cabinet office. It declares the policy which Her Majesty's Government proposes to carry out in the coming session and, in this somewhat inaptly feudal setting, it may well announce Socialist measures for nationalising steel, increasing taxes on the rich (the baron in the back row cups an anxious ear), for legitimising abortion, or some other radical measure. One emerges rather impressed with the devious poetry of the British version of government, as was intended.

The Queen descends to her coach for her journey back to the Palace. The lords disperse to their homes by car and taxi or, not impossibly, on the bus. Most of them are unlikely to be in Her Majesty's presence for another year; and this fact fairly represents the separation which has developed over the last few reigns between the nature of the monarchy and that of the aristocracy.

Logically regarded, the Queen should be the premier aristocrat. She and her predecessors have created the nobility. They are closely linked in the constitution. They share the magic and the pitfalls of an ancient hereditary system – continuity based on the luck of the draw. These and some other aspects of the royal establishment and its way of life do have a patrician flavour, the things one might expect to find in the head of an elite. The Queen has the status of great personal wealth and possessions. Her private fortune has been estimated at rather more than £50 millions. It includes the world's finest art collection in private hands (some of its items have passed down through the monarchy since Henry VIII's time) and a valuable assemblage of jewellery, stamps, and racehorses.

The Crown is the second largest landowner in the country. It owns 285,000 acres of Britain, including a good deal of lucrative property in the best parts of London. The income from this and from the quainter sources of royal revenue – like the sale of sturgeon caught off the coast (rather few), excise money from beer and wine, and treasure trove, is in practice handed over to the national Exchequer.

This amounts to some £2½ millions a year, and is supposed to offset almost exactly the cost of maintaining the royal establishment and the allowances paid by the government to its leading members. These allowances are: £475,000 to the Queen; £70,000 to the Queen Mother; £40,000 to the Duke of Edinburgh; £35,000 to the Duke of Gloucester; and £15,000 to Princess Margaret. In addition the government pays for such things as the Queen's private yacht, *Britannia*, and her flight of Heron aircraft. Critics of the monarchy as an institution challenge the idea that it pays for itself, suggesting that the so-called Crown lands and their income must belong to the nation anyway. That apart, the monarchy is rich on a level that would be warmly recognised as undoubtedly aristocratic by any of the greater noblemen of past times.

The Queen has the use of four residences. Besides Buckingham Palace (six hundred rooms: the largest private house in the country) and Windsor Castle, which is frequently used as a weekend retreat, the Queen personally owns Balmoral and Sandring-ham. Balmoral is a Victorian-baronial pile set in empty Scots moorland, and the Queen and her family regularly occupy it for two months of every year.

Sandringham is a large, brick, Victorian country house in Norfolk. It has a ballroom and a bowling alley; it is not known whether these will survive through the present reconstruction work. Its estate of 7,000 acres, set in a picturesque part of the county, has fine gardens, a deer park, and woods well stocked with game. Nowadays it comes into the news as a rule only in the shooting season when the Duke of Edinburgh with a party of friends is blasting off at the seasonable bird life.

The royal pastimes are the traditionally aristocratic ones. The Queen is keenly interested in anything to do with horses. She likes riding herself, is a well-informed spectator at show-jumping events, and she and her party occupy the royal box at big racing occasions like Derby day, Ascot and Goodwood, when several of the Queen's horses are often running. The Duke of Edinburgh finds horse-racing boring but prefers the even more distinctly elite-sport, polo.

Despite this background, the royal family tries to achieve a certain degree of flexibility in its image, seen in the context of the class structure. The Palace is said to attach much weight to this as one aspect of its role as a unifying symbol. A fair measure of success is achieved. A telling part of the evidence for this is that, to the aristocracy itself, particularly the more sophisticated section of it, the monarchy is quite plainly middle class.

'I think one of the cleverest things the monarchy has done is to keep a bit of distance from the aristocracy,' said one young marquess to me. 'I can get drunk, go to gaol, get a divorce and the Queen doesn't have to worry what I'm doing to the royal reputation . . .' It is a piquant thought. But the chances that the murkier doings of the nobility have ever really reflected badly on the royal image look doubtful. No doubt they might have had some effect had it not been for the sterling ability of the British public to breathe in large gulps of paradox without complaint.

As Head of the Church, the monarch has customarily been

expected to take a firm moral line on such things as divorce. Yet the peerage, the class supposedly closest to the throne, has always been one of the most-divorced groups in the country, relative to their numbers. This ambivalent position has been revealed in all its creaking awkwardness on such occasions as Royal Ascot when the sovereign, cast in the difficult double role of leading moralist as well as luminary of the turf, has been obliged to gaze down on the heads of the sporting nobility.

Until 1955 the rule was that no guilty parties in divorce cases could be admitted to the royal enclosure. When this rule was abandoned in that year a smaller enclosure called the Queen's lawn was created below the royal box, admission to which is by Her Majesty's personal invitation.

The idea of the monarchy as a 'middle class' institution is interesting, not only for the light it sheds on one group's conception of the monarchy. It also reflects the fact that the aristocracy has at least a vague awareness of what its own characteristics should be and what they are not. If the possession of large estates, of an art collection worth £15 millions which outshines anything in noble hands, of a pedigree that goes back to King Egbert and Charlemagne, of four stately residences, of a first-class string of racehorses – if all these and more, not to mention the possession of a Throne, do not automatically enrol the owner into the aristocracy then one is left curious about the reason why.

Certainly no member of the real middle classes, who see the Queen as a figure elevated well above the heads of the aristocracy itself, would venture to describe the monarchy as 'middle class', not purely out of reverence, but plainly because for them it would not be accurate. To the middle-class ladies who most habitually line royal routes, or turn up to cheer royal occasions – the ones who mostly give the idea of monarchy its old-fashioned emotional charge – the Queen descends from a great, remote height and evidently continually surprises them by being a human after all.

How does the Queen manage to avoid being immured at the centre of the aristocracy? The answer is that, for one thing, it is far easier to move out of an elite than into it. The so-called aristocratic attitude is a closely-integrated affair, a complexity of things all neatly carpentered together into a 'natural' manner. It is only necessary to exhibit a few symptoms of middle classness to get one's exit visa from the elite, though this does not necessarily mean that one arrives at the class below.

Either from temperament or a sense of duty, the Queen does not dress in a style that will bewilder the multitude with chic, or hint at a sense of taste that is in advance of theirs, or indicate an extravagance or flamboyance that might be alien to the bourgeois nature. It is hard to say whether this does, in fact, allow ordinary people to identify the Queen as someone who is, at least partially, 'one of Us' rather than 'one of Them'. It is not even sure that ordinary people want a monarch to come down and meet them half-way. It is evidently the view of the Palace that they do; and the Queen's friendly demeanour in public helps to bridge any remaining gap.

But it has a defensive look about it, and that is certainly not part of the aristocratic code. Many of the middle-class aspects of the monarchy arise from the nature of the job, as its requirements are seen from the Palace. It addresses itself to some vaguely-conceived, composite figure placed roughly half-way down the social scale. There is an emphasis on happy and respectable family life; though it is clearly a triumph of privacy in an age of publicity that so little is known about the royal family's more off-guard and human side, and what its personal views are on any particular subject. Compared to the White House, say, the Palace is a totally unknown domain. With the exception of the occasional resounding broadside from the Duke, it apparently keeps up its air of neutrality round the clock.

The Queen is highly conscientious, visibly mindful of her duties. This approach is not a traditionally aristocratic one. The aristocrat may well get his duty done; but he will take some pains to look a little casual about it, give the air of pleasing himself. Earnestness, one of the most glaringly middle-class qualities in the eyes of the elite, is strictly taboo for them. The aristocrat is one who essentially doesn't give a damn what the neighbours think. The Palace, on the other hand, works hard to project an image that will win the good opinion of fifty million neighbours in that sense, not to mention the ones overseas.

This popular and passive conception of monarchy, with its determination to fit in with what the unseen majority of the people are presumed to expect of it, had been developing over several reigns. Queen Victoria, for all her imperiousness of manner with her ministers, instinctively inclined herself to the values of the rising middle classes.

After the brief, gay breakaway of Edward VII from this conformity, it was resumed by George V with an even firmer emphasis on the notion of duty. He lived through the early years of Socialism, when it was sowing its wilder oats. He was not a little worried about 'extremism' in relation to the stability of the monarchy, having seen it topple not a few thrones in his lifetime. He was largely the originator of royal middle classness as the defensive attitude to this. But those were days, now departed, when it was not merely passive. He could still argue hotly with his ministers in private. As his biographer, Harold Nicolson, says, 'In private conversation King George was not wont to hide or understate his views; the language that he employed had about it the tang and exuberance of the salt sea waves'.[1] He could still feel strong enough to issue sharp memoranda to the Prime Minister about probity in public life or, unexpectedly for such a seemingly stiff person, urge his ministers to humanitarian methods in the treatment of German prisoners or victims of the Irish troubles.

Since his time, two or perhaps three traumatic events have had much effect in enjoining an attitude of fairly stiff and middle-class conservatism on the monarchy. The first was the abdication of Edward Windsor in 1936. He, though a King of undoubted social sympathies and by no means an undutiful monarch, was rather closer to the more easy-going and aristocratic attitudes of the international smart set than any of his brothers.

His confrontation with the Prime Minister, Stanley Baldwin, and the Archbishop of Canterbury, made it finally clear that the monarch did not have even a minimal aristocratic freedom. He

[1] Harold Nicolson, *King George V*, London, 1952.

had to conform to rules devised by middle-class morality and respectability, further enjoined by his position as Head of the Church. When it came to the crunch, it revealed how powerless, how very much a servant, the monarch was.

Inevitably his successor was required to demonstrate twice the sense of duty to restore the balance sheet of monarchy; and George VI, temperamentally unattracted to the burden of kingship, nobly sacrificed himself to this end.

The third event was the coronation of the present Queen when, on a wave of emotion partly engendered by the ups and downs of these previous experiences of the House of Windsor, for the first time 'a sustained effort was made to represent the coronation as a sacrament in which all the population are simultaneously communicants'.[1] This remarkable upsurge of sentimental-religious-patriotic feeling (engendered, oddly enough, largely through the new scope of television) seems to have astonished even the Palace. It apparently confirmed the impression among the senior advisers that any attempt to shed this aura in favour of something more modern and practical could be a dubious move. 'We must not let daylight in upon magic,' had been Bagehot's prescription for preserving the monarchy; and this was still largely the guiding rule at the Palace.

The paradox was that the monarchy had become more revered as its real powers had diminished and as the old Empire, which arguably needed some unifying symbol, fell away. The existence of the monarchy had become a reassurance, a popular focusing point for nostalgia, a reminder of past British greatness; and the existence of the nobility no doubt dimly shared this role in the public mind.

The House of Windsor (with the possible exception of Edward VII) had never aspired to be leaders of Society in the old sense of the word. In fact one had to go back to Charles II to find a monarch who looked as though he might qualify for the position and, more unusually, enjoy it. One of the few customs which kept up the link between the Palace and the smarter social whirl, and which had been kept going down the decades in the face of

[1] Kingsley Martin, op. cit.

crises of all kinds, had been the tribal rite of presentations at Court, the ceremony by which the daughters of the upper crust, having made their curtsey to the Throne, were passed out into society in what was presumed to be some especially glamorous nubile condition.

It was not until 1958 that the Palace found the nerve to terminate this ritual. No more the queues of limousines inching their way down the crowded Mall to the Palace, bearing ostrich-feathered Mums and nervous deb daughters, the amazed middle classes cooing through the windows at them. The rite had lasted to a surprisingly late date, a mark of the Palace's great caution about change of any kind. The debs continued their 'coming out' ceremonial, but in another place and without the monarch's blessing.

The royal household has been streamlined, but not nearly as much as some people expected when Queen Elizabeth succeeded at the age of twenty-five, looking very much a professional young woman. The Court keeps up its façade of ancient dignities and titles while, behind it, regular office hours are worked by a staff of largely untitled people. The staff numbers about three hundred in England and Wales and sixty in Scotland. Roughly seventy of these are working full-time; most of the remainder are honorary and take up little of the holder's attention.

The Lord Chamberlain (at present Lord Cobbold, former Governor of the Bank of England) is head of the household. He is presented with the traditional white rod by the Queen on his appointment as a token of the dignity. He and his assistants look after a remarkable range of jobs which, like a persistent and many-branching creeper, has grown up around the office.

The Lord Chamberlain supervises Court ceremonial, State visits, royal garden parties, investitures. By a quaint (and much-criticised) survival from the time of Charles II – the King wanted to protect himself and his mistresses from stage lampooning – the Lord Chamberlain was until recently in charge of the censorship of all plays. He is ultimately responsible for the royal swans, the Crown Jewels, the royal works of art, for the appointment of the Queen's bargemaster and watermen (who, maybe once or twice in a reign, will transport her on the Thames), for the selection of the Queen's chaplains and medical advisers. To round off this slightly Alice in Wonderland programme, he also has the task of appointing the royal warrant-holders (now numbering about a thousand), these being the traders and manufacturers who have been awarded the right to declare that they are the suppliers of the royal marmalade, riding boots, cutlery, jewellery, guns, biscuits, and so on.

Much the most important of the Queen's officials in practice is her Private Secretary (now Sir Michael Adeane). He arranges her engagements list, is her link-man with the government and adviser on her relations with the public generally. Apart from the Queen herself he probably has more influence than anyone in shaping the image of royalty.

The Keeper of the Privy Purse (Lord Tryon) supervises the Queen's finances, her private estates, royal patronage, donations to charity, and the accounts of the racing stable. Though he uses modern accounting methods, there is still a veritable 'purse' in existence which the Keeper carries at coronations.

Some of the more lordly appointments need less attention. The Lord Steward (the Duke of Westminster) is theoretically the supervisor of the royal kitchens and servants. In practice all the day-to-day work of the job is handled by the tall, elegant baronet (Major Sir Mark Milbank, Bt) who is Master of the Household.

Then there is the Master of the Horse (the Duke of Beaufort) who is nominally responsible for the Queen's safety when she is on horseback. He takes a keen interest in this and is often to be seen expertly scrutinising the mounts, the harness, and the equipages at the royal stables. Once a year the Queen is his chief guest at the big show-jumping event on his Gloucestershire estate. An ancestor of the Duke was Master of the Horse to the first Queen Elizabeth.

The Queen has ten Ladies-in-Waiting (also called Ladies or Women of the Bedchamber) who are often personal friends of the Queen and are either titled or otherwise associated with the nobility. They are headed by the Mistress of the Robes (now the Dowager Duchess of Devonshire) who occasionally goes on overseas tours with the Queen, accompanies her on bigger ceremonial occasions, and arranges the waiting-ladies' duty roster. Each does a spell of duty at the Palace for about a fortnight at a time, answering some of the Queen's correspondence, acting as hostess when the Queen is away, doing the personal shopping, and generally acting as superior maids of all work.

The whole household list is a very long one and, at least in print, looks a bizarre mixture of the medieval and modern. Keeper of the Swans, Examiner of Plays, Hon. Veterinary Surgeon, Hereditary Grand Almoner, Examiner of Plays (Welsh), Press Secretary, Apothecary to the Household, Chief Accountant, Clerk of the Closet, Consulting Engineer, Master of the Music, Land Agent, Librarian, and a number of Gentlemen Ushers and Equerries – it all has a peculiarly timeless and venerable appearance. But this, according to the Palace, does not prevent it working to their full satisfaction. No age-old dust has been allowed to gather where it might matter, they say.

Outside this central establishment are one or two honorific groups of people whose services are occasionally called upon. There is, for instance, the Honourable Corps of Gentlemen at Arms. This is composed of thirty-two retired senior officers from the Army and other services, a number of them in the landed gentry class. They are seldom seen actually in the Corps uniform and are usually called upon to act as discreet, gentlemanly stewards at royal garden parties and suchlike occasions.

Its equivalent in Scotland – a rather grander affair, in keeping with the romantic temperament of the country – is the Queen's Body Guard for Scotland, the Royal Company of Archers. It numbers four hundred strong, has numerous lords among its officers, and is altogether a profoundly loyal and nobility-conscious outfit. Members wear a dark green uniform with red piping and a Balmoral bonnet with an eagle's feather in it. They carry bows and have three arrows stuck in their belts. The Body Guard normally parades officially only when the Queen is visiting Scotland but – perhaps a token of their seriousness about the job – some practise their archery throughout the year.

In practice, the running of the royal system is in the hands of a number of not particularly elevated people who, like the Queen herself, are simply good professionals. But while some notion of class neutrality may be ultimately the Palace's objective, this lightly gilded palisade of ladies-in-waiting, lords-in-waiting, gentlemen ushers, nobly-born accountants and titled heads of the household services, armigerous equerries and baronial bowmen – these at least preserve the aristocratic connections and ensure that the vision of middle classness is not being too thoroughly realised.

He would, of course, be a pretty demented radical who suggested that these glittering attendants should be replaced by sound chaps with a grammar school background. It would hardly be a more exciting prospect. The interesting thing is the ambivalence of the Palace attitude. As Lord Altrincham (now Mr John Grigg) once put it, the problem of British royalty is that 'they have to perform the seemingly impossible task of being at once ordinary and extraordinary'.

Traces of this dilemma can also be detected among the aristocracy, exemplified by the complaints of the more active and modern-minded ones that the workaday world still declines to take them seriously as 'real people'. It is true that a few of the nobility have encouraged this popular belief in their phantom nature by their gift for making eccentric speeches in the House of Lords, and their apparently tenuous grasp of life as it is lived outside castles.

But the sense of unreality is also projected upon them from below. The attachment of the British public to primitive magic in their conception of a royal personage also imposes itself to some extent on the nobility. 'I was deeply surprised at the difference it made to me when I inherited the title,' the late Duke of Westminster said to me. 'When I was just plain Colonel Grosvenor nobody bothered about me and I was just another Gloucestershire farmer. Then came the dukedom and I felt that people were seeing me in a quite different light. Mostly just snobbery, I suppose, but there's also something mysterious about it as though they've transformed you into something superhuman in their minds.'

There is clearly a store of uncritical adulation in the British make-up which is constantly working to create or refurbish an

elite at the top. The shape of modern British society, as socio-
logists have described it, has changed from its former pyramid
shape into something like an egg. The much-expanded middle
classes form the bulge in the middle, with the smaller upper and
lower classes at each end. The facts of economics and jobs have
brought this about. But this other process which accompanies it,
the one of feeling, of aspiration and deference, is always engaged in
trying to restore the pyramid.

Many if not most lords clearly enjoy living on the heights;
they have both status and a wide freedom to be as they please.
Closer to the more revered circle of the monarchy it is apparently
not so easy and there have been symptoms of the difficulties
involved in being 'real' as well as worshipful. Prince Philip, a man
of some drive and talent, is said to have bridled at some of the
more archaic aspects of Palace protocol though – confusingly for
him – it is not at all clear that most ordinary people want the
mystery exposed.

Nor is it at all sure that the Palace itself knows what it wants.
It too, like the conception of the aristocracy, hangs somewhere
between mystique and reality. Prince Philip may dislike some of
the devious ways of protocol. But the imperious, Cap'n Henry
Morgan, walk-the-plank manner with press photographers shows
that some of us are a long way from being able to manage without
it. He has been allowed, between blast-offs from the butts, to
take a lead in such quietly royal things as nature preservation.
But as soon as he begins to become 'real' (i.e. controversial) – as
for instance in his speech about being 'sick and tired' of apolo-
gising for British exporting methods – his right to be more than a
figurehead was promptly disallowed by some exporters and trade
union chiefs. The lesson is that royal leadership is expected to be
essentially a passive one. No one could contemplate, for instance,
giving Prince Philip his own exports factory so that he could
demonstrate how to do it – unlike the lucky Prince Bernhard
across the water, who, partly because the Dutch have never felt
Trade to be unworthy for a gentleman, is an active company
director.

Princess Margaret and Lord Snowdon enjoy circulating with a

more swinging show-business group of friends; but the Princess is said to be capable of a lightning return to protocol when occasion demands.

Princess Alexandra and her husband, Angus Ogilvy, manage to look more relaxed and cheerful about the whole business. He enjoys working a long business day in a small, old-fashioned office in the City, and seems to have taken pains to prevent anyone sprinkling some of that ambivalent royal glamour on to him. He hails from an old Scots aristocratic background, but is understood to have declined the earldom offered him on his marriage – to the scorn of some of the grander Scots lords who feel that this tends to devalue the prestige of their own titles.

The Earl of Harewood has also managed to keep clear of the gilded royal cage as a hard-working, professional impresario. When the question of his divorce came up in 1967 he took the impressively intelligent step of issuing a frank and unashamed statement to the Press about it, thus denying newspapers and public the chance of moving it back into the area of royal mystery and bogus martyrdom.

All these signposts and symptoms together indicate broadly where the monarchy and aristocracy stands in the mid-1960s: and that is, in a state of suspense. The Crown and, to some extent, its vaguely-associated noble elite have increasingly felt obliged to take their cue from below, trying hard to sense public mood and direction.

Much of the country evidently wanted this traditional leadership to stay romantic and mystery-laden with its strongest attachments to the past. Critics thought this feudal drama an over-indulgence in the modern world, stimulating unreal attitudes to twentieth-century problems. In this sense Britain was still a developing country; and it looked as though it would take a long time yet to decide what kind of society it wanted to have.

6

LORDS OF PARLIAMENT

'The treatment you get here makes you feel a hell of a fellow,' said the Labour life peer, as we made our way along Gothic corridors, into the cathedral hush of the House of Lords. 'Even if you're behind with the rent.' Helmeted policemen and attendants dressed like eighteenth-century butlers twitched their heads deferentially, with a murmured 'My lord . . .' as he passed by.

We were just in time to see the Chamber arouse itself into one of its periodic flurries of activity. After an afternoon of debating Scottish water (reservoirs and suchlike) they were about to take a vote. One of the three bewigged Clerks at the central table gravely turned the sand-glass in front of him while ushers went flitting along the corridors crying 'Division!' with a note of urgency in their voices. The sand takes four minutes to run out (to suggest replacing this apparatus with a stop-watch would be ignoble), and any lord who isn't inside the Chamber by then will find the doors closed on him.

My peer hurried inside to abstain from voting. After some heart-searching he had decided not to support the party line on Scottish water. So, following the customary method, he would plant himself conspicuously on the Labour benches while the other lords filed out to vote. 'The Whip won't like it at all,' he said. 'One is being rather a bad lad. In the Commons they turf you out of the party for this sort of thing. All that happens here is that he'll gaze at me a little coldly for a week or so, take care not to buy me a drink. It's *such* a gentlemanly place.'

That is still one of the most noticeable things about the House of Lords. All its activities are cocooned in politeness, a fine and delicate casing which one raised voice might damage irrevocably.

Yet, behind this, over the past five or ten years, the House has seen some striking changes and now takes up attitudes which would have been unthinkable before that.

Typically, the changes have been little noticed outside its walls. After all, most people would somehow have guessed that they are still using the same sand-glass; and the ceremonial aroma of the peerage and the transcendent architecture of the place are an effective disguise surrounding the reality of its present nature and doings.

Built in 1847, at just about the time when the peerage was learning to listen more closely to the ominous murmurs of the lower orders, the House has had woven into its every fibre the idea of the almost religious nature of nobility. Everywhere around there are symbols of lordliness, crests, coats of arms, baronial statuary, heraldic floor tiles, armigerous stained-glass windows, a pungent air of Gothic mystery.

At the head of the Chamber the vacant Throne stands illuminated by spectral lighting. If an heir to a peerage wants to listen to a debate he may not do so unobtrusively from the gallery; he must sit on the steps of the Throne like some medieval court favourite – which is possibly why some heirs obdurately refuse to come. Below this is the Woolsack, a red-upholstered affair about the size of a double bed, its woollen stuffing being a reminiscent symbol of the landed wealth which created the parliaments. Upon this sits the Lord Chancellor, at present the Socialist Lord Gardiner, formerly a brilliant practitioner at the Bar, who must bring to his job a remarkable stamina for listening wakefully to speeches.

A mellow light filters into the Chamber through the stained glass. Gazing down from the gallery at the figures which half fill the red leather benches, the visitor tries to detect and bring into focus some elusive essence of titled rank. 'Ah!' he may say – as no doubt some have before him – picking out a face at random, 'how unmistakable are the lineaments of pedigree, breeding and tradition!' Only to find, quite possibly, that he is looking at a lately-ennobled trade union leader who spent his maturing years on a railway footplate. If one disregards the well-known faces, there is little at first glance to distinguish the Labour peers from the hereditary Tory noblemen. Both look fairly prosperous, comfortable, and utterly at home here. The Conservatives display a quite wide and noble variety, from the short and jovial to the aloof and aquiline but one eventually picks out some of the more-caricatured traits which provide an identity label for the gentlemanly classes: the cavalry moustaches, the trace of hauteur and the habit of command (now more defensively indicated, in inverted commas so to speak), the uncertain and well-bred chin (which, contrary to report, often goes with martial valour), the more countryfied air of some of the suits and neckties.

The elaborately formal and grand setting of the Chamber gives its activities a context of theatre. The effect of this can be seen, for instance, in the obligation which members seem to feel – and occasionally fulfil – to produce a speaking style which will outshine that of the Commons in courtliness. Experienced listeners here claim that they have heard arguments on deer preservation classically unwound as though they were passages from Racine.

Several times in a session the theatrical undertone is revitalised with a beguiling touch of ceremonial as a new peer takes his seat. The ushers fling wide the doors at the foot of the Chamber. The official known as Gentleman Usher of the Black Rod leads in a colourful little procession. Behind him comes the senior Herald, Garter King of Arms (now Sir Anthony Wagner), wearing his heavily-gilded tabard, that is a sleeveless jacket, his sword at his side.

In his wake follows the new peer, flanked by the two peers who are his sponsors, all three wearing their red robes and carrying black cocked hats. The peer's Letters Patent, the scroll issued by the sovereign which declares the lord's right to his title, is read out to the Lord Chancellor and then, presumably to allay any lingering doubt, is displayed to him by the peer himself. Then, at a sign made by the Garter with his baton, the three peers raise their hats and bow three times to the Lord Chancellor and he raises his own hat in acknowledgment. Finally the Lord Chancellor gives the new man a warm handshake and the other lords murmur 'hear, hear' by way of welcome.

On his admission to the House, the new peer has become a part of the cornerstone of aristocracy, the body which has traditionally given it its fundamental significance in British life. It is a part of the modern legislature which is most deeply rooted in custom. Here, with a little effort, the visitor can feel himself to be at some sort of pivotal point in the British mind upon which swings a sense of the past and the present, the traditional and the new. Viewed as a continuously-running piece of theatre, the House of Lords probably most clearly represents the character of the nobility at any one time.

All the audience has to do is detect the theme of the play. As the powers of the lords have become more uncertain so has this theme become more veiled and enigmatic. That air of determined vagueness which comes so naturally to the British constitution is seen at its most resolute in the House of Lords; and nowadays it is tantalising in the imprecision of what it can and cannot do, what purpose it serves, what exactly it stands for.

What it certainly has – to begin with the starkest simplicities – is a fraternal atmosphere, a thing that makes it (as members new and old do not tire of saying) 'the best club in London'. Like those other clubs, its accommodation would be swamped if all the members turned up at the same time. The biggest attendance there has been in the last two decades was 333 in 1956 for a capital punishment debate and then the Chamber was packed to the doors.

Out of the thousand-odd peers there are always about a hundred at any one time who are ineligible to take their seats for various reasons. The lord concerned may still be going through the often irksome process, which all inheritors of a title have to endure, of proving his claim to it. This not only involves producing documentary evidence that you are your father's rightful heir; but also that he was legally married to your mother. For some peers, this has involved seeking out some long-lost and ageing relative who was at the wedding ceremony.

Another reason preventing a lord from taking his seat can be bankruptcy (there are several cases). Lunacy, though a bar to membership of the Commons is, oddly enough, no legal hindrance to taking a seat in the House of Lords.

Under a scheme introduced ten years ago, peers can apply for leave of absence from the House for a period up to the five-year life of the whole Parliament. A further 200 peers take advantage of this. The scheme was brought in as one way of attempting to reduce the excessive Tory majority in the House, to give it a better political balance.

It is also a way of getting round the awkward fact that the Writ of Summons to Westminster which each lord receives at the beginning of each session is the Queen's command. It offers a loophole to those who are glad to be relieved of the duty of coming for various reasons – unable to leave their jobs so frequently perhaps, lack of interest in politics and diffidence about public speaking, or – a reason a surprisingly large number now give – because of their uneasiness about taking up a right that is purely hereditary.

Thus there are about 700 peers who are qualified to come. About 300 of these are Conservatives, 100 Labour, 45 Liberal, and the remainder, who claim to have no party line, sit on the cross-benches at the foot of the Chamber. Unlike members of the Commons, a peer is not paid for his services. But he is entitled to £4 14s 6d a day expenses when he attends.

One hereditary peer, Lord Milford, who farms in Gloucester-shire, is a Communist. His maiden speech urged, inevitably, the abolition of the House of Lords. It is entirely characteristic of the House that it should wear its extremist rather comfortably, like a badge of merit. I asked one veteran peer how he reacted to this revolutionary presence and he said, 'Very decent chap. I only wish he'd explain this Marxist business more clearly.'

In practice the work of the House falls upon a hard core of some 150 regular attenders – if one allows speaking and listening to be a major part of the work. The number of those who apply themselves really diligently to the study of Bills and amendments is probably nearer thirty or forty. There are twenty-six Lords Spiritual (bishops and archbishops) and nine judges who are the Law Lords. The House is the highest court of appeal; five of the judges normally represent it in deciding a case.

The House can be in session so long as there is a quorum of

E

three lords present—that is, the Lord Chancellor, one speaking and one listening. It has not been reduced to that in living memory; but occasions are recalled when a speaker was left to argue with completely empty benches opposite. The lords possess enough sang-froid, unlike some actors, not to find this kind of situation disturbing.

Members wander amiably in and out in the middle of speeches. The House is fond of declaring its pride in the quality of its debates, claiming that they are more knowledgeable, less politically biased, and show more breadth of mind than those in the Commons. This is largely true. But brevity is not always the key-note and, by late afternoon, there is often a distinctly somnolent atmosphere.

One life peeress, Lady (Barbara) Wootton, has written that 'after eight years of careful observation I have concluded that about ten per cent of the audience are obviously asleep'.[1] This tallies very closely with my own count on occasions when I have gone to see the lords in action. Others claim that appearances are misleading, and that these peers are merely concentrating intently with their eyes closed. If so, one can only say that they maintain the same concentrations on the silence between speeches.

The sense of style is important to the lords and they are very partial to all the grace-notes of parliamentary speaking. 'As the noble Earl so pertinently says . . .', 'If the noble Lord will forgive the correction . . .', or 'I will not detain your Lordships at this late hour . . .' (you glance at the clock and find that the sun still has some way to go to the horizon).

This seductively relaxed and polite atmosphere is the first thing that strikes the new member and, more often than not, captivates him. One peer recalled to me how, before he was raised to the peerage, the ferocious old Socialist member of Parliament, David Kirkwood, used to denounce the House of Lords. But after a spell here he became lamb-like in his loyalty to the House.

The newly-ennobled trade-unionist will indeed find the Tory

[1] Barbara Wootton, *In a World I Never Made*, London, 1967.

leader, very possibly a man of well-crusted pedigree, seeking him out and enquiring earnestly after his well-being. It is so much more *civilised* than the aggressive hurly-burly of the Commons, they all say after a few weeks. Newcomers also appear to be impressed to find that a speech by a leading duke is accorded no more attention, or inattention, than goes to the most fresh-faced young baron. 'It is the most egalitarian place on earth,' concluded another Labour life peeress, Lady Phillips, after two years in the House.[1]

This emphasis on tolerance and gentlemanly relationships between parties, while it may be pleasant for its own sake, is also an interesting pointer to the present state of the House. Politeness has never been a particularly valuable ingredient of realistic and active politics; indeed, it can get in the way. The clubman's atmosphere has replaced the real, political steam which was formerly raised by the tension between the mainly reactionary, land-owning nobility and the radicals of the House of Commons.

The last real attempt at a showdown between Lords and Commons was in 1909 when the peers threw out Lloyd George's Liberal budget, and King George v was left for some days in great anxiety that the Prime Minister would ask him to create five or six hundred peers all at once to defeat the Tories.

In recent years there have been only occasional upsurges of this old Tory mood in the Lords. In 1956 there was the record turn-out against capital punishment already mentioned. When the question of sanctions against Rhodesia came up there was a mass advance of Tory 'backwoodsmen' peers (the big landowners from the shires) on the House, some of whom had not been seen for years.

The Lords can still speak as forcefully as they like on contentious subjects and, so long as they get reasonable newspaper coverage – which happens only on special occasions – they may have some influence on public opinion. But there remains to them scarcely a shred of that power which alone commands respect on conflicting issues. The Lords' power to delay legislation on its way through

[1] Quoted in *The Times*, 21 June 1967.

the pipeline, which used to be its reserve strength, is now hypothetical.

The Lords cannot now delay a Bill that is concerned with money at all and can only hold up other Bills for a year. In practice they are unlikely ever to use this. The Labour government has made it clear that it would not accept stonewalling tactics from the Lords. Now and again one has had the impression that the Labour leadership would not really mind a dramatic showdown with the Lords, as a theatrical diversion from its own more real difficulties – a last-ditch struggle when there is hardly a real ditch left.

Still, a Tory-dominated House of Lords has to move rather gingerly when there is a Labour government well established in the saddle. Under the able and tactful leadership of Lord Carrington, the Tory lords make their critical speeches, chew over amendments, study the clauses – and then co-operate.

This evaporation of the political character of the House, as many members on both sides ruefully recognise, has removed most of the tension that relates an institution to people's convictions (as distinct from high-minded thoughts) and to outside reality. The Tory peers, who have naturally suffered most from this, react in various ways.

The grander rural lords are not content to be part of a sideshow to the main action and they are now seldom seen at Westminster, especially if they have other jobs as Lords Lieutenant or council chairmen. For them, the centre of interest has moved back where it began – out in their own territories where they have some importance and where the anomaly of their hereditary position does not feel so obtrusive. Possibly because a too candid liking for power is not one of the gentlemanly virtues, few of these noblemen are inclined to reveal their true feelings about the diminished role of the House. But certainly a number that I met appeared to be rather sad and aggrieved about it.

Another group of peers – not a very numerous one, I would estimate – stays away from the House for a different reason. These are the ones who are convinced that the hereditary right to a seat in the legislature is indefensible and they demonstrate this by their absence.

The hereditary peers who remain as active participants in the business of the House include a high proportion of the landless, London-based lords, some of them the younger, professional men. Divorced from the older conservatism that is inherent in land-ownership, these tend to have a more flexible political outlook and their views on most social questions is often individualistic and liberal, even if they sit on the Conservative benches; and the party Whips often complain of the nightmarish time they can have in trying to rally support for the party line on some question.

Ironically enough, the House of Lords has acquired a new lease of energy just at a time when the uncertainty about its proper function has become most apparent, and when its maligned, reactionary nature is being largely discarded.

Some of the hereditaries show more enthusiasm for the work of the House than it has seen for a long time. They must make the more languid of the club members feel a trifle guilty. The decline of the House's real power seems to have been paradoxically one of the stimulating factors. As the twilight comes down the active peers seem anxious to prove that the hereditary luck of the draw does produce the right sort of man to be a senator.

Viscount Colville, who is one of the younger and more dedicated peers, dismisses the doubts expressed by some other lords about the value of the House. He is thirty-four, a barrister, and looks after the legal side of things for the Tory peers. He points to the wide variety of professional experience which the landless lords now bring to bear on legislation. 'For instance,' he said to me, 'we were once wrestling with a clause in a Copyright Bill, wondering how on earth you could judge the royalties due on a wallpaper design. Suddenly, up popped a peer who revealed that he'd been in wallpaper for years and we got some sound and practical advice from him.' Lord Colville believes that the wider experience of life which the House now possesses enables it to do its job better than ever before.

The introduction of non-hereditary life peers from 1958 has also helped to give Lords' debates more lustre and ideas than they used to have. It brought in a good stock of intellectual ability, and people with recourse to a wider knowledge of such things as science and technology than the landed classes could ever claim. This has done most to change the House – behind its medieval veneer – into a sort of Senate of the Professional Classes.

Voting on some issues shows how rapid the change has been. In the 1950s the Lords showed a majority voice against pretty well all liberalising measures, like the move for the abolition of capital punishment. But by 1965, a measure to abolish hanging was *supported* by 204 votes to 104. In the same year, the Lords were ready to give support – by 96 votes to 31 – to Lord Arran's private member's Bill on Sexual Offences, whose main provision was to legalise homosexual acts in private. In this case, analysis of the voting shows that it would have been approved by the hereditary peers alone, without the support of the life peers. This showed a remarkable change of outlook.

The House has also floated liberal-minded Bills on such things as legalising abortion, easing restrictions on Sunday entertainments, and raising theatre censorship. None of these would have been conceivable ten years before. The House now takes a certain pride in such peripheral measures of social reform, legislation which the House of Commons does not find time for.

The pride is justifiable and would be more so if, perversely, these Bills did not somehow go to the bottom of the pile of statutes awaiting Commons attention. Lord Arran's Bill lay in the stack for three sessions – and by then the Commons' own Bill on sexual offences had overtaken it.

The value of some of the other functions of the House is arguable. Traditionally, one of its main jobs is to 'tidy up' Bills sent up to it from the Commons – that is, to be a House of Correction. Once upon a time the Lords could and did affect the force of a piece of law-making by introducing amendments. Now it is more innocuously non-political, mainly a matter of seeing that badly-worded clauses do not get past which might put a judge in a quandary.

Certainly, some of the more conscientious peers do burn the midnight oil in giving second and third thoughts to the most obscure and unexciting legislation. Lady Wootton, on the other hand, thinks that the usefulness of this is much exaggerated. 'These amendments, as everybody knows, have not the slightest chance of success unless they commend themselves to the government, and it is only a few of the minor ones that even manage that. The lordly mountain brings forth rather small mice . . .'[1]

A number of the newer peers who come fresh to the ways of the House find them puzzling. Everything appears to work very well, like an efficient theatrical production; but all the time there is a doubt about how well-linked it is to reality.

I sat in the House of Lords bar with a group of peers who, in a desultory way, tried to elucidate the mystery of its nature for me. There had been a break in the business of the Chamber and, in ones and twos, the lords were drifting in for a drink. In one corner, a trio of Scottish noblemen who between them owned (I calculated) about 200,000 acres of Highland terrain, brooded together over their whisky. A pair of young Tories, both of them in the public relations business, engaged themselves in a conversation which needed a fair amount of dramatic gesture: business, I suspected.

Faces known and half-known looked in or passed by. Lord Snow diligently pacing the corridors of non-power. Lord Saltoun – or so they said – who is the House's authority on botanical matters. The Earl of Dundee and the Duke of Atholl. Another peer who was a quite famous politician until he took his title: now his name escaped me. Viscount St Davids, the resident expert on inland waterways, dropped in. He lives by the side of a canal in North London and even goes shopping by boat. During a lull, he explained to me how it was possible to navigate all the way from his home to the river steps of the House of Lords. It sounded complex. 'Only 23 miles and 12 locks!'

'When I first came here,' the Labour life peer began, 'I found the routine quite bewildering. Then when I began to understand it, I felt frustrated. One has the feeling – no, the conviction – that while the government keeps up the pretence that the House of Lords matters, they never bother their heads about it. Then here

[1] Article in *The Observer*, 10 June 1962.

we are, congratulating ourselves on all these fine speeches we make. They're certainly pretty good these days, but who hears them? You're lucky if enough gets into the papers to make sense. Sometimes I just think we're talking to ourselves.'

A colleague of his, a Labour viscount, sadly agreed that this might be the case. Which was a pity he thought considering the expert knowledge they could muster on any subject, ancient or modern. 'In my first few days here I dropped into the Chamber for a few minutes, and stayed for three hours. The Diseases of Fish Bill, I think it was called. But they knew simply everything about it. Really fascinating.'

'The great thing about us,' said another, 'is that we argue things on their merits without much of this silly political bias. That doesn't work here but some of these new chaps promoted from the Commons don't seem to realise it. There was Lord —— last night, trying to do a "Lloyd George" on us. All that tub-thumping! You could tell it didn't work. *He* was talking to himself all right.'

This fairly recent 'anti-political' feeling is an example of the way in which this aristocracy is continually trying to renew its meaning and status, as it always has done, by making a virtue of necessity. It loses political power; so it discovers a more high-minded purpose in *not* making political speeches. One reason for the inattention of newspapers and the wider public is clearly the removal of the political steam and of those less 'civilised' and polite reactions to affairs which engage ordinary interest.

One or two seem to find that this makes for an unnervingly rarefied atmosphere. One young Liberal lord described the feeling of getting up to speak. 'It's the politeness that's overwhelming. I doubt whether there's anywhere else in the world where people will sit listening to speeches for hours without any special re-action. So you start pepping up, speaking more and more emphatically, but you never know whether you're getting through. Of course, they always congratulate you afterwards.'

The Labour government's announcement in 1967 that it proposed to reform the House of Lords came as something of a surprise to the reading public since it had not regarded this as one of the most urgent matters on the national agenda. Sceptical Tory commentators suggested that the government was trying to whip up some factitious, out-dated drama in a bogus confrontation between Commons and Lords, purely to distract the eye from sterner problems.

It seemed that the government feared that the Lords' power to delay a Bill for twelve months might be used to stall legislation in Labour's last year of office. It planned to curtail this privilege. Secondly, it looked probable that the automatic right of hereditary peers to a seat in the House would be ended, though some might be elected into it on their own merits. A House with its membership thus reduced would consist predominantly of life peers and its function would more conspicuously become that of 'a talking shop of the professional classes', and would only confirm the way the House had been changing in character over the last few decades.

It remained to be seen whether the Lords could make anything out of a debating academy without much power. In the shaping of public opinion it is obviously valuable to have a group of leading men, free from election fears, discussing tolerance for homosexuals, the need for theatre censorship, and so on, or to hear the bishops' view of divorce or the judges on crime.

But these matters are argued thoroughly in the Press these days and, between the big occasions, the mountain-sized apparatus, as Lady Wootton says, tended to produce rather small mice. It is much the same with the Lords' legislative work. Their job of scrutinising Bills is useful but gets an exaggerated esteem largely because the parliamentary system is out of joint and the Commons so over-loaded with business. The opinion of informed observers is that the employment of twenty more counsel on the drafting of Bills could do as much in the way of revision as now occupies the time of several hundred peers.

With the virtually total exclusion of the hereditary land-owning class in prospect, the trend towards liberal attitudes in the Lords is likely to be expedited. The ironic situation might thus conceivably arise that the Upper House would prove to be a more radical body than the administration currently governing the

E*

country; that liberal legislation devised in the Lords might be stonewalled by the elected democrats along the corridor – which would be a strange reincarnation for this ancient Valhalla of the parliaments.

7

POLITICS AND PARTY

In principle Britain is a democracy. In practice it is a peculiar mixture of democracy and elitism. The old idea and fact of a ruling class still cast a long shadow, more especially on the affairs of the Tory party, clearly not by any underhand chicanery but with the active approval of a majority of its supporters.

It is true that no single aristocrat (Sir Winston Churchill is a special case) has wielded special power for a generation or more. Perhaps the last was the late Lord Derby, the uncrowned political 'King of Lancashire'. Control of party affairs has moved a little way down the social scale to take in the managerial men, the self-made rich, the occasional ambitious and able grammar-school product. But the leadership, in the country as well as at the centre, shows the traditional partnership between the gentry, the old and new men of property, and the professional and mercantile class. As one recent study has shown they retain a virtual monopoly of offices within the party.[1] At the top the flavour is intensely public school and upper-middle to upper-class. The proportion of Etonians involved has dropped only very slightly in the last half-century. When the battle for the Conservative party leadership took place in 1965, six of the nine conceivable contenders were old Etonians. (I do not mean this to be a reflection on the school; admiration might well be a more correct response. Simply that the range of choice in educational background is remarkably narrow.) The basis of this continuing elite position is that the decline in the proportion of wealth owned by the upper class and the redistribution of income by taxation has been extremely slow – as a number of writers have pointed out. What has also happened in Britain,

[1] W. L. Guttsman, *The British Political Elite*, London, 1963.

as in other democracies, as one sociologist reminds us, is 'not so much a reduction in the power of the upper class as a decline in the radicalism of the working class'.[1] As lower classes improve their own position slightly they become more rather than less tolerant of inequality. This is especially true of the middle class which, in numbers and effectiveness, carries most political weight. Since many commentators on the British scene often work on the assumption that the public at large is actively looking forward to a classless society and fuller democratic responsibilities, I think it important to stress that there is always an impulse, at least equally strong, working from below as well as above, towards preserving the hierarchy where everyone 'knows their place'.

The confusion in the Tory Party, which has become annually more apparent over the last twenty years, lies in precisely this state of chronic indecision about the virtues of the new and the old. Bagehot's statement that the English 'want to be ruled by sensible men of substantial means' still holds true for a large mass of Tory supporters. They do not want to be governed by their equals but by their betters. They like the irrationality of the hereditary principle partly because it is a simulacrum of the monarchy. Old Etonians do not rule simply because of their personal conviction that they are the most-desired leaders. The Tory voter is also impressed by their self-assurance and is made to feel paradoxically *more* secure by the genial awareness of inequality, as part of Mother Nature's handiwork, which they convey.

The Tory leadership is perfectly aware at the back of its mind – and now and again at the front – of the old-fashioned or even 'feudal' character of much of its support, the partly unconscious desire for a ruling class to continue in being. The dilemma arises when it has, at the same time, to present itself as the liberalising, free-enterprise party which is dedicated to the claims of personal merit. It wavers between the two, never quite forsaking the one, never quite grasping the other. Conservative Central Office looks desperately about for a couple of cloth-capped meritocrats to put up as parliamentary candidates – only to be spurned by local committees who wonder what they're playing at. A Tory politician

[1] T. B. Bottomore, *Elites and Society*, London, 1962.

who is promoted too far above his class expectation can apparently have an uncomfortable time. Mr Reginald Bevins, a 'working-class Tory', who became Postmaster-General in a Macmillan administration and then fell into party disfavour, later wrote bitterly about his experiences. He wrote of 'a power group operating behind the scenes' – largely aristocratic in its affiliations – and urged that 'the notion that some people are born to rule must be destroyed'[1] – an idea which, if carried into effect, would I believe, remove a very large slice of the public support for his party.

When it comes to the public shaping of its policy programme the Tories are at their most ostensibly democratic. The sight of a man with titled connections speaking from the floor at the annual conference is as rare as a snow-goose. It is in the back-room area where personalities matter that they still count. This was clearest in the 1965 leadership struggle when what Mr Ian McLeod, another minister of non-elite origins, described as the 'magic circle' (of Etonians etc.) was not only seen to be writing the script of the show but also producing it, doing the casting, acting its leading roles, and handling the stage lighting. The choice flitted like a will-o'-the-wisp from one head to another – this peer (Hailsham) or that peer (Home) or managerial type (Maudling)? In the end, in this state of muddle and indecision, it is significant that the party should have played safe by choosing Sir Alec Douglas-Home, the aristocrat of quiet charm and apparent modesty, who was to claim that he did his economic calculation with a box of matches. It was clear that he was not setting out to be a technocrat. Sir Alec proved to be no shining success in uniting this two-sided party; so, in 1966, they swung to the other end of the spectrum and chose Mr Edward Heath, the able, middle-class, grammar-school product. This may have restored some confidence among the go-ahead, managerial section of the party. But by 1967 it was clear that he had rapidly been losing support, and it is a reasonable guess that the defectors included a large section of those voters who prefer to be led by a patrician, who still think in terms of a ruling class.

Much of the trouble was that the Tory party was like a person

[1] R. Bevins, *The Greasy Pole*, London, 1965.

who has some inner conviction but was too timid to speak it out, afraid that his audience will find it odd. This statement, if it came, would be an admission that the party still believes in the theory of a ruling class, and the philosophy of Burke and Disraeli which go to support it. Two political journalists of Conservative sympathies made this very point at the last election. Writing in the *Sunday Telegraph*, Mr Peregrine Worsthorne urged that in a free society authority must be associated with privilege; that the Tory party would never convince anybody of its special understanding of social leadership if it 'did not have the courage to admit, without fudging the issue, that the only way to guarantee [it] in a free society was through property and privilege.' Similarly, in the *Observer*, Mr Henry Fairlie suggested that such things as private education and private medical treatment – which implied freedom of choice for those who could afford them – could not be protected in isolation. 'They imply privilege and they can be defended only by a defence of privilege as such.'

As both writers indicate, the reason the party does not own up to this part of its philosophy is that there is felt to be something shameful about believing in inequality; and I would add that it is because many or most Conservatives are only dimly aware of their belief. I am not concerned with its political merits. It is simply a good example of the way Britain likes to become unconscious of things. It supposes it is heading towards a meritocracy. But all the time this underground stream of tradition draws it back to older, half-forgotten patterns.

8

LORDS AT WORK

The aristocracy's attitudes to work and to the ways in which a living may decently be earned have always provided some of the group's strongest taboos and protective devices. The fact that these were at their most rigid during a period when Britain was striding ahead as an industrial and commercial nation has been one of the more curious and irrational aspects of the aristocratic outlook.

The roots of the taboo against 'trade' – a term which would include most productive and commercial processes – go deep into the past; they were not simply, as they sometimes appear, a genteel-poetic reaction to the satanic mills of the nineteenth century. The taboo had its origins in the belief and practice of medieval times that the nobleman was essentially one who was supported by the manual labour of others. The Christian theory of the 'dignity of labour' was not much canvassed until the time of John Wesley and other Nonconformist propagandists and the ruling class, of course, hardly needed to lend an ear to it. For some centuries before, the aristocracy had been intent on developing the theory and practice of the dignity of leisure; and the terms of this code were much more precisely recognised and understood by the people at large than any such revolutionary idea as that the productive worker was the subject of some special heavenly blessing. The status of gentleman was a closely delineated one, and there were various statutory enactments during medieval and Tudor times to ensure that people did not dress above their station in life.

In 1649, one case that came before the Court of Chivalry – the body which decided heraldic matters, who was entitled to coats of arms, and so on – was that of Lawrence Twentyman, a litigant who wanted to prove that, though he was a goldsmith, he was also a gentleman. The Court disputed his claim on the grounds that he sometimes worked at the forge and anvil himself and therefore could not be considered a gentleman. He answered this by producing evidence that he always wore an apron at work, the implication being that he had clothes underneath of a quality worth protecting. In the eighteenth century, Addison and Defoe were deriding – as the former once wrote – 'those sprigs of nobility who would rather be starved like gentlemen than thrive in a trade or profession that is beneath their quality'. But they were rare sceptics. There was much more support for the other point of view. 'Trade,' wrote John Locke, 'is wholly inconsistent with a gentleman's calling.'

Taboos about work have historically been one of the commonest aspects of elites everywhere. Veblen, in his *Theory of the Leisure Class*, mentions the example of the Polynesian chief who would rather starve than convey food to his lips with his own hand. It was essentially a servant's task to undertake this effort. A more sophisticated, present-day example occurs among the Bedouin who live in the marsh country of southern Iraq. This is a very old, stratified society, strongly attached to tribal traditions, but now having to meet the challenge of new trade outlets and economic temptations. On its minute scale it bears a passing resemblance to the situation in nineteenth-century Britain. As it was for the aristocracy then, the challenge presented to these Bedouin tribal elders is that money is clearly there to be made in commerce – will they come out into the open and be seen to be making it? The answer, according to an anthropologist who has studied them,[1] seems to be No. The new trade has been taken up by a class of nouveau-riche marsh dwellers and they have thereby become wealthy shopkeepers, moneylenders and exporters. They enjoy the new wind of competition, but they find it hard to win recognition as notables despite their wealth. The prestige still goes to the heads of families of long lineage, and these notables 'scorn the pursuit of personal gain and restrict their economic activities to the ill-rewarded mat weaving necessary for a bare livelihood . . . the old Bedouin values

[1] S. M. Salim, *Marsh Dwellers of the Euphrates Delta*, London, 1962.

are still asserted in an attempt to stem the tide of commerce and external influence'.

The analogy is, needless to say, only a glancing one. The English gentleman was seldom obliged to undergo economic hardship for the sake of preserving his status. He usually had a reasonably prosperous estate behind him, and the younger sons of the noble family could readily avoid 'trade' by choosing such prestigious and traditional professions as the law, the church, and the Army. But judging by the comments of Addison, Defoe and others, there was a class of poor-genteel in the eighteenth century who preferred to keep their hands clean and go short. In more recent times there has been an ex-officer class, particularly between the wars, which has chosen to decide the job-hunting problem largely on the basis of what is gentlemanly and what is not, quite apart from the merits of the post as an earner of money.[1] This attitude not only derives from the old taboo against certain occupations but also from the fact that the gentleman could not allow himself to get into a directly competitive situation with others, especially people of a lower social class. His outlook, in past times at least, has been unsuited to the aggressiveness of the market-place. Though he might strongly deny it, there is a fear-of-losing in him somewhere; and it is significant that the theory of 'the good loser' should have been developed on the playing-field, where it does not matter.

In rejecting the contamination of 'trade', no doubt the gentleman believed that he was preserving old values, like the Bedouin patriarch today. What these values were and are can only be guessed at. The idea of cultivated leisure is a nobler aim of life perhaps: the avoidance of any sign of living for money for its own sake. But again this involved a measure of theatrical pretence, a tendency to think of appearances as more important than reality. Most prestige has gone to posts in which money is not *seen* to pass, so that the gentleman can create, for himself and others, the illusion of being supported without visible personal effort, by powers out-

[1] Compare and contrast the lack of inhibition of the White Russian and Czarist nobility who became familiar as cab-drivers, waiters, and night-club doormen in Paris and elsewhere after 1917.

side himself, as in an act of levitation.[1] The gentleman enlarges his own rationalisation by presuming that anyone making money in trade was a bit of a shyster, carrying no responsibilities and not to be trusted, a poor thing compared to his own patently incorruptible self.

Whatever the merits of the values he imagined himself to be protecting – and there were one or two genuine ones there perhaps – the defence effort was entirely vitiated by the snobbery it induced.[2] It also encouraged disdainful attitudes to certain kinds of work, especially those involving *visible* money, or a *visible* productive process, which are still only gradually being eroded. One can see how deeply the gentleman's credo has bitten by comparing the American situation. In the United States, anyone – whatever his social standing – who is not actively engaged in work, who does not have a workshop, desk, or office suite to go to, is regarded as slightly odd or inadequate, a poor fish out of the swim. No prestige attaches to having nothing to do. In Britain, a 'gentleman' is still, technically speaking and in law, someone who has no occupation, and the implication is that this carries more status.[3]

The taboos against that sector of the economy which, for the gentleman, was too close to the making and selling of things inevitably involved a good deal of hypocrisy. While snob attitudes to those who were directly involved in trade flourished throughout the nineteenth century and after, the gentle and noble classes

---

[1] Hence the old aristocratic taboos against even talking about money. Another survival of this is the fact that barristers – one of the oldest gentleman-professions – get their fees through an intermediary, the solicitor, and cannot sue for non-payment. Shopkeeping, where cash changes hands all day, is the lowest of the low, no matter how palatial the shop.

[2] Examples from English literature are limitless, of course; it is one of its main themes. One specimen mentioned by E. M. Forster in his semi-autobiographical *Marianne Thornton* is interesting because it had a lasting effect on his own view of society. A favourite aunt of his wanted to marry her music teacher. But the other womenfolk in the family would not hear of it at any price, even when she developed a severe emotional illness about it. The man whom they spurned was a distinguished musician of some international repute and was grand enough to have been twice Lord Mayor of Shrewsbury. Their objection to him was that he kept a music shop.

[3] I think one could go some way – perhaps not all the way – in framing a theory that the Labour Party's regard for producing the leisure-using citizen is an example of absorption from the old ruling class. Certainly a laudable aim, but it carries the slight implication that work in itself cannot be interesting. Party supporters have perversely shown that they can't take too much leisure. They want shorter hours, but this is a different thing, usually seized as a chance to earn more overtime pay.

were all the time becoming more caught up in it as shareholders. As in the case of the aspiring Lawrence Twentyman, dignity was maintained so long as one kept one's apron on – in this case the apron of distance. It became common for peers to become directors of railway companies whose lines ran through their estates, and about 1880 there was an outburst of positive enthusiasm among the peerage to get directorships of all kinds. By 1896 there were 167 noblemen – over a quarter of the peerage of the time – holding seats on boards in industry and commerce.[1] At this time probably three-quarters of the peerage also had substantial estates as well. It became customary, as agriculture went through this shaky end-of-the-century period, for landowners to spread their assets into a wide variety of stocks and bonds.

Table I shows the occupations of a random sample of one hundred members of the present House of Lords, which is roughly ten per cent of the total. It shows how the variety has widened. The main feature of the occupational pattern is the very close balance between land-ownership and business interests at director level. If one combines the groups one gets a total of 43 per cent whose income is wholly or partly from estate ownership and 46 per cent whose income is wholly or partly from business director-ships. The other significant feature, as the fourth group in the table shows, is that about one-third of the peerage is now engaged in a variety of professions or, in a few cases, gets its income from service pensions and suchlike.[2] Most of these professionals are landless peers holding a title of fairly recent creation. They cover such a variety that it is hard to see much pattern in the choice of jobs except to note that science and technology do not get much of a showing. With only one liner-steward in the list (a younger lord needless to say) the proportion of eccentricity is evidently lower than the gossip-columns sometimes suggest. Virtually all the others appear to be normally earnest earners of money and very few would describe themselves as 'gentleman' in the old sense of

[1] *Complete Peerage*, Vol. V, App. C.

[2] All noblemen who qualify appear to draw their state old age pensions of roughly £4 10s a week (or £7 10s for a married couple) with no false modesty about it. Lord Montgomery was recently pictured in the papers drawing his in person from the local Post Office. Some others appear to get it quarterly by cheque.

TABLE I: OCCUPATIONS PER 100 PEERS (1967)

Occupation	number	notes
1. Company director only	27	(8 in banking, finance, insurance; 12, industry and commerce; 7, TV, newspapers and miscellaneous)
2. Company director also landowner	19	(variety of board-interests roughly as above)
3. Landowner only	24	
4. Various professions or income sources	33	(3 diplomats, 2 airline executives, 2 barristers, 1 solicitor, 1 hospital physician, 2 film directors, 2 authors, 3 members of Lloyds (insurance), 1 university professor and 1 lecturer, 1 newspaper publisher, 1 book publisher, 1 building engineer, 1 trade union secretary, 1 advertising copy-writer, 1 stockbroker, 1 'writer and liner-steward', 1 ex-railwayman and 1 ex-miner, 5 retired service officers).

Notes:
The acreage of the estates in Groups 2 and 3 is not ascertainable precisely. My impression is that only one-third of the peerage have major estates (see Chapter 9); the others in the landed groups will own a few hundred acres at most with their country house.

The total in the second column exceeds 100 because in a few cases a peer's income may come equally from more than one source.

being jobless and living on private means (though they will often have that sort of income too).

One can only make a guess at the sort of income range the House of Lords represents. It is clearly on the high side even for upper-class standards. One could estimate from the occupations represented as well as other evidence in the sample (e.g. ownership of more than one house) that no more than eight per cent of the peerage have an income of less than £4,000 a year. In the first three groups incomes must range from about £4,000 a year up to several times that figure. The landowner is particularly hard to define in income terms because, as I explain in Chapter 9, what he has is a 'way of life' which he tends not to think about in terms of hard cash. While the occupations listed suggest that there is not much elbow-room now for an old-style leisure class, the idea of an aristocracy which is 'broke' is a myth.

But the most interesting thing about the occupations, it seems to me, is the way they strike a balance, so that the aristocratic quadruped has a footing in just enough of the right places to give it stability and a look of social reality. Though some of the estates represented among the landowners will be small and possibly of fairly recent vintage, the connection with the land is strong enough to give an impression of continuing local roots and old traditions. Next there is the smaller businessman-landowner group which might be said to act as a bridge or communications link with the world of commerce, and the company directors proper cover a wide enough field of interests. If one subtracts the seven 'retired' men from the sample it would seem that about a quarter of the peerage could be described as professional men in some degree, outside the company director class. Therefore it is hardly true to claim, as some peers do, that the peerage is 'indistinguishable from the professional classes'. The land ownership is at least one thing that marks it off. Again, the professional element is just enough to demonstrate contact with modern life.

While it might be difficult to provide chapter and verse to back up the theory it would seem that the composition of the aristocracy has always been just about 'right for the time'. There are now about nineteen lords per million of the population. In Henry VII's

time it was fifteen per million. Between those times there have
been many highs and lows in the number of new lords created.
But, broadly speaking, the proportion has kept fairly steady in
relation to the population as a whole. At times the taboos of the
elite have imposed a big time-lag on the speed with which it has
managed to catch up with reality. For much of the nineteenth
century they dragged their feet socially, politically, and in terms
of what part they were ready to play in the way the country
earned its living. Again they woke up just at the last moment;
and one might say that to have a quarter of the peerage actively
connected with commerce and industry by 1896 was also about
'right for the time'.

I think it unlikely that this nicely-balanced tightrope walk can
be pure accident since it is obviously one of the main preservatives
of the aristocracy as an institution with some glimmer of real life
about it. The Prime Minister and the Honours Committee in
office at any one time clearly do not deliberately set about creating
a balance between land, business, and professional interests in
recommending new men for ennoblement. The nature of new
creations depends on a variety of seemingly arbitrary factors such
as the colour of the party in power, political expediency, not to
mention the unpredictable chances of what sort of people are
inheriting established titles. If any Prime Minister wanted to let
the aristocracy die off as an archaic joke much the best way
would be to insist on choosing – if new titles have to be made at
all – only the very wealthy or only the much-landed. This does
not happen. Public instinct, I suggest, operates in making or
approving the sort of fairly balanced selection which has promise
of a continuing life-span. The reason it does so is that the British
continue to need an aristocracy. It needs it, not for its glamorously
coroneted appearances which are, after all, highly infrequent. It
needs it because the aristocracy acts as the keystone of the class
system. It needs the class system because, being so ingrained, it
acts for most people as the framework of their security about social
status; and ultimately it needs it because the public has not yet
been able to imagine what life is like without class. It is a step into
the dark. True, some degree of social and economic levelling

continues. But underneath this there is always some instinctive pressure engendered by all classes to keep the social pyramid in being.

Leaving aside whether this is a good or bad thing, whether the security of the class system is real or bogus, it is fairly evident that the aristocracy is still shaped for continuity. It can afford its feudal fancies, its antique heraldry, its portly parades, all the things which lend the traditional aura, simply because there are enough lords who are sceptical about these things. It can afford stately-homes, showmen-peers, and the gadding about with lions and round-abouts, simply because there are enough ultra-grand lords who find such things disturbing. And the showmen and the professionals of all kinds perform the same service of making sense of the lords who still hanker for feudal dignity.

Big Business

As one would expect of an elite with any claim to serious regard, the nobility has a large stake in business, not only in its aggregate number of directorships but also in its representation in the major enterprises. Ninety-one peers have seats on the boards of Britain's top hundred companies and thirteen hold chairmanships among them.[1] Most of this group hold directorships outside the top companies as well. One of the interesting points about this group – and this may well apply to most of the peers who are exclusively company directors – is that they are quite clearly the newer titled families. This is shown in Table II. For convenience, those fifty-nine lords who have been the first in the family to get a title have been omitted. Those listed are the thirty-one peers whose title is second generation or older.

The big business group is essentially comprised of men whose families have risen to prominence over the last century or commonly a much shorter period, and there is little connection among them with the older landed class. In only half-a-dozen cases in the group does Burke's Peerage trace back a pedigree before 1800. These few representatives of the older families include Lord

[1] Top hundred companies as listed by The Times for 1966.

Halsbury, a branch of the Giffards who were at Hastings and settled here in the immediate post-Conquest period. He is unusual in the peerage in being a well-qualified scientist. He has led a number of bodies concerned with research and has been governor of the BBC. Lord Brocket is one of an Ulster family of ancient lineage though the title did not come until 1933. Viscount Hampden's family acquired a barony, their first step up the ladder, in 1321. The Earldom of Perth dates to 1605. The Earl of Rothes is the 20th Earl, the barony dating from 1445. Lord Verulam's family came to prominence in medieval times. Lord Bicester is of the Smith family, one of the old banking dynasties.

TABLE II: DIRECTORSHIPS IN TOP 100 COMPANIES

Note:

Table shows the thirty-one second-generation or older peers holding seats on these boards. Figures in brackets give total number of directorships held in these and other companies. Chairmanships (chs) are also mentioned where these are numerous. The date preceding each peer is the date the family first acquired titled rank. Each peer's main business interests are given but the list is not meant to be exhaustive.

1881	Lord Ampthill	(1)	tobacco
1938	Lord Bicester	(8)	merchant banking; Shell; Vickers
1935	Lord Blackford	(13)	(5 chs) banking; brewing; insurance
1933	Lord Brocket	(9)	(5 chs) brewing; insurance
1939	Visc. Caldecote	(12)	aircraft manuf; electronics
1936	Lord Catto	(9)	merchant banking
1914	Lord Cozens-Hardy	(1)	glass
1929	Lord Dulverton	(2)	tobacco
1918	Lord Essendon	(4)	shipping
1917	Lord Forteviot	(6)	whisky; chairman Dewars
1942	Lord Geddes	(12)	(5 chs) shipping; finance
1911	Lord Glenconner	(9)	mining; merchant banking

1944	Lord Gretton	(3)	brewing
1885	Lord Halsbury	(6)	distilling; chemicals
1321	Visc. Hampden	(7)	merch. banking (man. dir.); insurance
1929	Earl of Inchcape	(31)	shipping; banking; oil
1919	Earl of Iveagh	(2)	brewing
1941	Lord Kindersley	(6)	merchant banking; chairman Rolls Royce
1947	Lord Layton	(4)	steel
1945	Lord Lyle	(4)	sugar
1932	Lord Moyne	(4)	brewing
1960	Lord Nelson	(11)	electrics (chairman and chief exec., English Electric)
1605	Earl of Perth	(6)	sugar; banking; insurance
1919	Lord Rothermere	(10)	newspapers; TV; films
1939	Lord Rotherwick	(28)	shipping; finance
1445	Earl of Rothes	(6)	electrics; insurance
1937	Lord Runciman	(14)	(8 chs) banking; insurance
1917	Lord Southborough	(4)	petroleum (man. dir., Shell transport)
1935	Lord Tweedsmuir	(10)	finance
1633	Earl of Verulam	(10)	engineering; metals
1918	Visc. Weir	(6)	rubber; banking; TV

Otherwise it would seem that these captains of industry are generally from families who rose from relatively small beginnings in the nineteenth century or later. They moved ahead possibly because their attention was not so much divided by estate owner- ship and, too, because they had fewer of the landed class's in- hibitions about trade and technical matters.

Titles as such within the business world probably have less significance than almost anywhere else, though they may well induce outsiders to believe – as some lords complain – that any nobleman on the board is bound to be there for decorative pur- poses only. This belief has been encouraged by some of the companies themselves, either through their own superstition about titles or their resolve to play up to other people's. Many, perhaps most, of the lords on boards are outside directors who do not play a vital part in the day-to-day running of the show. Banks and insurance companies have especially tended to have two or three peers on the board to impress shareholders. I met only one peer who candidly admitted to being a 'wallflower'. He said he 'enjoyed the meetings' (of a bank board). City people have the impression that these decorative appointments are less common than they were ten years ago. As business becomes more specialised the redundant amateur becomes more obvious and less impressive even to the shareholders. Even the 'wallflowers', it is claimed, usually pay their way by introducing new business through their connections, by acting as snappers-up of political gossip or as useful go-betweens with old school friends or club-mates on other boards.[1]

It can be financially helpful to the lord concerned. One peer told me how he had been struggling (when he was merely heir to the title) to keep a large family on a middling salary. As soon as he inherited the title he got a seat on several boards, his earnings tripled, and he was able to pay off his old mortgage and move to a big house in a smart neighbourhood. A success story, if you like. I asked him how he felt about it. 'It released my talents,' he said, with touching simplicity. He had a point, at that. He found that he was as capable as the other board members, and by no means a passenger. There must be a number of other examples of talent-release by a simple injection of titled rank.

The Warrior Elite

The idea of an aristocracy thus means little in the business world. A peer with ability is on the same terms as any other professional, though he probably has a certain edge over rivals in making contacts, particularly overseas. Otherwise the titles of the able and the not-so-able are exploited where they can be as just another kind of business asset.

[1] Appearances can also be deceptive, a City expert reminded me. 'Take the case of Lord So-and-So,' he said, mentioning a peer vaguely attached to several boards in the financial world. 'Quite clearly one of the least intellectually endowed lords we have. But an impeccable judgment on money. He's got a nose for it. Sniffs it like Burgundy.'

To find an employment area where an aristocracy or special class elite still counts one has to turn to one of the older professions traditionally favoured by gentlemen, the Army for example. Up to fairly recent times the officer-corps recruited itself from the wealthier landed classes. The reason was a mixture of tradition, deliberate policy, and the fact that a military career was far too expensive for almost anyone else. Up to 1914 being an officer was impossible without private means. For most of the nineteenth century the majority of officers purchased their commissions. In 1870 a first commission in the Foot Guards cost £1,200. Promotion had to be bought, too. It could cost £10,000 to get from subaltern's rank to lieutenant-colonel.[1]

The exclusiveness was justified, or rationalised, by two theories. First, the landed gentlemen were rightfully in command because of their stake in the country – they 'had more to lose' (there was a degree of myth-making in this since the Navy, a much less upper class body, took most of the defence burden in the nineteenth and twentieth centuries). Second, that their self-assurance and habit of command made them the best 'natural' leaders. There was obviously a good deal of truth in this; but there were few aspirants from outside the class who wanted to challenge the theory. On the other hand, the myth that being a 'gentleman' inevitably signified all-round capability invited some disasters and did as much as anything to delay serious professional training. 'Efficiency', in the sense in which a modern industrialist might use it was (and still largely is) quite alien to the nature of the English gentleman. They put their trust in personal qualities; and it is certainly not hard to detect in it a rather uncritical faith in the natural superiority of the breed. 'They asserted the primacy of the aristocratic values in military life – courage, honour, dash, as opposed to expertise, rational calculation, and bureaucratic efficiency.'[2]

There is no doubt that it is an outlook that has produced many remarkably brave men, many heroes. Patriotism and readiness for

[1] For this and other background information I am indebted to a thesis entitled *The Origins and Recruitment of the British Army Elite, 1870-1959*, by Dr C. B. Otley of the University of Sheffield.
[2] Otley, op. cit.

sacrifice on the battlefield have remained distinctively aristocratic attributes. It is also arguable that the outlook has, on occasions, led to some dire shortcomings in preparedness; and the unsung infantry, not always shaped so much in the heroic mould, shared in the heavy price paid for dash and honour when some bureaucratic efficiency would not have come amiss.

In peacetime the profession of arms has been seen as a fairly leisurely occupation in which time could be devoted to cultivating the traditional qualities and pursuits of the gentleman. In wartime, too, on occasion. The Duke of Wellington, a great zealot for aristocratic leadership, kept a pack of hounds available for officers' use during the Peninsula War. Robert Graves once related how, when he joined the Royal Welch Fusiliers in 1915, he found its two battalions playing polo and riding lessons were still obligatory. Graves asked one of the officers if there wasn't a war on, and the reply was, 'The battalion doesn't recognise it socially.'

Professionalism developed very slowly through the nineteenth century, always with this emphasis on breeding at its shoulder. Some of the costly errors in the Crimea, the Boer War, and in 1914–18, induced a growing public scepticism about the special talents of the aristocratic leadership and helped to hurry along more professional attitudes. But a degree of exclusiveness in the officer-corps remains; the sources of recruitment have not greatly changed. Between 1870 and 1959, with very little variation over the whole period, roughly a third of all members of the officer-elite were closely related to major figures in the upper classes; and, according to a sample in 1959, eighty-three per cent of army officers were public-school educated.

But public-schools vary, and the leaning towards true aristocratic connections is far more noticeable in the so-called 'smarter' regiments (i.e. socially smart) which are those which form the Household Brigade. The Brigade is made up of five Guards regiments – the Grenadiers, Coldstream, Scots, Irish and Welsh Guards – with the first two carrying the most *cachet*. There are two cavalry regiments, the Lifeguards and the Royal Horse Guards (the 'Blues'). In the latter, which are regarded as top of the league for smartness, between five and ten per cent of the officers are titled or heirs to titles, and there are close connections with the landed gentry. In school background they show a much higher proportion of recruits from Eton than from other public schools. They particularly outnumber the products of those newer public schools which developed on Dr Arnold 'character-training' lines and whose alumni, while they may be 'gentlemen' in the sense that a mother would recognise, are not necessarily *gentlemen* in the traditional and purist sense of the word. In 1963 the Colonel of the Coldstreams said that half his officers were old Etonians. The Household Brigade as a whole has only a handful of officers with a grammar-school background, and a high proportion – as much as forty-five per cent in some regiments – are the sons of former officers in the regiment.

In trying to give the Army officer corps as a whole a democratic appearance – the main burden of the recruiting campaign over the last few years – the Army finds itself up against difficulties similar to those of the Conservative Central Office in its attempts to place candidates of a wider class background in some of the Tory strongholds. The plain fact is that most peope in Britain of a conservative temperament (found in all classes) insist on voting for, or being led by, individuals of a higher class than their own. This presents the recruiting department with one of those pretty layer-cakes of dilemma which are typical of the class system. The trouble is that they cannot discuss the class aspects too bluntly and openly. The recruiting campaign is almost plaintive in its egalitarian message, urging the grammar-school lad that he cannot fail to get to the top. This may be true for the especially able in most regiments. One thing that is not mentioned is that most esteem in a military as well as a social sense still goes to those Household regiments which are officered largely by a class elite. It is also true, strangely enough, that the state-educated aspirant with a heavy regional accent would find more acceptance in the socially-secure cavalry or Guards mess than he might in regiments lower down the scale. But the look of class solidarity about the officer corps is one thing that makes the outsider disinclined to try to get in. In the Household Brigade and a number of other smarter regiments a private income is needed if the officer is not to feel a poor relation. For the regiment based in London £200 a year is about the minimum and, according to former officers, between £500 and £1,000 a year is 'helpful'.

Senior officers tend to speak in cloudy terms when discussing the elite aspects of the Army. 'The troops are just tickled pink to be led by a lord,' said one Colonel. 'They're the biggest snobs going – and good luck to them.' In choosing his officers he said, 'What I'm looking for is good chaps, whoever they are.' I am sure he sincerely meant it. But what, it turned out, he meant by 'good chaps' were 'people who are going to fit in' which, in practice, meant drawing them from a fairly narrow class spectrum. I would doubt that there is any deliberate policy of excluding middle-class aspirants. An elite of this sort is self-perpetuating simply because its differences are strong enough to be recognisable by, and daunting to, outsiders, even before they have to consider their lack of private means and so on.

The philosophy of these 'smart' or aristocratic regiments is distinct from that of other army units. The assumption is that officers are primarily gentlemen and therefore give their orders as a personal right rather than as a professional concession. In the officers' mess – indeed, on the battlefield too – there is more emphasis on personal relationships, less on protocol and rank (one of those odd reversals of the expected, typical of any area where the aristocratic element intervenes. In the Royal Navy the opposite is the case: the higher the prestige of the unit, e.g. a battleship, the greater the formality, the fiercer the saluting.) In a cavalry mess, officers of all ranks are on Christian name terms. The commanding officer, that is the Colonel, is the only one addressed by rank, but he addresses all his officers by Christian name. The only saluting an officer normally expects to do is a click of the heels on first meeting his company commander in the morning; but at the same time he greets him as 'Tommy', 'Harry', or whatever it is.[1] The most disliked things are earnestness or, as

[1] Non-commissioned officers observe protocol in their own way, of course. A friend who served in the wartime Guards recalls hearing a sergeant-major yell at the recruit standing next to him in the ranks (he proved to be a duke), 'For Christ's sake wake your ideas up, Your Grace!'

it is sometimes termed, 'efficiency', a word invariably used in a derogatory sense, in heavily inverted commas. The cavalry elite look down from a great height on the officer-corps of the ordinary line regiments and include them all under the generic nickname, 'Charlies', which implies earnestness, 'efficiency', and other leaden-footed attributes. Evelyn Waugh's war trilogy, *Sword of Honour*, while it is imbued with an extra dash of Catholic fatalism, perfectly catches the spirit of it. His fictional regiment, the Halberdiers, with its strong regard for personal relationships (warm or cool), its recognition of muddle as a regrettable (there was, after all, a war on) fact of nature, clearly reveal it to have been a regiment of high social prestige (Waugh himself was in the Royal Horse Guards). Characters who show any square-jawed liking for 'efficiency' are exposed as frauds.

Mess rules in a smart regiment are far more flexible than in others. There is rather more tolerance of individual quirks of character than would be the case lower down the scale. Since the assumption is that all the officers are 'honourable' (and, implicitly, with the financial means to support such a code to its full extent) the Colonel would not dream of setting a stake-limit for mess gambling, whereas this would be common in other regiments. Infantry regiments often have some mess taboos, as for instance that shop, religion and politics are banned as subjects of conversation. Cavalry regiments usually have no such restrictions. I asked a regular cavalry major whether this freedom opened up the talk to the challenge of the bigger subjects. 'Well ... not exactly. It's horses and women mostly, in that order. A few little islands of culture here and there, set in a sea of aristocratic indifference.' While it is quite obvious that any officer who commands a modern tank has to be a serious professional, there is still a decided preference for preserving attitudes in the effortless, amateur context, and there is a bias against too heavy an attachment to technology. Tank maintenance, for instance, the very basis of their war-effectiveness, is usually in the hands of a specialist engineering officer who is 'borrowed' from a technical regiment which obviously cannot afford to look down on 'efficiency' even in the worst sense of the word. Some of the lustre of gentlemanly status can thus only be preserved by little glosses of this sort.

Summing up the general effect of this elite is not easy. It is rather like having to divine the influence of Buckingham Palace or Nelson's Column on architecture. The only certain thing one can say is that it is there. The emphasis on the personal and gentlemanly code at the top of the military tree, the attractive dislike of bureaucracy, is a defence against Prussianism. When it comes to war, though, this subtle regard for individuality, honour, and the old romanticism of the battlefield, may only help to disguise the impersonal juggernaut that it has been since 1914. Perhaps a greater service to humanity is done by those who do not behave like gentlemen and, instead, run away. But in peacetime, this military elite still wins regard because of the nature of the class system; it is one small corner where memory of an aristocratic order is openly kept green.

PART THREE

F

9

THE GREAT ESTATES

The extraordinary tenacity of land-ownership within the British nobility and gentry is one of their most striking characteristics. Despite wars, agricultural depressions, the inroads of estate duties, family misfortunes (everything from gambling losses to the lack of an heir) the lordly classes remain easily the biggest private and individual landowners in the country. So far as an aristocratic group survives, with a personality distinct from that of the merely rich, it is due to this continued rootedness of much of the nobility in inherited land, and to the various social influences which flow from this.

Of course, a good many of those families which once owned a great estate no longer have so much as an acre left. It has often dwindled, even within the last fifty years, to little more than the garden of a town house. The minor landed gentry have suffered most in the decline of estate-ownership; the landless ones are chiefly noticeable for their insistence on keeping their names in the gentry reference books.

Since there is no central registry which can say who owns how much of Britain – an omission which is rather typical of the mystery surrounding property-ownership – it is hard to say exactly how much landed character the nobility has left. From my own experience of the field I would estimate that about a third of the total peerage, say 350 lords, still own enough land to provide a significant element in their income and outlook. This figure is composed about equally of those who combine estate ownership with active business interests; and those who live off the land alone. There are perhaps another 1,500 untitled landed

TABLE III: TABLE OF LAND OWNERSHIP

(1) The table gives some examples of the estates owned in 1967 by the nobility and gentry and compares them with the acreage owned by the family in 1873. Most of the figures in the 1967 column were communicated to the author by the owner concerned; a few others were derived from recent press reports and other sources believed to be reliable. In some cases the land has been passed to the heir; but, for consistency, the name of the head of the family is given throughout.

(2) A blank in the 1873 column means only that there is no corresponding entry in the source-book for these figures, *The Great Landowners of Great Britain*, by J. Bateman (1882 edn). In some cases the land has been acquired since then.

(3) The estates mentioned in the table represent about one-seventh of those owned by the titled nobility, according to the author's estimate. It should be stressed that they are not necessarily meant to indicate which are the biggest or most valuable. They are simply examples from the large to the small; and while they are not a 'random sample' in the precise scientific sense, the author believes that they give a fair picture of acreages owned by the 'landed classes' for the country as a whole.

(4) The simple acreage, as such, is no indicator of the value or earnings of an estate unless the character of the land is taken into account. Estates in Scotland and the moorland areas of the north of England may have a book-value averaging between £3 and £10 an acre. Good arable land in England is worth £240 an acre. So a 10,000-acre estate in the south may be worth twenty times as much as one in the north; and a hundred acres of London will earn far more than either. Even the smallest of the London estates, the Duke of Bedford's thirty acres, is worth at least £20 millions.

ENGLAND AND WALES

	1873 (acres)	1967 (acres)
Abergavenny, *Marquess of*	28,000	1,000 (Kent)
Anglesey, *Marquess of*	29,700	3,000 (Anglesey)
Aylesford, *Earl of*	19,500	5,000 (Warwicks)
Ailesbury, *Marquess of*	55,000	6,000 (Wilts)
Brocket, *Lord*	—	4,500 (Herts)
Brassey, *Lord*	4,000	4,000 (Northants)
Bath, *Marquess of*	55,000	10,000 (Wilts)
Beaufort, *Duke of*	51,000	52,000 (Glos)
Bolingbroke, *Viscount*	3,300	4,000 (Hants)
Bolton, *Lord*	29,200	18,500 (Yorks)
Blakenham, *Viscount*	—	580 (Suffolk)
Brudenell, *Mr E.*	15,000	10,000 (Leics and Northants)
Brabourne, *Lord*	4,100	3,000 (Kent)
Bromley-Davenport, *Sir W.*	15,600	5,000 (Cheshire)
Brownlow, *Lord*	58,300	10,000 (Lincs)

	1873 (acres)	1967 (acres)
Bristol, *Marquess of*	32,000	16,000 (Suffolk)
Carnarvon, *Earl of*	35,500	6,000 (Berks)
Cawdor, *Earl of*	34,700	30,000 (Wales)
Clinton, *Lord*	34,700	26,000 (Devon)
Cobham, *Viscount*	6,900	400 (Worcs)
Cowdray, *Viscount*	—	17,500 (Sussex)
Crathorne, *Baron*	5,600	4,000 (Yorks)
Craster, *Sir J.*	2,800	750 (Northumberland)
Durham, *Earl of*	30,000	30,000 (Durham, Northumberland)
Derby, *Earl of*	68,900	5,000 (Lancs)
Devon, *Earl of*	53,000	5,000 (Devon)
Devonshire, *Duke of*	138,500	32,000 (Yorks) 40,000 (Derbyshire)
Egremont, *Lord*	109,900	20,000 (Sussex, Cumberland)
Exeter, *Marquess of*	28,200	22,000 (Lincs)
Ferrers, *Earl*	8,600	250 (Norfolk)
Feversham, *Lord*	39,300	47,000 (Yorks)

	1873 (acres)	1967 (acres)
Fulford of Fulford	4,000	3,500 (Devon)
Grafton, *Duke of*	25,000	11,000 (Norfolk)
Harewood, *Earl of*	29,600	7,000 (Yorks)
Huntingdon, *Earl of*	13,500	None
Hertford, *Marquess of*	12,200	8,000 (Warwickshire and Worcs)
Iliffe, *Lord*	—	10,000 (Berks)
Iveagh, *Earl of*	—	24,000 (Norfolk)
Legh, *Mr Charles*	5,800	2,000 (Cheshire)
Leverhulme, *Viscount*	—	99,000 (Cheshire)
Lonsdale, *Earl of*	68,000	71,000 (Westmorland, Cumberland)
Marlborough, *Duke of*	23,500	11,500 (Oxfordshire)
Middleton, *Lord*	99,500	13,500 (Yorks)
Newcastle, *Duke of*	35,500	9,000 (Dorset)
Northumberland, *Duke of*	186,300	80,000 (Northumberland)
Pembroke, *Earl of*	44,800	16,000 (Wilts)
Portland, *Duke of*	64,000	17,000 (Notts)
Redesdale, *Lord*	26,400	1,000 (Northumberland)

	1873 (acres)	1967 (acres)
Richmond and Gordon, *Duke of*	17,000	12,000 (Sussex)
Scarsdale, *Viscount*	9,900	6,000 (Derby)
Somerset, *Duke of*	25,300	5,700 (Wilts and Devon)
Spencer, *Earl*	27,100	15,000 (Northants and Leics)
Verulam, *Earl of*	10,100	5,200 (Herts and Norfolk)
Waldegrave, *Earl*	15,400	5,000 (Somerset)
Weld, *Col Joseph*	15,500	11,000 (Dorset)
Westminster, *Duke of*	20,000	18,000 (Cheshire and Shropshire)

SCOTLAND

	1873 (acres)	1967 (acres)
Airlie, *Earl of*	69,800	40,000
Argyll, *Duke of*	175,100	96,000
Atholl, *Duke of*	201,000	120,000
Balfour, *Earl*	87,000	3,500
Breadalbane, *Earl of*	438,300	None
Buccleuch, *Duke of*	460,100	220,000

	1873 (acres)	1967 (acres)
Cameron of Lochiel	126,000	130,000
Cawdor, Earl	101,600	50,000
Dalhousie, Lord	138,000	44,000
Haig, Earl	—	1,500
Hamilton, Duke of	157,300	13,000
Home, Sir A. Douglas-	106,500	60,000
Leverhulme, Lord	—	37,000
Lothian, Marquess of	32,300	30,000
Lovat, Lord	181,000	160,000
Mansfield, Lord	49,000	37,000
Moray, Earl of	81,600	44,000
Moleyns, Andrew Eveleigh de	—	120,000
Polwarth, Lord	10,600	6,000
Portland, Duke of	118,000	47,000
Seafield, Countess of	305,900	213,000
Sutherland, Countess of	1,358,000	138,000
Westminster, Duke of	—	60,000

F*

LONDON: PROPERTY

	1967 (acres)
Duke of Westminster (Grosvenor Estates)	300
Lord Howard de Walden	100
Earl of Cadogan (Cadogan Estates)	90
Viscount Portman (Portman Estates)	100
Duke of Bedford	30

families who still own big estates and who are still recognisable as gentry or 'squires' in the old sense.[1]

The most noticeable thing about those noblemen who still own land is that they nearly always do so abundantly. There are no half-measures about it. Either they have left the rural scene for good and become totally urbanised; or they own estates of several thousand acres.

This looks a significant point. It means that the nobleman expects to have an estate big enough to allow him to live on rents paid by tenants rather than on primarily farming the land himself. In other words, the nobility's traditional attitude to the land is still basically there. One can see this more clearly by considering how it avoids the alternatives to this time-honoured role.

If a family crisis comes up which obliges him to sell the greater part of the estate – to pay death duties, for instance – he will prefer to sell the lot and find another source of income, probably in the city. This is a little puzzling. One might suppose that he would try to hang on to a few hundred acres of the ancestral land,

---

[1] The position of the landed gentry is slightly different to that of the peerage, and is more fully dealt with in Chapter 10.

to retain the family foothold in the district and to indulge an interest in farming.

Again, if he were as closely attached to country life for its own sake as is claimed he might reasonably become that hybrid-sounding thing, a titled yeoman farmer. There is nothing materially wrong with this. From a mixed farm of three hundred acres he could reasonably expect an income of £4–5,000 a year, the attractions of country life, and very sound professional status. Yet, according to my findings, the nobleman even these days seldom seems to do so.

Most lords with big estates also keep a large home farm 'in hand' these days (looked after by their agent) because farming earns good profits now and there are many tax reliefs attached to it. But in the course of personally visiting about fifty landed lords and gentry, I met only one who could simply be described as a farmer. (There are others, but this indicates the proportion.) This was Earl Ferrers, whose family, the Shirleys, has roots going back to the Conquest period (the pedigree, woven into a silken banner, is thirty feet long) and in 1873 owned 8,000 acres of land. The family seat, Staunton Ferrers in Leicestershire, and the last of the family land was sold in the 1930s. The house is now a con-valescent home. Lord Ferrers, who took an agricultural degree at Cambridge, now runs a farm of 250 acres in Norfolk.

I heard of no case where a peer has completely reversed the traditional role and become someone else's tenant. If this situation exists it must be extremely rare. To see the meaning of this it should be made clear that being a tenant is not a position which lacks material or even social status. There are tenant-farmers whose rented land in the southern counties runs up to ten thou-sand acres, and they are rich men with ample farming prestige to match.

I think one may conclude from all this that, for all the talk of the common peer, things are different in the country. There are still felt to be strong inhibitions about how a nobleman may earn his living from the land. It is evidently important that he should be in some squire position. Simply to be an agricultural producer is less acceptable to the group than to take a job right outside the landed circle, as a member of the Stock Exchange or as an insurance underwriter, for instance.

Just as hereditary wealth itself has shown great durability, so there would appear to remain a large measure of the tradition that the lord has a special relationship with the land: that the noble landowner has a particular status and function to maintain which goes beyond being a mere agriculturist. The estate owners have, in fact, made their home farms bigger these days for sound economic reasons, so that they are personally somewhat closer to the activities of the pigs and the poultry than they used to be. But very few are apparently ready to operate without a tenantry system, a rent-roll, and estate-owning status.

The significance of this, in estimating the survival of aristocracy, is that land-ownership has always been regarded as the primary source of its prestige. It was always (and still is) the most durable form of property with a certain pagan magic possibly attached to it. A gift of land was the monarch's customary way of rewarding military service and, at the same time, of establishing a baronial peace-keeping system in the shires, one which would also be a source of soldiery for foreign wars. Later it was granted as a bonus to administrators, to recognise men of local eminence, or to set up court favourites and royal bastards.

Land gave the nobleman a fixed domain where he was the privileged master who also had duties. Out in the shires, the assumptions of a national ruling class were acquired. The people continued to recharge their allegiance to the hereditary principle, seeing the Big House as the centre of affairs for generation after generation. Out in the shires the lords developed their paternalist attitudes and, incidentally, learned how to run an empire. In the rich and cultivated life that circulated round the great noble houses was developed that unique product, the English gentleman, with his enormous self-assurance, his readiness to take command without any self-questioning about his merits or talents, his antagonism to urban 'progress', and his own complex code of manners and habits.

This old landed class had a grandeur and character all its own. V. Sackville-West has given one of the best pictures of it, as it was sixty years ago, just before the break-up of the greater holdings:

'They all belonged to the same solid, territorial aristocracy that took no account of "sets" or upstarts, jargon or crazes, but pursued their way and maintained their dignity with the weight and rumble of a family coach. They had genealogical tables at their fingers' ends; they thought more of a small old family than of a large new fortune; they were profoundly and genuinely shocked by the admission of Jews into society ... Their solidarity was terrific. They had a way of speaking of one another which reduced everybody else to the position of a mere petitioner upon the doorstep. Too well-bred to be arrogant, too uninspired to sneer, they were simply so well convinced of their own unassailability that the conviction required no voicing, but betrayed itself quietly in glances, in topics, in the set of shoulders, the folding of hands, and in the serene assumption of certain standards and particular values as common to all. They moved all together, a large square block in the heart of English society, massive, majestic, and dull.'[1]

The old solidarity has broken up to a great extent; but there remain a number of ways in which the landed class still acts as the caretaker of what remains of the aristocratic system. There are many peers, both land-owning and otherwise, who will say that 'a title is meaningless without land' – that simply to be a baron in advertising, sportswear, or journalism, is to have become a sort of honorific ghost. In the case of the House of Lords, the irony is that the landless peers are among its most regular attenders and hardest workers, whereas it was the idea of the hereditary stake in the land, of thus being 'born to rule', which gave the House its sense of absolute legitimacy.

The idea that land-ownership was automatically implied by noble rank persisted in the nineteenth century. In 1873, only sixty of the 585 peers and peeresses who then existed had no land. The mystique attached to it was exemplified by the case of Disraeli who, though it is hard to think of anyone less suited to the pastoral scene, had to be set up with his 750 acres at Beacons-

[1] V. Sackville-West, *The Edwardians*, London, 1930.

field to make him respectable. Gladstone, too, arch-foe of the Tory landowners, was himself a dutiful member of the landed gentry, with no fewer than 2,500 tenants on his 7,000 acres in Cheshire and just as keen a sense as his opponents of being 'born to rule'.

The table on p. 150 gives some examples of the size of present land-holdings compared with what they were in 1873, when most estates were probably at about their peak size. The survey from which the 1873 figures are taken[1] was called the New Domesday Survey since it was the first assessment of land-holdings since 1086. It was ordered by parliament, on the encouragement of Lord Derby and other aristocrats who wanted to demonstrate to critics that land-ownership was relatively widespread. The outcome rebounded on their heads. It revealed that four-fifths of the land was owned by seven thousand people, that about ninety per cent of the peerage owned sizeable estates, and that more than twenty peers owned more than 100,000 acres each.

From the acreages in the table (and I emphasise that these estates are only a random sample) it can be calculated that in the last ninety-five years the estates of the titled nobility – the gentry were not included in the calculation – have shown an average decline of seventy-six per cent in England and Wales, and sixty-nine per cent in Scotland. These figures are broadly confirmed by the numbers of country houses which are estimated to have closed in about the same period, allowing for the fact that many which are still lived in have only their gardens left.

Of the peers in my list who still own land, only twelve, or about a quarter of the total, own less than five thousand acres. The list is slightly biased towards landed families which have been historically prominent and who thus might be expected to own more land than others. Allowing for this, I think it would be a fair estimate to say that two-thirds of the landed nobility in England and Wales, or just over two hundred families, own a minimum of five thousand acres.

Nearly all of these estates have been in the family for some centuries. It is rare to find a landed lord holding an estate which

[1] J. Bateman, *The Great Landowners of Great Britain*, London, 1882.

has been wholly or partly bought by the present owner, or by a predecessor in the last two or three generations.

The holdings of the landed gentry are harder to assess, because they have become a rather loosely definable class. My impression is that those who are still established on old family land, and are getting most of their income from it will have an estate averaging about 1,500 acres. But the range across the average is wide. Some gentry have estates of ten thousand acres or more, a size which rates their untitled owners well up with, or even ahead of, their lordly neighbours – down to holdings of a few hundred acres or so, the last gasp of the old patrimony.

The decline of land-ownership was an abrupt and not a gradual one. One authority calculates that between six and eight million acres changed hands between 1918 and 1926. A number of present lords can vividly recollect, like a sombre passage in the family saga, the day that large stretches of the family territory came under the auctioneer's hammer. Lord Ferrers recalls 'the terrible wrench, the feeling of losing family roots' which he experienced at the time, in the 1930s, when the last of the Ferrers' land in Leicestershire had to be sold. By the date of the sale it was down to 1,700 acres. Lord Ferrers' father, who had made strenuous efforts over a long period to find a buyer who would preserve the family mansion, Staunton Ferrers, died the night before the auction.

Lord Pembroke told me how 'whole valleys and villages' had to be auctioned out of the sometime sixty thousand acres of the Wiltshire estate. The Marquess of Anglesey, whose nineteenth-century forebears were reckoned to be the richest men in England, owning 100,000 acres, most of it in the Staffordshire mineral country, now runs a shrub nursery on the three thousand acres which is left of the estate on the island of Anglesey.

Despite the decline, a sufficient number of noble families have managed to hold on to large acreages – to an extent that, in out-line at least, still strikingly preserves an historic elite-pattern of ownership. The pattern is still the varied thing it always was. In Wales, peers' landholdings are few but large, mostly in sheep-and-timber country. In Scotland a very high proportion of the nobility have land. Because of the terrain, estates are almost invariably very extensive and of ancient connection with the same family. In Perthshire, still one of the most aristocratic of counties, no fewer than thirty families have been landowners there since before the Battle of Flodden (1513).

The greatest change in the last half-century is that the land-holdings of public bodies and corporations now easily dominate those of any of the remaining territorial magnates. The biggest single owner is now the Forestry Commission, which has acquired 2,500,000 acres since it was founded in 1919. Other big public owners are the Crown Commissioners (285,000 acres), the Church Commissioners (180,000), the armed forces, the railways, and so on. The insurance companies and such bodies as the Oxford and Cambridge colleges also hold large parcels of land as a sound form of investment.

What is surprising, however, is how far the old pattern of indi-vidual noble ownership has survived, and how far the gentlemanly classes still keep some measure of their former country position because of it. Lords and old-established gentry are still easily the biggest individual landowners in every county which is mainly agricultural.

A handful of the dukes are still among the most affluent land-lords in town and country; the capital value of their estates makes some of them millionaires several times over. The Duke of Westminster's estate, now a family trust like many others, is reckoned to be the richest in the country and it is one of the most remarkable in the way it has been built up.

The Grosvenors (the family name of the Dukes of Westminster) were minor gentry in Cheshire from the twelfth century to the early seventeenth century, deriving their position from the few thousand acres granted them by the powerful Earls of Chester. Now the earldom of Chester is extinct; but the Grosvenors prospered.

The big step forward was the marriage of Sir Thomas Gros-venor to the heiress daughter of Alexander Davis, a rich Middlesex farmer, in 1677. This brought into the family some of the best grazing land within the London boundaries, the fine meadowland between the Thames and the present Oxford Street. When it came under building it provided a handsome income from the rents of Mayfair and Belgravia. Besides this, the estate now covers 12,000 acres in Cheshire, 6,000 in Shropshire, and 60,000 in the north of Scotland, and the Grosvenor Trust's agent has to run a private plane to supervise these territories.

The estate is one of the very few which has extended itself into overseas property. It now has land in South Africa, Canada, and Australia, some in Bermuda and, for some odd reason, owns one house in Nairobi, Kenya. The family had to pay £11 millions estate duties in 1953 on property valued at about £50 millions.

The Duke of Beaufort's 52,000 acres of Gloucestershire is the heart of what is known as the Beaufort Country, a famous fox-hunting area over which the Duke runs his private pack of hounds. On paper, the value of the land itself must approach £15 millions and, renting out at about £6 an acre, it probably has one of the biggest rent-rolls for a predominantly agricultural estate.

The Duke of Northumberland (the celebrated Percy family, traditional protectors of the northern border) has 80,000 acres in his home county, including valuable land which stretches through the mining areas to Newcastle-upon-Tyne. The Duke of Devonshire has 40,000 acres of Derbyshire and a Yorkshire grouse moor (none at all in Devonshire itself). In its variety of moor, woodland, and arable, it is possibly the finest-looking of the dukedoms. The Duke of Portland owns 17,000 acres in Nottinghamshire and another 47,000 in Scotland.

The estates of the Scottish dukes are much the biggest in sheer size, but because they mostly consist of rough hill grazing, their capital value and the profit from them is proportionately a good deal less than those in the south. The Duke of Buccleuch is top of the list with 220,000 acres (part of the estate is in Leicestershire). He has three country houses and a town residence in use and has one of the best private art collections. Three other large ducal estates – those of Sutherland, Roxburghe, and Hamilton – complete a tight little covey of dukedoms on the Scottish border.

The reasons why the dukes are still so pre-eminent in land-ownership varies somewhat from one to another. In most cases they were territorial magnates before they acquired the senior title. The fact that they reached such eminence is a sign of the family's former standing in royal favour, and this often opened the way to fabulously lucrative court offices. In the days when rank was more significant, the dukes were expected to live with more 'port' or style than their juniors. Inevitably they were always a great marriage target for heiresses with ambitious parents; and the dukes, realistic men, have seldom flinched from the altar when it meant the financial betterment of the dynasty.

The much-landed dukes are particularly disinclined to sell their titles short by any false humility. Some of their estates, like those of Devonshire, Beaufort, and Northumberland, can still be seen as little rural kingdoms, relatively grand in size and large with a number of estate workers and servants to keep them going. The families on the estate have a strong sense of continuity about their small world.

The annual tea-party for the tenantry on one of these estates can be a striking sight, with perhaps three or four hundred estate dependents and their families milling about the trestle-tables which have been set up and victualled on the customary patch of grass between the stable block and the family chapel. Here, one can feel that one is in one of those private domains that existed more commonly in the nineteenth century. The Duke moves through the throng, shaking a hand here, a word there. It is all very friendly and informal; but in it there is also a hint of very special status, the air of an old-time princeling moving among his loyal subjects.

The estates of the rest of the landed peerage and greater gentry are also outstanding, far exceeding in size the holdings of property-owning commoners. There are very few independent yeomen, or even many of the new farming syndicates, which can approach their acreages. Over the last half-century a great many more people have acquired a share of the soil. About 265,000 people now own some agricultural land, but it averages only a hundred acres for each of them. If one were to share out the land equally among the whole population it would provide just over one acre apiece.

In England, the estates of the nobility are fairly evenly distributed over all the southern and midland counties, though they become scarcer, but correspondingly bigger, as one moves north. In the neighbourhood of industrial centres, especially in the north, there are gaps in the pattern, showing where the nobility have sold up and fled in face of the advancing factories and the urban sprawl, evidently preferring to take their profits rather than attempt to live a shop-soiled version of the gentlemanly life. In such places one often finds that it is the bigger territorial magnates who remain, possibly because their lands are wide enough to allow them to keep a lucrative foothold on the fringes of the industrial belt, while their own country seat is still far enough away not to have a speck of soot on the lawns.

The picture one gets of a typical county is of the existence of between six and a dozen really big landowners, both peers and major gentry, invariably with a historic attachment to the district; while below them come a larger number of long-established minor gentry, yeomen farmers and tenants, the two latter groups mixing the old-established and the relatively new.

In Northamptonshire, for example (and including the fringes of adjoining counties), the bigger owners include Earl Fitzwilliam (25,000 acres), the Marquess of Exeter (22,000), Earl Spencer (15,000), the Duke of Buccleuch (12,000), Lord Brownlow (10,000 in neighbouring Lincolnshire), and Mr Edmund Brudenell (10,000) – the Brudenells being a branch of an old and ennobled family which has lived in the same country house, Deene Park, since 1514.

Noble and gentry families inhabiting a particular region are often linked by marriage somewhere back in their pedigrees. One can dimly make out some sort of pattern in it, partly related, I suppose, to the development of the railway. In counties not too distant from London, territorial marriages frequent in earlier times, are becoming fewer as better transport allows more trips to London and a wider choice; though in the case of heiress marriages (like the Grosvenor-Davis one), pedigree and money beckoned to each other across the distances, however doubtful the stagecoach service.

The further one goes out from the centre, to the west and north of England and (especially) Scotland, the more localised become the marriage ties. In some of these remoter families these links recur, though possibly with gaps of generations or centuries, from medieval times up to the present.

Except in the case of the more pedigree-conscious peers, like the Scots, these remoter cousin-relationships are not taken very seriously by the lords concerned. At least the last generation to take a real interest in all these side-branches of the family tree seems to be gradually disappearing.

Another part of the old pattern whose outlines are still visible is what one might call the baronial satellite system. In early times it was the custom for the knights and gentry of a particular shire to march to war, with their men, under the banner of the leading local baron. This again created a close network of family ties.

Though traces of the system have become blurred with the departure of so many old families from the land, one can still find a good many cases of lords and gentry still living as neighbours in the same area, whose ancestors went off to Crecy, Agincourt, or some other battle together, linked by this feudal arrangement.

More surprising, to my mind, is that they so often seem to have kept the same relative status which they had, say, five centuries ago. The baron whose family once led the county contingent to the service of the King is still the leading local peer; the gentry (who may nowadays join him on a grouse shoot) are still at about the same level in relation to him.

This sort of thing demonstrates the peculiar durability of the land pattern. As to what significance it has for the present nobility, I think one could hardly claim the existence of anything so cohesive as an Agincourt Old Comrades Association. These ancient military links are merely part of the subconscious background of the landed classes (the Scots, again, are more aware of them); and nowadays they only show on the surface in the form of a common interest in the Territorial Army, the county regiment, and so on.

But I did hear of one or two piquant survivals. The Earls of Devon, for example – the celebrated Courtenay family whose pedigree connects with the last Christian emperors of Constantinople – settled in Devon in 1152 and once owned great stretches of land along the south coast of England (it is now down to 5,000 acres). The Courtenays were powerful enough to be the liege lords in medieval times of a number of gentry and minor lordlings' families whose descendants still own land in the area.

Among them are the Fulfords, also of old Crusader stock,[1] who live about ten miles away from the Earl's seat, Powderham Castle, as they have done for centuries.

Until a few years ago, I am told, the Fulfords insisted on sending the Earl a small sum of money each year. This was a token that they still owed him the feudal duty of half a knight's fee, which was the obligation to provide so many horses and men for military duty. This payment, which had been kept up for centuries, one scrupulously-loyal generation after another, continued until the Earl wrote and said, 'Seriously, I think we should call a halt to this . . .'

A somewhat similar relic is that the Earl of Mansfield, who lives at Scone Palace, near Perth, still receives a few shillings a year in 'protection money' from his tenants in Dumfriesshire. This payment, a consideration for defending them against rapacious barons round about, has been going on since medieval times. The present Earl gives rather more back to local charities than he gets; but there is no indication on either side that the custom will be stopped.

The hereditary feeling for the estate is still paramount among the nobility. I asked the peers and gentry I met what they saw as their main objective. They invariably replied, in so many words, 'to keep the estate intact and pass it on'. Ordinarily, this makes good business sense too, since land is an appreciating asset. But even in cases where it hardly does so, because of a chronic shortage of capital or because country life has no appeal for the present incumbent, there is usually a strong notion of a duty to posterity which acts as a deterrent against selling up.

Most families have had at least one holder in the past who let the estate slide, either through incompetence or dissipation. The family speaks of 'the bad 'un' – the 4th Marquess who neglected his acres for the sake of actresses and baccarat, the 7th Earl who was a recluse, that 12th Baron who was careless enough in the eighteenth century to mortgage away what is now a prosperous city centre and a landlord's dream of rents,

[1] See also Chapter 3.

They refer to the black sheep with wistful regret if he happened long enough ago; with distinct vexation if he was the one responsible for the mess they inherited. There he is, in the portrait on the stairs, dark eyes gazing out of noble and forthright features. 'Hardly put a penny back into it,' observes the Earl, as we pass by his predecessor.

Several told me how they had been instructed in youth about the importance of the hereditary duty to land. One elderly lord recalled his uncle saying to him frequently, 'Look after it, boy, or God will never forgive you and I'm damn sure the family won't.' But most heirs seem to have picked up the lesson as a matter of course, like breathing.

The greater fortunes among the landed classes were seldom made from the land itself, either from farming or the rents of tenant agriculture. In earlier times wealth came as much from court offices and sinecures as from an estate. Later, those who became really rich and survived best were the ones who had minerals under their land like the Dukes of Devonshire, the Marquesses of Anglesey (land in Staffordshire) and of Bute (South Wales coalfield), or the Earls of Durham and of Derby. Or there were others who had big rents from town property like the Dukes of Bedford and Westminster. From the mid-nineteenth century onwards, landowners increasingly tended to invest in commerce and industry as a form of income insurance, no matter how disdainful their attitude to the parvenus who ran such enterprises.

The richer lords are still those whose estates have produced a consistent enough surplus to enable them to invest in the business world and who manage to combine an estate with a number of city directorships. Others, particularly the younger ones, have gone in for law, banking, and other professions, and take a supervisory stroll round the estate with their agents at weekends.

Those who combine in this way appear to lead very busy lives. They may be richer but they are hardly a leisured class. The Marquess of Exeter (Sir David George Brownlow Cecil, sixty-two, the former Olympic hurdler), for example, is in the territorial magnate class with 22,000 acres, an estate that includes seventeen villages – largely owned by the family – and the right to appoint the vicar in seventeen church livings. With an agent to supervise, Lord Exeter farms 4,500 acres of his land himself.

In addition he is a director of one of the major banks, of a hotel company, and of six other companies mainly involved in engineering in the Midlands (he is chairman of four of them). In the week I met him, which seemed to be a fairly normal one, he was commuting from his estate to various board-rooms in the Midlands and London; also fitting in an Olympic Committee meeting, various business talks, the ceremonial opening of a swimming bath, and a spell at the House of Lords.

While the typical noble landlord still sets great store by his estate for its background value, with its undertone of family tradition and social place, he now takes its economic well-being much more seriously than most of his forebears ever have. Up to recent times the standard of management was mixed. A good many jogged along on the force of habit and very little was done about improving the tenants' cottages or the farm equipment. So long as the landlord got his surplus he was content enough.

Now it is fair to say that the bigger estates are better run and more productive than they have ever been. Day-to-day management is in the hands of well-trained agents; and it is common to find that the heir to the estate, after doing his spell in the Guards or the Cavalry, is working for a diploma at an agricultural college. He will often do a few years as an assistant on some other big estate before taking over his own.

The old amateur tradition is rapidly disappearing. In its place there is a readiness to exploit the patrimony on businesslike lines. I doubt that there was ever a great deal of sentiment applied in running the big estates. There is certainly little now. As old tenants die off, their land is incorporated into other tenants' farms, to make bigger units that make more economic sense. Some of the lords whose estates adjoin urban areas have shown themselves stubborn bargainers when it comes to selling land for housing.

There is also rather more resourcefulness. The Earl of Lonsdale is an example of the new professionalism. When he succeeded to the title in 1953 he inherited a 365-room Gothic palace in Westmorland, 40,000 acres of farmland, and 45,000 acres of common lands; 'but his high-sounding titles were about the only financial asset he had'.[1]

His great-uncle, the swashbuckling peer known as the Yellow Earl, owned coalfields in Cumberland, several country houses, two steam-yachts, a fleet of yellow carriages with liveried postillions, employed a hundred servants, and lived on the £80,000 a year pocket money allowed him by his trustees (£3,000 a year went on cigars alone).[2]

His successors had to find £2 millions in death duties and the present Earl was left with a major problem. He had the huge and unusable palace demolished for a start. Then, by intensively developing the estate, going in for such lines as broiler chickens, timber, and servicing agricultural machinery as a business, Lord Lonsdale managed to restore a reasonable state of prosperity in a quite short space of time.

Other estates have also found a healthier future in commercial development. The Duke of Hamilton's estate in Lanarkshire includes two industrial towns where development land is worth £3,000 an acre. The Hamilton Estates company owns eighteen businesses ranging from hotels to sawmills, and the 13,000 acres owned by the present Duke earn more than the 157,000 owned by his predecessor.

Since 1945, when the outlook was bleak the landed classes have steadily been recovering in economic strength. The value of agricultural land has increased four-fold over the last twenty years to its present average of £240 an acre in England and Wales; so that the landowner whose estate approaches 5,000 acres (roughly 200 titled families, according to my estimate) can describe himself as a millionaire, in the unlikely event that he wanted to.[3] These landlords would consider it hypothetical anyway, since they do not intend to sell.

Considered purely as background assets the value of these

---

[1] Article by Macdonald Hastings, *Weekend Telegraph Magazine*, 2 December 1966.
[2] D. Sutherland, *The Yellow Earl*, London, 1965.
[3] Because of the greater acreage of rough hill-grazing in their estates, the proportion of Scottish landowners in this 'land-millionaire' category is much lower. If such assets as growing timber, fishing rights, and so on, were included then the proportion might be about one-third of the owners.

estates is enormous and extremely durable. Writing in 1946, one authority calculated that over much of the country the value of land remained relatively the same as it had been in 1086, the year of the Domesday survey. That is still broadly the case. Over the past twenty years it has also proved to be a better investment than the stock market.

But it is not easy to get a very clear picture of how truly prosperous or otherwise the landed classes are. In the great days of 'conspicuous display' it was perfectly simple: through the magnificence of his house, his picture collection, even his expenditure on cigars, the nobleman wanted to impress on the world how rich he was. Now that the nobility is going through a long phase of what might be called 'conspicuous modesty' it is necessary to distinguish between the landowner who is genuinely having trouble finding capital, and the sort who regards being a 'hypothetical millionaire' as a sort of hard-luck story.

Several landed lords took pains to emphasise to me that outsiders got a false impression of their wealth, failing to perceive the difference between the high capital value of their land and the relatively small percentage return on it. The truth seems to be that the prosperity of the big estates covers a fairly wide range. The lord who is living solely off the rents of one of the smaller estates, having to put some surplus aside to provide for death duties, possessing little capital for development, may well be (by lordly standards, that is) 'just jogging along' or 'just about breaking even' – as they so ruefully put it.

On the other hand, the estates which run an efficient farm of their own besides drawing a rent-roll from tenants, which can draw on extra capital from business interests and apply it to land development, are making large profits.

The landowners disagree about whether outside resources are needed to make an estate thrive. Earl Bathurst was one I met who emphasised that the land itself did not produce enough of a surplus. The Earl, a young-looking forty (he succeeded to the title when he was sixteen), runs a 15,000 acre estate in Gloucestershire where the family has been since 1648. Three villages and three church livings go with the land.

On paper, his land is worth about £4,500,000 at current prices
in the county. But he contrasts this with the £5 an acre (say, a
total of £75,000 gross) which he receives in rents. Out of this he
has to find most of the capital for improvements; but he thinks it
essential to have some from other sources too. Having explained this,
Lord Bathurst, who had obligingly come out of his way to see me,
gave a subtle emphasis to his economics by ignoring passing taxis
and hopping on to a London bus for the fourpenny ride to his flat.

Much depends on how much the landowner applies his earnings.
One might take the example of a ten thousand acre estate on good
land in the south of England. Farming a thousand acres of this
himself, the landlord will make a turnover of about £45,000 a
year, leaving him a surplus of £10,000 on the year's operation. On
the remaining nine thousand acres he will probably have about
twenty tenants, renting their land at an average of £6 an acre,
giving him a rent roll of £54,000.

Considering that the total value of his land is about £2,500,000,
this return on fixed capital of around two-and-a-half per cent
compares badly with stock market interest rates. Most landowners
I met were making, they said, between one and three per cent
profit on the operation. There is no reason to doubt the figures.
But there is some self-deception in seeing the mathematics of it in
these terms, which seem to assume that the lord has recently paid
this enormous purchase price for the land whereas it has usually
been in the family for so many centuries that the purchase price, if
any, has long since been written off. The return on the working
capital, that is the equipment he has installed himself, is probably
nearer – or so a farm economist estimated for me – to fifteen or
twenty per cent.

Two of the bolder spirits among the noblemen I visited were
able to reassure me that times were not hard. 'Anyone who says he
isn't making money in farming now,' said one of the younger
marquesses, 'must be telling himself fibs or be really incompetent.'
And the heir to one of the bigger estates and an ancient title said,
'It really does need capital. But if he's got it, the estate-owner
hasn't had such a prosperous time for years. For instance, on our
land we've got one stretch of hill-grazing, under a thousand acres,

and we made £3,000 profit with the subsidies on that alone last year.'

Both of these were younger lords with an active professional life beyond their estates. They are especially interesting because they probably represent the direction of future change, even among the much more solidly conservative landed peerage. By contrast with the older members of the nobility, who are often groping for the shadowy aura that has traditionally gone with inherited land (some finding a little of it, some not), these up-and-coming younger lords actively shy away from it. Both of them could certainly be described as rich and successful. They spend much of their week on business in London and circulate around Parliament. Besides their big estates they also have country houses and a close association with a tenantry. But they make it obvious that they do not want to lean too heavily on their landed background. They would regard this as quaintly old-fashioned. They would much rather be accepted on their own merits as professionals.

The noblemen whose exclusive interest is their estates are far more inclined to have the time-honoured characteristics of the class. This certainly need not mean that they are less efficient than the two peers I have mentioned. But they are more plainly pinned to a rural locality and to the assumptions of lordly status and lordly duty which have always gone with the position. Possibly because they have more time to brood, they have more often convinced themselves that being a 'hypothetical millionaire' is part of the sadness of the human condition; and they are forever mentally comparing themselves (unfavourably) with this or that new-rich businessman who has just bought himself another yacht. Speaking of their income, they are more inclined to say that all they get out of it is 'a way of life'. This is often true enough. But since the phrase conjures up images of flute-playing shepherds, gypsy rovers, and other exponents of devil-may-care, a sharper definition is needed. One might sum it up by saying that they are granted an opportunity to worry about money in surroundings and comfort which are so far enjoyed by a fraction of one per cent of the population.

The special burden of estate or death duty looms much in their minds. So it may do with anyone who wants to provide for his family. But their intense desire to avoid selling any of the land which may have been in the family for centuries, not to be the failure in the dynasty, does mean that they have to take a steadier look at their own mortality prospects than most other people. I was impressed when one of the younger estate owners, a man with nearly ten thousand acres, said: 'If I fall under a bus tomorrow, the estate begins to crack up . . .'

His heir would have to find about £1 million to pay the forty per cent estate duty, and this would inevitably mean selling much of the land. Those with the means try to build up stock investments to provide for this; or else, given reasonable luck, duties can be avoided by forming a trust or by passing over the estate as a gift to the heir. But the latter must be done five years before the owner's death to avoid tax. This has its snags. The present Duke of Devonshire's father died four months before the five-year period was up, so there was £2,500,000 duty to pay.

On the other hand, it can be passed over to the heir perhaps too soon. I met two landed noblemen who had done this in their middle fifties to be sure of staying the five-year course. Both had lived well beyond it into the hale and hearty mid-sixties. Both evidently felt a certain chagrin at having been needlessly 'unemployed' for so long, and no longer taking the ultimate decisions on the estate management.

Can the big estates survive? Some of the greater landowners seem very confident that they can; others doubt that they can last more than another generation, especially if a Labour government were to impose more taxes on the class. But I am sure there was just as much head-shaking on the question a century ago, probably by the same families who are sceptical now. While there may be a very gradual annual decline in acreages, I think that most estates are well-placed enough to last a long way into the forseeable future. There will certainly be enough to give the aristocracy a strong enough semblance of the old, landed character, for a good many generations yet; which is one good reason for thinking that reports of the disappearance of this elite have been premature.

IO

THE LANDED GENTRY

The landed gentry of Britain have been called 'the only untitled aristocracy in the world'. As a historic class they have possibly done more than the peerage itself to encourage acceptance of the naturalness of an aristocratic order since they have demonstrated down the centuries that the local status and duties which have formed the basis of the system depend very little on the possession of a title.

The person inhabiting the Big House in any rural locality, whether sensitive, paternal-minded gentleman or impervious dunderhead, has automatically assumed local leadership without any special need for the central government to jog him into it. The villagers and the tenantry have just as automatically accepted it. In this ancient two-way relationship, I think, as much as in any more recent social development, can be found the original elements of that 'deferential society' which is apparently irremovably ingrained in the English character. In the rural areas one can still see how a semblance of this relationship exists in the present.

Before the major break-up of the big estates in the nineteen-twenties the houses of the gentry formed a network, fitting in between the greater palaces and castles of the lords, which covered the country at intervals of a few miles or so. Many have disappeared or been abandoned but a good number are still there. Though there were some very rich gentry, they seldom went in for the grand or grandiose structures which the nobility often preferred, as settings for self-display.

Gentry houses are the sort you glimpse from the train-window: the Manor, the Hall, the Grange, just along the road from the village; big enough to indicate the family position, but not flamboyant enough to show off, except in the discreetest way. They may be little Georgian or Jacobean mansions, or perhaps a piece of leaning black-and-white Tudor, where they are still gamely fighting the ancestral dry-rot.

Who exactly can be counted as landed gentry now has become less easy to assess. At one end of the scale the class shades off into the yeoman farmer category, a stock from which about half the gentry originally sprang, and at the other it merges with the titled nobility, a group with which the gentry families often have marriage connections.

To be regarded as gentry does not entirely depend on the size of a man's estate. Some could not be described as 'well off' by urban standards of income. On the other hand, there are still major gentry whose estates are big enough to elevate them to somewhere near the territorial magnate class, equal to or better than most of the neighbouring nobility, and with a social standing no less than theirs.

Out in the country, there is no really significant difference these days between the landed lord and the untitled gentleman who owns a roughly similar acreage. They share much the same educational background, army experience, political outlook, clubs, and conventions, and they both tend to have the same large families. Now that so many of the landed peerage, the celebrated backwoodsmen, stay away from the House of Lords the similarity is even closer.

Where there seem to be exceptions the difference is chiefly that of higher peaks which stand out of a fairly even mountain chain. There are the titled territorial magnates, for instance – possibly no more than thirty or forty of the nobility – whose local position is conspicuous mainly because of the great size of their estates, the ownership of one of the historic houses, or the fact that some of the most exalted ranks, like the dukes, still take their status very seriously.

The other difference between nobility and gentry out in the country is the sadly ironic one that far more of the titled noblemen now find themselves saddled with the burden of a multi-roomed stately home, thanks to the vaulting ambition and penchant for

display of their forebears. They have often been pushed un-
willingly into the half-crown stately-homes business to keep them
in repair. The result is that you find Lord Portcullis up at the
Castle, mildly cursing the lack of privacy and extra work involved in receiving the public; while his neighbour, Major
Fitzsmythe, whose family had more pedigree but less ambition,
can potter undisturbed around his smaller Grange.

The fact that one can now see the titled men and the gentry as
forming one landed class, fairly homogeneous in all the important things, is worth noting, partly because it is a development of
comparatively recent times, say the last century or so.

In Tudor and Stuart times, economic jealousies divided the
'mere gentry', whose only resources were their estates, from the
greater gentry and noble courtiers who, by string-pulling, aggressiveness, and good fortune, had got hold of the lucrative court
offices and dignities whose income largely took them to the top.

The envy and division of interests between the aristocrats and
merchants circulating round the busy bee-hive of the court, and
the lesser gentry who were stuck on their little domains out in the
shires, increasingly burdened with taxes, did much to give shape
to the two contending sides in the Civil War.

From the Restoration onwards nobility and gentry continued in
some sort of loose partnership, sharing many of the elements of a
common outlook, often having marriage connections. But a certain difference of attitude and temperament continued to distinguish one group from another. Though fortunes fluctuated a good
deal, with the great declining and minor men winning promotion,
it is strange how often this difference of outlook can be seen in family pedigrees, running through from the distant past to the present.

Some gentry seem to have been firmly and irrevocably ordained
to be nothing but gentry from the very beginning. A surprising
number of these families have remained almost perfectly in station
for six, seven, or eight centuries. The sheer, dogged conservatism
of it is almost absurd if one considers all the honours and prizes
which they demurely failed to try for, all the potential disasters
they managed to avoid, as history rolled on and on, bearing these
even-tempered, unruffled local worthies on its back.

The family had so many acres not long after Domesday; they have, give or take a little, roughly the same now. Some one or two ancestors, almost forgetfully, may have married the younger daughter of a local baron who was not too far above himself; but they have consistently avoided acquiring a title in the main branch of the family. The modesty, lack of aggressive impulse, reserved pride, or whatever motivated these families, has possibly been their salvation. They never aspired too high, and were never struck down.

The mass of the gentry, of course, allowed themselves a fairly wide variety of style over the years. By the eighteenth century, the descendant of the Cromwellian gentry had become the rollicking English squire. He somehow got through his traditional duties as administrative handyman for his rural spot, Justice of the Peace, estate supervisor of sorts. But he liked to spend much of his day in the hunting field, at the races, nourishing himself at his groaning board, cracking a bottle of port or two with the parson.

In fact, says one writer who has studied him closely, he was inclined to be a bit of 'a bumpkin, bonehead, and barbarian'; and 'the practically unanimous contemporary verdict was that the Old English Squire was conspicuous by nothing so much as his complacent lack of intellect.'[1]

Cobbett, on his rural rides, found him 'the most base of all creatures that God ever suffered to take human shape'. It was not until the early nineteenth century that popular imagination romanticised him into the fine, archetypal, and gentlemanly John Bull figure.

The intellect may have varied. But one thing that marked him, for good or ill, was his lack of pretension to any aristocratic mystery or any of that streak of imagination that might have reached out into the wider world beyond his own fox-hunting acres.

In his politics he remained blissfully contemptuous of, and separate from, the more go-ahead landed magnates who were more enterprising, avaricious in a more adventurous way, possibly more intelligent than himself. 'And here's a confounded son of a

[1] E. Wingfield-Stratford, *The Squire and his Relations*, London, 1956.

whore of a lord,' says Squire Western in Fielding's *Tom Jones*,
'. . . he shall never have a daughter of mine by my consent. They
have beggared the nation but they shall never beggar me . . . I'll
ha' no lords nor courtiers in my vamily.'

He formed the solid bedrock of the Country or Tory Party,
standing for the land, some idea of the past and tradition as the
crowning glory of English life, insular, suspicious of new ideas,
often dutiful after a fashion, intensely loyal to his own county and
parish. He remained jealous of that grander Whig aristocracy
whose wealth, wider enterprise and self-seeking, more capitalist
outlook, appeared to have divorced itself too far from that
parochial way of life which the Tory squire treasured. It was not
until about Gladstone's time, and the assault on the landed interests,
that greater nobility and smaller gentry found a defensive position
behind which they could unite.

In looking at the landed gentry as they are today the first difficulty is to decide who can count as belonging to it. There has
always been a certain amount of English vagueness about it,
exasperating to visitors from the Continent or Scotland who are
used to a little more precision on such vital matters as who is
'noble' and who is not. Rightfully, a 'gentleman' should be
identifiable by his possession of a coat of arms, and virtually all the
older gentry have this insignia.

But the term was extended in England to include those who
behaved in a 'gentlemanly' way, or had that style of life. A court
case reported in the London *Observer* on 13 April 1806 suggests
both how confident people were then that the word had a precise
meaning, but also how much it was left as a matter of social
judgment.

The report says that a gentleman farmer had been summoned
before the magistrate for the offence of 'profane swearing'. He
had had an argument with the village curate and had 'damn'd the
clergyman's eyes'. For this offence he was fined five shillings. The
farmer contended that since he was not a gentleman he ought to
pay no more than one shilling. This objection was overruled by
the magistrate 'as it appeared that he kept his sporting dogs and
took his wine after dinner'.

G

One of the qualifications for being landed gentry in the stricter sense should at least be the ownership of some land. The last complete edition of the standard reference book, *Burke's Landed Gentry*, 1952, contained the names of 4,500 families and their pedigrees; and one of the criteria for getting into it was not only possession of an ancestry of some interest but also ownership of at least three hundred acres. Even that amount would hardly be enough to allow the owner to have tenants on it or, unless he were very proud and short-sighted indeed, to regard himself as much of a squire figure.

The new edition is coming out in three volumes, such is the clamour of people for a place in it, and the complete work will contain 21,000 families. Would-be entrants must now simply have an 'interesting' pedigree, one which goes back at least four generations. Ownership of some land supports an entry, but it is no longer an essential.

The curious fact that the leading reference book to the gentry will thus contain – by popular demand, and no fault of the publishers – about five times as many names as it has ever done, even in the hey-day of land-ownership, has a touch of light-headedness about it. One suddenly seems to be confronted with a whole new class of neo-gentry. Where on earth can they have come from? Part of the answer is that a large number of town-dwellers, possibly once landed, are taking advantage of the dropping of the property qualification to rush forward with their pedigrees, treasured all these years in the bottom drawer. A good many others will still be on the land, if only in a small way: the more socially-sensitive farmers and their wives (especially the wives), who cannot be quite classed either as 'yeomen' or 'old gentry' in their districts, but whose background is rooted enough to make them feel a cut above the company directors and tele-vision executives who are now getting to predominate at the Hunt Ball.

One can also see in it the reverse side of the coin to that other phenomenon, the upsurge of the London Season.[1] In periods when England looks least concerned about class as in a period of

[1] See Chapter 14.

post-war economic recovery, all the while the pressure is building up behind the scenes. New money ultimately finds a breach and streams breathlessly into the world of the well-bred in massive numbers. Gentility, or its least secure elements, looks about for handholds of reassurance; and getting into *Burke's* is one of them.

In one sense even these landless claimants to a place in *Burke's* have some backing from tradition. Since 'social recognition' as such was always a major part of being gentry, a fairly numerous but rapidly dwindling group of people has managed to go on conveying the rather special aura of this status, without so much as a square yard of land left under its feet. Tweedy, defiant, conservative, proud, denizens of the spas and the cathedral towns, they are a vanishing race.

One of the last of them was Mr Crouchback, the father of Evelyn Waugh's hero in his trilogy, *The Sword of Honour*, the landless descendant of an old Catholic family.

'Only God and Guy knew the massive and singular quality of Mr Crouchback's family pride ... He was quite without class consciousness because he saw the whole intricate social structure of his country divided neatly into two unequal and unmistakable parts. On one side stood the Crouchbacks and certain inconspicuous, anciently allied families; on the other side stood the rest of mankind, Box-Bender, the butcher, the Duke of Omnium (whose one-time wealth derived from monastic spoils), Lloyd George, Neville Chamberlain – all of a piece together.'[1]

Pride apart, the number of true landed gentry can hardly be more numerous than they were in the nineteenth century.

In 1873, J. Bateman's survey of the country, *The Great Landowners of Great Britain*, calculated that there were about a thousand 'greater gentry' (families owning between three thousand and ten thousand acres); and roughly two thousand minor gentry or 'squires' (owning one thousand to three thousand acres). At that time the areas occupied by the gentry ranged from forty-four per cent of Shropshire down to seventeen per cent of Middlesex. In thirteen counties the gentry as a whole owned more than twice as much as the titled aristocracy. The most gentrified areas were

[1] E. Waugh, *Men at Arms*, London, 1952, p. 36.

Shropshire, Herefordshire, Gloucestershire, Oxfordshire, and the eastern counties.[1]

Since that time, the successive blows of war and taxation have hit the gentry more severely than the landowning lords. The main reason is that the bigger estates of the latter were able to cushion them better, and accept reduction without disappearing. True to character, far more of the landed peerage also had outside resources in business and investment which enabled them to take the strain.

While the number of landed lords has declined by about forty per cent of what it was in 1873 – to the present (estimated) 350 estate owners – the gentry who were then in the more-than-1,000-acres class have been reduced by about two-thirds. This would give a present figure of three hundred greater gentry and six hundred squires. The 1873 standard of estate-sizes for these two categories has almost certainly been reduced too. The untitled gentry seem much more ready and able to stick it out with a severely reduced acreage than the nobility who, once the ground needed to support rent-paying tenant farmers has gone, tend to change occupations entirely. There are a good many gentry, another five hundred or so, left with only perhaps a few hundred acres of the old domain, who have moved out of the Grange into a smaller house, and gone on farming the land themselves. The disappearance of their country houses continues steadily. In Shropshire, for example, of the ninety-odd country seats which existed in 1873, no more than about forty appear to be still lived in; and most of the remainder have been demolished.

But a number of the gentry still show an astonishing rootedness in one place. The Swinton family, for instance, owns land in Berwickshire which it has held since Saxon times. With the Ardens, and the Berkeleys (of Berkeley Castle, Gloucestershire, where they still live after 800 years), they are the only families which can trace their ancestry in the male line to before 1066.

A few other gentry families still own land granted to their forebears in the immediate post-Conquest period. Among them are the Berkeleys; the Shirleys of Ettington; and the Dymokes of Scrivelsby, Lincolnshire (a family whose head always inherits the

[1] F. M. L. Thompson, op. cit.

post of Queen's Champion as it has for six hundred years: theoretically to take on any challengers in the lists, but there are few duties attached outside coronation appearances). A few years ago the coincidence occurred that the Lords Lieutenant of three adjoining Welsh counties were living on estates which their chieftain-ancestors had owned in the eleventh century.

Others have lived on the same land since the twelfth century. These include the Giffard family, who still have 4,000 acres at Chillington, Staffordshire (the first Giffard in England was William's standard-bearer at Hastings). There are the Lucys of Charlecote, Warwickshire, whose seventeenth-century ancestor was satirised as Robert Shallow by Shakespeare; and other equally durable families like those of Fulford, Saltmarshe, Tremlett, Tichborne, Plowden, and Medlicott.

But the chief characteristic of the gentry is not necessarily their venerable age but their variety, the way they symbolise the rise and fall of fortune. The Scropes, of Danby, Yorkshire, were statesmen of some grandeur long before most of the present nobility came to notice; but they reverted to being modest landed gentry. The pedigree of the Elmhirsts, of the West Riding, is traceable back to a serf who lived on the same land some time before 1350.

Families in the older trades, like brewing, have nearly all sprung from old-established rural stock. The Whitbreads, for instance, were yeomen farmers in Bedfordshire in the fourteenth century and remained so until the eighteenth when the founding of the brewery business made the family fortune. They transformed themselves into gentry in the customary way by buying land – eleven thousand acres in the same part of the county where they had begun; and this is still intact in the family.

II

NOBLESSE OBLIGE,

RURAL LIFE AND DUTIES

The place of the landed gentry as local leaders and unpaid administrators is one of the older parts of the social system. Beginning as lords-of-the-manor in medieval times, they were gradually enrolled as magistrates, captains of their local militia, and general factotums on whom the government depended for the good order of their districts.

A good many families have been performing these functions for century after century in an unbroken line to the present. Just how far the aristocracy is still engaged in them has become one of these characteristically vague areas of its existence. *Noblesse oblige* is a sterling motto; but how far the elite still feels bound by a sense of obligation, how much people in any locality expect of it, has become a foggy area.

I should add that in this context landed peers can be regarded as 'gentry'. While one or two of the grander dukes and more venerable earl's might demur at this styling, it is generally true that a title has no special meaning in a country setting, where a landed gentleman can have much the same prestige, fill the same posts, as someone of titled rank.

The idea that the bigwig had the ultimate voice in running the local show was widely accepted well into the present century. Even after the 1880s, when county and rural district councils came into being, an approving nod from the man at the Big House was necessary in most areas of local decision. The fact that he was the biggest local landlord and employer – of house servants, gardeners, gamekeepers – in times when wages were a pittance and jobs hard to get naturally made him the kingpin of the economic system in his district.

It was both autocratic and paternalist. He or one of his family represented the locality in the House of Commons. He and his fellow-gentry predominated on the magistrates' bench. He built the village hall and had his name immortalised on its foundation-stone. He paid for the repair of the church steeple and, since he had usually appointed the vicar, his taste decreed the length of the sermons. Sometimes he stood back benignly; sometimes he meddled. But generally speaking more got done through his presence than would otherwise have been managed.

When I asked various peers and gentry how they expressed their local leadership today some could recite an impressive list of jobs – county councillor, Lord Lieutenant of the county, school governor president of this or that – which cannot have left them much spare time. Others had to think hard to find concrete examples of local lustre: 'Let me see . . . Patron of the Young Conservatives – they like me to give them a little speech once a year. My wife runs the Red Cross and the flower show and we let them have the Park for the annual fête. That's about the size of it.'

Sometimes one gets the feeling that the custodian of the Big House needs the villagers quite as much as they need him. Gazing down the empty drive, he would dearly like to see more petitioners arriving with requests for him to do this or that. It would exercise his latent sense of duty to be done; it would reassure him – this applies more to the older generation – that an aristocracy is still wanted. Younger lords, usually more active in the professions, more often tend to see *noblesse oblige* as something of a false quantity. 'I rather resent being asked to open a charity fête,' said one of the younger marquesses. 'It's a bit insulting, as though you had nothing better to do all day than snooze in the library. Same old idea that a lord is bound to be a bit of a wallflower . . .'

The most obvious area to look for continued influence is the political one. Before the break-up of the big estates the pull of the landed class was roughly proportionate to the size of their estates and the vigour of their personalities.

A classic example of what the rich landowner could be, given enough zeal, was the late Lord Derby (1865–1948), styled 'King of Lancashire'.[1] His income was about £300,000 a year. He was 'the undisputed Tory spokesman' of his county; no party candidate could succeed without his blessing. He was in his time a self-appointed arbitrator in industrial disputes. His insistence that any proposal of titles and honour for Lancashire people should pass through his hands was not gainsaid.

Influence of this order became rare after about 1910; and Lord Derby, on this level, was the last of his kind. My impression is that this kind of influence out in the shires is now one of the most diminished things; that it would be uncommon to find any *individual* landed lord who could much influence any constituency against its natural inclination – which is not to say that he is ignored. I asked several peers who are on local Tory constituency executives what sort of weight they thought they carried and they said, credibly enough to me, that it was not noticeably more than that of middle-class members.

Political Pull

Only one peer was ready to acknowledge that he was politically influential in his county – where his family has been very long established – saying that 'my presence on an election platform means a thousand votes for our candidate'. Perversely enough, this was one of the hereditary Labour peers.

Members of the landed classes naturally do count more as a *group*. This tends to emerge in the occasional argument over a candidate between Tory Central Office in London and leaders of the county interest. Headquarters, in its persistent effort to find candidates from a wider range of social class, to give the Conservative Party a more apparent streak of Common Man appeal, have at times been frustrated by the county committee which insists on a local man, at least someone of the gentry type.

It is true that the son of the local landowner, especially if he is armed with Etonian self-assurance, has a far easier ride into politics

[1] Randolph S. Churchill, *Lord Derby*, London, 1959.

than the possibly more able grammar-school man sent up from town. But even this hardly involves anything so crude as 'fixing' by the landed elite. Mr Randolph Churchill gives an explanation which still applies. Recalling that the late Lord Derby claimed never to have exercised influence to get a friend or relative nominated for Parliament, he observes: 'There was no need for him to do so. There was hardly a Conservative Association in Lancashire or Cheshire which, confronted with the necessity of finding a candidate, did not instinctively wonder whether there was any member of the Stanley family [i.e. the Derbys] available to carry their banner.'[1]

In other words, why 'fix' when there is so little need? Even where the local selection committee is predominantly middle class, there is a well-known tendency for Conservatives to go for the man who shows more of the traits of the traditional ruling class, whatever the comparable weight of his ability.

As one writer puts it: 'The reaction from Socialist egalitarianism has made the conservative English probably more class-conscious than they would otherwise have been and by and large they prefer to be represented in Parliament by Public Schoolboys.'[2]

I believe that it is an underestimate to see it purely as a modern reaction to Left-wing ideology. It seems to me that it is simply another facet of that far older underground stream of tribal custom which continues to bubble up into English life, affecting it in a hundred ways. It is a stream which has been flowing, with varying force, for centuries rather than decades. It shows itself in that still manifestly strong English preference for a graded social order in which everyone 'knows their place' (the flip-side of the coin of snobbery); in which deference is not only a matter of ingrained custom but is seen as positively 'good' or 'right', or otherwise beneficial, since to defer to a class Above implies a set of rules which must also be observed by the class Below, thus preserving the Middle from change, invasion, or other appropriation of status. This pattern is often described as 'social stability'.

The fact that habitual Conservative voters include a large

[1] R. Churchill, op. cit.
[2] Christopher Hollis, 'The Conservative Party in History,' (*Political Quarterly*, July–Sept. 1961, p. 222).

G*

number of lower-paid workers who should, by the canons of
revolutionary psychology, be Socialist – the 'working-class Tories',
as they are called – seems to me to be another little inland lake fed
by the same underground stream. Many of them, of course, are
urban workers and their motives may be complicated. But I think
it significant that so many of them are found in rural areas where a
clear paternalist relationship between noble landlord and villagers
has been most obvious and most accepted as 'natural' over the
centuries.

What seems to me to lend weight to the point is that agricultural workers were, until fairly recent times, one of the most
notoriously under-privileged groups in the labour force. There is
still a fair degree of rural poverty, though it is disguised because it
is 'clean'. Yet the amount of Socialist zeal aroused among them by
these conditions has been so relatively slight that only half the
country's agricultural workers bother to belong to their main
trades union.

It would be missing the point – and inaccurate – to suggest that
this had been brought about by any covert anti-union pressure by
the landlords. The reasons for the conservatism and Tory-voting
habits of so many of the country workers are no doubt complex.
They probably have much to do with rural loyalties seen in
opposition to those of the towns (these are still very strong); but a
constant element is the tradition of deference developed in a
locality and the feeling of security that seems to be derived from it.

The County Jobs

In computing membership of county councils, the titled peerage
and baronetcy is the only part of the whole group that can be
counted very accurately. Thirty of the fifty-two county councils in
England and Wales have some titled person on the strength and a
number have several. The Greater London Council has only one,
a peeress; and noble membership of town councils is generally
slight.

The titled county councillors in England and Wales include
four dukes, one marquess, eight earls (one a chairman), two

viscounts, eighteen barons, five peeresses, twenty-seven baronets (one a chairman), making a total of sixty-five. This means that the titled group is represented on these councils some 260 times more often than the average person on the voting list. But as a proportion of the total peerage and baronetcy it is small (about three per cent); and as a fraction of the landowning category among them (I estimate it at about ten per cent) it is still not notably high in a position where one might have expected it to be influential, if anywhere at all.

Peers and gentry occupy most of the posts of Lords Lieutenant in each county. Since part of this job is concerned with ceremonial – arranging the Queen's tour on county visits, and so on, and with supervising the Territorial Army – it has normally gone to the ex-officer gentleman class. Even Labour governments have done little to try to infiltrate Socialists who happen to be gifted with the ceremonial touch and officer-like qualities.

Out of fifty-five Lords Lieutenant there are three dukes, one marquess, eight earls, three viscounts, seven barons, and nine baronets – total thirty-one, and nearly all the remainder are gentry.

The most serious part of the Lord Lieutenant's work is in acting as chairman of the local committee which recommends to the Queen (represented by the Lord Chancellor) which persons are worthy to be appointed magistrates in the district. They have naturally tended to choose a preponderance of other 'gentlemen'; but readiness and ability to find spare time has possibly been as important a reason as prejudice in deciding that the so-called leisured classes get a bigger share of this work.

On the magistrates' bench the peerage shows up more strongly. Roughly forty per cent of the three upper grades of the peerage (dukes, marquesses, and earls) are Justices of the Peace, that is thirty-eight out of ninety-five. For viscounts and barons the average is about six per cent. The (Labour) Lord Chancellor recently urged local selectors to try to achieve a wider class representation on the Bench, a sign that by the mid-1960s still too much was being taken on by (or left to) the class which had traditionally run the show.

Choosing the Vicar

Another more curious area where the aristocracy carries weight – one which puzzles foreigners who are trying to understand how and by whom the Church of England is run – is in private church patronage. Since early times the right to appoint a vicar to a church has often been hereditary with the local land. In 1830 over half the church appointments in the country were in the hands of private persons. This has diminished, but remarkably slowly.

The total number of livings is now about 12,000 and approximately 2,300 of them are owned by private persons. Of this total, about 800 are held by peers and their children; and one would estimate that at least seventy per cent of the remainder are held by the landed gentry class.

Some have many. Earl Fitzwilliam has twenty-eight livings and shares three ('shared' means that two or more patrons take turns at appointing the incumbent – an even odder arrangement). The Duke of Devonshire has seventeen livings with three shared; Lord Lonsdale, sixteen and five; Lord Derby, fifteen. Eight other peers have seven or more livings and many have three or four.

Church law is very broad-minded about the system as it stands. Perhaps it has to be. Agnostics and atheists are not specifically barred from being patrons. Only Roman Catholics, aliens and lunatics are ruled out. The local man of estate is presumed to be the touchstone on religious matters, as on everything else.

The noble patrons have some strange bedfellows. Smiths Potato Estates, the crisps manufacturers, appoint to one living; and Cornish Manures Ltd share turns with a bishop in another. The company directors no doubt take this duty seriously; but the board-room scene in which they turn from the earthy side of their work to the spiritual is hard to picture.

The members of the aristocracy I met obviously take great pains to fulfil this duty, even more so now that it is one of the few specific tokens of overlordship left to them. Some find it an onerous task; the risk of choosing 'the wrong chap' for a small community weighs on them and they conduct far more interviews up at the Big House than would seem necessary if they were choosing someone to run Imperial Chemicals.

Lord Middleton is one who has had great experience of the task. One of the big Yorkshire landowners, now aged eighty, he has presented fifty-two vicars in forty years. He once had to appoint five in one year. 'I once advertised for a vicar in *Horse and Hound* [the field sports journal],' he told me. 'The Archbishop found it a trifle unorthodox but I satisfied him it got me the right man.'

In the past, richer patrons often helped to pay the vicar's stipend. Now this seems rare or non-existent. The candidate with a private income is, I fancy, often very welcome. On a religious level, noble patrons show a strong unanimity in what they are looking for – and that is, not too much 'religion'. As one nobleman put it, 'The village needs a practical chap. None of this swinging incense around our heads.' To their credit, the patrons do not shirk facing the result of their selection. Most landed lords read the lesson on a Sunday morning and, so the vicars claim, help to keep the dwindling congregations together by their presence.

Acting the Squire

Even where the custodian of the Big House cannot produce a very impressive list of positions of command, one gets the sense that the villagers are quite glad that his lordship still lives up at the Hall, even if he is no more than an invisible presence much of the time.

This is particularly true of the more out-of-the-way country places. Here the villagers feel an uneasy sense of being almost 'too equal' without some greater personage in sight. He need not do a great deal to justify his place. His presence seems to reassure them that the rural parish still counts for something, is worth living in, otherwise the lord himself would not be there. And it is as though the class inequality which he represents reassures them about their own identity. It again gives them a sense of 'knowing their place', which appears to be a necessary kind of protein in the English diet.

In the North of England, with its longer feudal memory and habit, the popular feeling in rural areas virtually demands that the local worthy steps in and takes charge of things, and makes no bones about his superior position. (One of the now-landless London earls told me about a visit he had paid to another lord in north Yorkshire: 'All the forelock-touching up there, milord this and that! I came back quite staggered.' In short, a nice reversal of the nursery story of the visit of the country-mouse to the town-mouse).

What country people seem most anxious to avoid here is, again, that uneasy sense of equality where village jealousies would spring up if the grocer or the garage proprietor were elected chairman of the parish council rather than the neutral gentleman who is presumed to be above it all.[1]

Fulfilling this need for the neutral man or minor 'constitutional monarch' remains one of the more common aristocratic duties. Even in the most Welsh part of Wales, where I had imagined the English nobleman would be somewhat isolated by barriers of language and culture, this need for one who is detached and out-side factions is the very thing that can keep him busy.

The Marquess of Anglesey, for example, is in this position. He is Sir George Charles Henry Victor Paget; is the 7th Marquess; educated at Eton; aged forty-five; was a cavalry major in the last war; and is one of the few peers to live in the place of his title.[2]

The house, Plas Newydd (New Place), is a long rectangular block magnificently set on the edge of the Menai Straits. The dark and stormy November evening when I went there brought out its dramatic possibilities very well. The blue and white Anglesey banner, with its four eagles, flew stiffly in the wind over

[1] It would be unrealistic to pretend that the village's relationship with the Big House is always an amiable one. I encountered two cases in which a state of minor feud existed between the local lord and rural district council; and another two cases, one in the south, one in the west country, in which the local 'squire' was not allowed into the village public-house, for being too 'lively' or other reasons. Both are gentry of ancient residence in the place; and one has to endure the irony that his name and coat-of-arms swing on the pub sign. Neither of them is the subject of an interview in this book, by the way.

[2] The Pagets have an interesting ancestry. Sir William, who became the first Baron in Henry VIII's time, had risen from nothing to become a very able Secretary of State. It is believed that his father was a humble Staffordshire nail-maker, but the lineage cannot be traced before the sixteenth century. After this flash of talent there was no one of particular distinction until the Paget who became first Marquess in 1815, having shown himself a brilliant cavalry leader at Waterloo. His biography, entitled *One-Leg*, has been written by the present Marquess.

the sombre waters of the Straits. In the distance the black and massy peaks of the Snowdon range were ribbed white with early snow. The rocky shores about have strong associations with the early Celtic church, saints, anchorites, and pilgrimages.

The house has thirty-six rooms. In the last century, when the Angleseys were reckoned one of the richest families in England, this was regarded by the family as 'just a summer sailing lodge'. Lord Anglesey, who had been working on his history of the British cavalry regiments in the library, broke off to tell me something about being, so to speak, an English squire in foreign parts.

He agreed that the language barrier meant some loss of contact with local people (this is a very solidly Welsh-speaking area); but he thought the titled man was found very acceptable because he could be seen as not personally ambitious, impartial, and therefore trustworthy. He has been a county councillor, is president of the Conservative Association, and sits on various Welsh bodies concerned with the arts, museums, and churches, and is a magistrate. He admits to taking *noblesse oblige* seriously, as 'a duty owed to the community in return for inherited position'.

Frequently one comes across the odd contrast – I mean that it is odd if you have forgotten that noble ranks have little meaning in rural areas – of a man of eminent title playing the paternalist role in a remote-seeming part of the English backwoods, so that the dutiful aspect seems all the greater.

The Duke and Duchess of Somerset live in a middling-sized country mansion just along the lane from the village of Maiden Bradley, a small, pale grey village of a thousand people deep in the heart of Wiltshire. It is the sort of place where the highway system is much as it was when it was sketched out by the wandering feet of the peasantry in Piers Plowman's time or thereabouts. The road ambles off confidently towards some farmstead, finds to its great surprise that it disappeared a couple of centuries ago, then shoots off three ways at once in a state of dilemma which the council has tarmacadammed but not solved.

The Duke, fifty-seven, amiable, quietly military in aspect (he is a retired major of the Wiltshire Regiment), is one of the celebrated

Seymour family, a descendant of the Lord Protector Somerset who could once ride to London from his west country properties with 150 liveried servants in his cortege.

In the front hall are a few family portraits and in a glass case (with light switch for illuminating as necessary) is the ornate saddle used by Sir Thomas Seymour, Speaker of the House of Commons, when he rode to greet William of Orange on his landing in 1688. The Duke lit up this little fragment of history for me; then, economising, switched off and went in to carve the chicken for lunch.

Beneath his serious concern about rural life is a more spry streak of personality. Carving, he wore a joke pinafore made up to look like a dinner-jacket with a false bow tie on top. He is reckoned to be a good amateur conjuror. He is a fan of Duke Ellington, who is also a friend of his, and that evening he rushed off to hear him playing at a place thirty miles away.

'No,' he said. 'We don't go to London much. All our loyalties are to the neighbourhood.' The Somersets have an estate of 3,700 acres here and another 2,000 in Devon, which is just enough, he says, to offer 'a way of life'.

After lunch the Duchess was going to drive herself in the small car up to the church hall on the hill for the Mothers' Union meeting. There would be the usual short talk by the vicar; then tea, cakes and gossip. All just as you might find in a hundred villages. But it did not quite fit my preconceptions of what Duchesses did, and I wondered why – not to mince words – she bothered. 'It's expected,' she said, 'anything you can do to keep a community together is very worthwhile.'

The Duke spoke regretfully of the way young people were drifting away to the excitement of the town. He clearly felt a nostalgia for the days when the aristocracy had more demands on their services. 'All the things we could do without reward are disappearing and that is bad for the character of the nation.'

One of the Duke's voluntary posts is to be President of the British Legion for Wiltshire. When they have a committee meeting the Duke and his fellow-members – the old chauffeur and the local woodman among them – discuss policy over a glass of beer in the ducal dining-room. In this setting, with the marble busts of the Tudor-period Seymours gazing down from the chimney-piece, the light flickering on the tapestries and the portraits, it must be a piquant scene.

Noblesse oblige, the supposed aristocratic duty to the community, seems to be a many-gendered thing. If it is a question of remorse and guilt, then it is also the case that some of those who collect a great list of jobs and duties, almost as a form of addiction, sometimes seem to enjoy it. This is more common among the very old-established gentry, especially in those really remote places where they are so relatively thin on the ground that they have had to provide whatever local dynamism there has ever been since the Conquest.

Sir John Craster, whose family has lived at the village of Craster, Northumberland, since about 1160, is an example of that old multiple-job tradition. On first approaching this gaunt and unpopulated part of the north-east coast one gets the impression that there cannot be many obligations for a *noblesse* to fulfil. It is a place seemingly more attached to past than present; but without a great deal of either. One of those places which the more well-matured gentry seem destined to inhabit, so that if they did not exist then perhaps neither would the land under their feet.

Driving east between green and misty fields in autumn, one at last makes the coast road. Out on the North Sea, on this calm day, a little collier saunters north to Tyneside, moving over the long swell with a sleeper's rhythm. On the beach are drawn up a few bright-painted cobles of the old Norse design that they use here still. The tide nonchalantly knocks the pebbles. It is a place where even the sounds are grey.

The road swings beneath a Gothic arch, as though one were about to enter some medieval city state; then, quickly throwing off the suspenseful disguise, delivers the visitor to the tiny harbour at the bottom of the hill and the kipper-curing factory which is the palpable heart of the village.

Sir John lives in a small mansion house higher up. Craster Towers has been vacated for economy reasons. He has 750 acres left of the estate, which is just under half the original twelfth-

century grant of land, and he runs it without an agent, as it always
has been. He owns the harbour; the fisherman's dues just about
pay for its upkeep. As Lord of the Manor he is entitled to a share
of the value of the flotsam and jetsam and wreck-salvage money
which this part of the coast (of Grace Darling fame) produces.
The coastguard service sends him 'a postal order' once a year for
his share; the envelope is double-sealed and marked 'Private and
Confidential'.

In his dark-brown plus-four suit Sir John looks every inch the
confident squire. A great deal of background has been built up to
support the position. He is an alderman of the county council, a
local magistrate, president of the Conservatives. He has been the
eighth Craster to be High Sheriff of the county. He is still chairman
of the national sea fisheries committee and, locally, is on committees that deal with lifeboats, carrion crow control, bird
protection on the Farne Islands, and so on. At any one time he
is on about twenty committees.

He likes to keep closely in touch with what the local fishermen
are anxious about. Recently he got out the car, did a private tour
of 94 small harbours in England and Wales, and slapped in a
report and suggestions to the Minister of Agriculture. 'Did they
act on them?' 'Oh, I should think so!'

Sir John is people's warden at the local church, a place girdled
by high and mossy elms and circling rooks, and inevitably full of
memorials to the Crasters. Like most of the gentry, they have
been an intensely localised family. Heirs have looked after the land;
younger sons have gone soldiering in India. Though so prominent in running the local show the family has never risen to a
hereditary honour. There have been three or four knighthoods
since Edward I's time (Sir John got his in 1955 for political
services). But even these have been decently spaced out at
intervals of some centuries to indicate that the Crasters were
making no headlong rush for mere grandeur.

The overall impression is thus one of variety. Out in the field
one can still find examples of most of the roles which the aristocracy has played in its time, though at a diminished voltage. One
or two peers have functions which defy category. Historically

quaint they may be; but they add a dab of colour to the corner of the total picture.

The Marquess of Ailesbury, for instance, is 29th Hereditary Warden of Savernake Forest, one of the oldest woodlands in the country. Driving west, you see its bosky clumps rising above the rolling north Wiltshire downland. The wardenship has been hereditary over nine hundred years, since it was granted after Hastings to Richard Esturmi, one of Lord Ailesbury's forebears. The forest was kept as a royal game preserve through medieval and Tudor times so that the King could find supplies of venison on his progresses to the West Country.

The setting helps to lend some credence to the reality of the job. The forest is a place of gnarled and knotty oaks, the sort that appear in illustrations of Hansel and Gretel; there are great elm clumps, ranks of beeches, a tangle of holly and elder. The village place-names on the signposts through the forest are not so much an attempt to state a direction; rather a piece of Norman-Saxon blank verse: Milton Lilbourne, Wootton Rivers, Collingbourne Kingston, All Cannings, Oare, Collingbourne Ducis, Burbage, East Everleigh.

Lord Ailesbury (Sir Chandos Sydney Cedric Brudenell-Bruce, sixty-three, educated at Eton and Oxford) has no difficulty in believing in the job. He is an enthusiast. 'We've got records going back to 1067,' he says. 'There are messages from the King ticking off my early ancestors for not taking sterner measures to deal with the poaching.'

There are still a number of deer to look after. Lord Ailesbury classifies them as 'official', that is the ones who live-in as steady residents; and the 'unofficial' or wild ones who wander in and out of the Forest. I forgot to ask how the wardenship would handle the breach of protocol of a mating between residents and visitors.

How did he see his job, I asked. Duty? Pleasure? 'Well, after nine hundred years, more of a habit I'd say . . .' He keeps up the planting in the four thousand acres of woodland he owns, as the old timber is cut. He speaks of the need for a sequence of 'really sound marquesses' (he sadly acknowledges one past 'dud' who left a great acreage and no money to run it) who will keep up the sequence.

He likes to maintain the decorative silviculture all around the estate, and he has one novel planting method. He bought a length of railway cutting on a now disused branch line nearby. He has a small French vintage car, a solid-tyred model with frowning windscreen and bulbous horn. He drives it along the cutting with a load of shrubs in the back and, at intervals, gets out and plants one. The spirit of this would be hard for an outsider to render but I found that he had obligingly dashed off a short lyric for me about it, which deftly caught the mood, beginning:

> In my de Dion Bouton,
> I motor out and back
> Where the gradients are easy
> On my private railway track . . .

12

THE STATELY HOMES

The houses of the greater nobility are both a testament and an enigma. They set out to tell us the whole story but, at the last moment, the key to it is withheld. They seem to say so much about their past occupants: who they were, the assumptions they lived by, their pride in possessions.

But having completed the circuit of the state apartments, explored the orangery and the music-room, admired the magnificent library of unread books, gazed at the lawns, the amazing frontage of the house, the string of ornamental lakes which Capability Brown deployed there, beyond the beech grove, to reflect the placid harmony of his lordship's life – having absorbed so much one finds, at the exit, that there is something about it which imagination cannot quite grasp.

What we see is the triumph of a family's aspiration; a dynasty on its best behaviour, suddenly standing still in time and describing itself in superlatively ideal terms. It was not merely a place for a family to live in. It was a piece of self-expression, composed with the help of an army of builders and craftsmen, one or several architects, and often occupying six, seven, or even ten years of his lordship's life to see it erected.

For the sake of the house, the nobility stretched their resources to the very limit, and a number ruined themselves in the process. In these magniloquent arrangements of stone, and the wide and splendid parks they are set in, one can see the burning desire of their creators to see a dynasty established once and for all: to demonstrate that the family had gained this foothold on the commanding heights and would never be moved from it. It was an outlook that was grandly, serenely sure of itself; and it showed a touchingly misplaced faith in the immutability of human affairs.

So the house is a testimony of sorts. But should we believe every word of it? Could they have been as good and as grand as this all the time? Unlike some of the more modest country mansions, a good many of the statelier homes say very little about what their past occupants were really like. It is hard to picture the sort of person who could live up to the scale of the grander ones; who could accommodate himself to such vast fantasies of stone as Seaton Delaval, Blenheim, or Castle Howard, and apparently wear them comfortably, like a good suit.

Even with the help of the commanding portraits of the 1st, 2nd, and 3rd Earls in the hall, or even that of the wastrel 6th, it is hard to conjure up the sort of man who could think or build on this scale. The present custodian is unlikely to project the sort of clues that might help to fill out the picture. It is not only for practical and economic reasons that the 15th Earl has retired to a small apartment in the west wing. It is a necessary adjustment on the symbolic scale as well. Out of season the state apartments are closed up; they are left to their oil-heaters, dust-sheets, and past echoes. No servants flit through the rooms. The great ship rides on; the noble admiral's still there in his cabin under the poop-deck; but most of his crew seem to have gone . . .

The other difficult thing to grasp is what kind of relationship the Big House had with the world just outside its gates. It became the boast of the nobility that they were close to the people and, geographically, the truth of this is generally clear enough. With the exception of some absentee coal-owners and suchlike, who preferred to live far from the drab scene of their profits, the landed families did entrench themselves in a locality, right among their tenants and workers. It was the basis of their claim to be paternalists; it was one of the things they pointed to if ever, in radical times, the generosity of their performance as landlords was called into doubt.

It is still a point made by the landed classes. As one peer recalled, 'My father used to tell me, "If you want to make money, the only way is to move out of the district. You can't be greedy *and* look the people in the eye . . ." That's why the aristocracy can't be bad landlords. We live here!'

So they do. It has been one of the hallmarks of the British aristocrat, whatever he does in the wider world of affairs, always to have some small corner of the countryside to which he was primarily attached. If he ever felt thwarted in London politics he could always come home and restore his sense of being an eagle among the sparrows. Even if he were a bad landlord – and I imagine there must have been some – there appears to have been hardly a whisper of challenge to his supremacy. The lord and his dependent countryfolk evidently accepted their different places on the scale, presumably with hardly a second thought. It is at least easy to make such a presumption. But it is when one gets out into the field and sees just what this mutual acceptance involved, the remarkable contrast between the lord's way of life and that of his villagers, that the relationship between the two becomes mystifying.

The magnificence of the great house speaks for itself. The lord who built, and the descendants who added and improved, all did so with a striking prodigality. But it is the self-confidence of their outlook that is breathtaking. Extravagance was an essential of the era of conspicuous display, the more whimsical the better. It was not only necessary to have enough money to throw away; the fact had to be demonstrated. Yet while these palaces, halls, and castles were shooting up, while the great picture collections were being amassed – and hung, purely for private pleasure, miles away from the metropolis – the people down the road were living in rural slums. To mention this inequality is merely to repeat a pale historical truism. But to grasp the real strength of the roots of the aristocratic system it is worth recalling just what both sides accepted as natural.

For the richer dynasties, not merely one or two but numerous houses were felt to be necessary.

'The Devonshires . . . grew richer with each passing generation. Hardwick Hall, Chatsworth, Bolton Abbey, Holkham Hall, Lismore Castle and Compton Place and Devonshire House – all vast, all costly, all crammed with pictures, statuary, furniture, and teeming with servants – gave them security and comfort during their peregrinations. At one time the Dukes of Buccleuch rejoiced in eight country houses (five gigantic) and two London houses (both palaces).'[1]

A dash of the whimsical was found useful in indicating that money was of not the slightest consequence. Lord Lonsdale gave Lowther Castle 365 rooms, and Knole, home of the Sackvilles, is believed to have the same number, though no one has had the stamina to complete a count (one of the Dukes of Bridgewater, offering the same sort of homage to the calendar, had 365 pairs of shoes). A similarly extravagant effect was achieved with far greater subtlety at Chatsworth where they gilded the window frames not only inside, but outside as well. Utilitarian standards hardly applied, of course. But what was Wentworth Woodhouse doing with its own skating rink, why did Lord Exeter need four large billiard rooms, and why the twenty pianos at Woburn which nobody ever played?

The wealthier families of the eighteenth century took it as a commonplace that no effort should be spared. In landscaping the Park they created plantations, dug canals to make decorative waterways, even diverted rivers on occasion. At Kedleston, to make a more spacious setting for the Hall, the Curzons moved a whole village half a mile. When it came to the Gothic revival period, a note of desperation crept into the urge for display. At Fonthill, the millionaire William Beckford had an entire mock-abbey created for his pleasure, including two 300-foot towers which collapsed twice during the building. The money to do all these things came from a variety of sources, from the law, the offices and sinecures of the court, banking, merchant venturing, and so on. But even the greatest resources sometimes ran out. Some families ran into such heavy debt with the moneylenders that they took generations to recover. The family which created Stowe, an enormous house with fine landscaped grounds, could never afford to live in it once it was up.

A number of the very rich families did their best to maintain some semblance of the extravagant style until fairly recent times.

[1] J. H. Plumb, *Men and Places*, London, 1963.

The present Duke of Bedford has recalled how, in the early 1930s, his grandfather was still surrounded by masses of servants. His income was then well over £200,000 a year. He had not one, but two, big houses in Belgrave Square which were kept fully staffed and ready for occupation though he visited them only twice a year. Four cars with eight chauffeurs were in use in London. At Woburn, with fifty to sixty servants, a footman stood behind each guest at dinner. In the winter some seventy wood fires were kept going to warm the house. The old duke himself never bought a suit and slept on a brass bed with a bumpy mattress.[1]

Apart from this unlimited capacity for conspicuous waste – of money, time, and other people's effort – one of the most striking things about the old aristocracy was its complete lack of timidity about anything to do with stone. They set down their follies, grottos, pagodas, pavilions with a negligent air; but even their lighter gestures had to be in durable material. One example of this casual attitude to throwing up permanent structures on any pretext – one that sticks in my mind for no particularly logical reason – is not one of the great palaces. It is the fact that Frances, Countess of Warwick, had a railway station built at Easton Lodge, near her home in Essex, so that Edward VII, whose mistress she was, could come and visit her. It is not easy to picture the sort of love affair which could proceed on any serious-minded level when it has to be supported by a whole railway station, signals and signal-boxes, a station-master and porters, and all the paraphernalia of steam locomotion. The trains still whistle by there, but Easton Lodge station has dissolved, leaving not so much as a stone to remind us of the sublime feat.

So, as far as one can tell, this extraordinarily lavish way of life was accepted as normal by the lesser tenantry and the £2-a-week farm labourers who were in sight and sound of it day by day. The landscaped Park gave some measure of insulation no doubt. From an upper window of the castle you can just make out the chimney pots of the village across the lawns and the tree-screened grassland. Reminders of the outside world are not excessively frequent; and, even now, outside visiting hours, to be in one of

[1] John, Duke of Bedford, *A Silver Plated Spoon*, London, 1959.

the greater park-girt houses can feel like being on one of those far-flung islands where the trading schooner calls once a month with stores. 'Yes,' the owner is saying, 'it is a curious fact that the aristocracy and the working classes have always got on extremely well together. A lot in common in a way ... neither of us go in for that horrible social-climbing ... we're both pretty relaxed, not too bothered about appearances like the middle classes ...' An intriguing and, to a large extent, perfectly valid theory perhaps. The only flaw I could see in it – looking out to where the drive curved in a wide arc around the former deer park, before striking out for the far lodge gate – was that few strange, urban sons-of-toil can have come up that way lately to put the reality of this relationship to the test.

An even more important part of the insulation, or perhaps one should say the system of acceptance, was the servants. It is well-known that butlers of the old school were almost invariably more aristocratic than their masters. Perhaps they still are, where they exist. A fairly recent example of the style was the sudden departure of the butler, a Mr Cronin, from the service of the Earl of Snowdon when, according to his own account in the press, he discovered to his dismay that his master preferred to dress like a photographer rather than in a style more becoming, in his view, to high baronial rank.

The rules of the hierarchy below stairs were often more strictly observed than in the state rooms over their heads. Servants often took the family title for their own name – so that Lady Moat's nanny would become Nanny Moat; and, when visiting other houses, the Duchess of Fontwater's maid, say, would get the precedence at the servants' table deserved by her mistress's august rank. Thus preserving all the aristocratic niceties, suffering as best they could their masters' sad inability to match their own standarts of *hauteur*, the butlers and their cohorts formed a ring-fence which may have prevented too critical an examination of the greater complacencies of noble life.

I doubt whether even this really solves the puzzle of the relationship entirely. There are places, particularly in the north, where the placing of the great house reveals the exalted, untouchable position of the lord and what must have been the totally deferential, dependent attitude of the tenantry at full strength. The house or castle is set in the middle of the village; the little, grey terraced houses and fishermen's cottages press up closely all round it. Inside the castle – tapestry-hung corridors, portraits by the fashionable artists of the time, cabinets of Sèvres and Dresden and fine glass, furniture of the best vintages, a library of thousands of books. Outside, a tired and stoic memory of bread, herrings and hope, all in pretty small quantities in past times, I imagine; a memory now buried somewhere under the bustling feet of the morning shoppers.

From the villagers – total acquiescence. From the castle – an apparently untroubled and cultivated peace of mind. How did they manage it so well? One startling possibility is that, up at the castle, they did not know the people were *there*.

Evelyn Waugh may have accidentally hit upon this solution in his first meeting with Sir George Sitwell, aristocratic owner of Renishaw Hall. Waugh later recalled how they had stepped out on to the terrace one evening before dinner to enjoy the sunset. Sir George was a tall, impressively-bearded figure in long-tailed evening coat. 'In the valley at our feet,' wrote Waugh, 'still half hidden in mist, lay farms, cottages, villas, the railway, the colliery and the densely teeming streets of the men who worked there. They lay in shadow; the heights beyond were golden.' Sir George turned and spoke in 'the wistful, nostalgic tones of a castaway, yet of a castaway who was reconciled to his solitude. "You see," he said, "there is *no one* between us and the Locker-Lampsons." '[1]

The size and insulated nature of the stately home no doubt played a big part in moulding the typical lordly personality; but it is not easy to separate this from all the other factors that went to create it. In *The Edwardians*, V. Sackville-West saw the stately home as a prison or mausoleum which would ensure that the custodian would end up as a stuffed image. The lord (says one character to another) is not the master of his house, but its victim. He would be held down by the weight of the past, venerate ideas merely because they were old, and inherit a ready-made code in

---

[1] Quoted in Osbert Sitwell, *Laughter in the Next Room*, London, 1949.

all things. 'That waxwork figure labelled Gentleman will be for ever mopping and mowing at you ... Even should you try to break loose it will be in vain. Your wildest excesses will be fitted into some pigeon-hole ... "An eccentric nobleman". That's the best you may hope for ...'[1]

Really full-fledged eccentricity – I mean the sort that another nobleman of the time would also recognise as slightly odd – was probably not as common as might be imagined by a close student of the doings of Bertie Wooster and some of the eighteenth-century worthies. If they all do it together, and at the same time, this might be said to lend it an air of group-normality. It is worth recalling George Orwell's point that P. G. Wodehouse was not, as foreigners believed, satirising the English upper classes. He approved of them far too much to knock them. His chronicle of the activities of Lord Emsworth, Wooster, Jeeves, and so on, was more evidently a job of conscientious reportage; the Master was letting the world have the brutal facts straight from the shoulder.

The most consistent sort of eccentricity was a chronic restless-ness – perhaps thus confirming Miss Sackville-West's theory of the stately home as prison. The house itself was often the bene-factor – or victim – of this mood. Few generations went by in any dynasty without some successor adding or subtracting a wing, entirely remodelling the gardens of the park, importing more statuary or – moving into a severely practical mood now and again – deciding that one lavatory simply was not good enough for a house with a hundred rooms, and going to the lengths of getting something done about it.

The sheer size of the house also imposed its demands. It had to be filled somehow – with people, servants, objects, diversions. In the eighteenth century, the Renaissance-like exuberance of the aristocracy attacked the problem with energy and confidence. In fact, it was no problem. House parties assembled for long periods, changing their composition slightly from week to week and month to month. A century later, at a time when the first hints of the decline of splendour had already reached keener ears, the more sound-proofed and world-proofed of the great houses were

[1] V. Sackville-West, *The Edwardians*, London, 1930.

still carrying on in something like the old style, but now with a note of solemn determination about it. An early version of Parkinson's Law seemed to be operating, turning the simpler business of life into an affair of unfathomable complexity.

The present Duke of Bedford has recalled how, as recently as thirty years ago, his grandfather's regime at Woburn Abbey approached the logistics of moving one guest with luggage from London to the house, a fifty-mile journey. 'You never travelled with your suitcase, that was not considered the thing to do. It had to come in another car, so you had a chauffeur and a footman with yourself, and a chauffeur and a footman with the suitcase, with another four to meet you. Eight people involved in moving one person ... This regime went right on until my grandfather died in 1940.'[1]

One or two noblemen appeared to be trying hard to recapture the devil-may-care eighteenth-century spirit. There was Lord Lonsdale, who once set off on an expedition to the frozen wastes of Canada (he had been asked to collect specimens for a naturalist society), taking as his only companions four spaniels and a valet. In the early days of flying, Lord Londonderry liked to do circuits round the house in a light plane before breakfast. Another early aviator was the Duchess of Bedford herself. She took up flying lessons when over sixty, partly intending it to be a cure for a 'buzzing in the ears'. One day she flew out over the sea, and was not seen again.

Since those days there has been a steady decline in the numbers of occupied country houses. *Burke's Landed Gentry* recently computed that in the twelve years since 1952, over 400 houses of some architectural interest had disappeared. The many that remain are undergoing some rather mixed experiences. A few odd ones seem to have edged quietly out of time, holding their owner quietly encapsulated like a fly in amber. I recall visiting one castle, the home of a gentry family for some centuries. The ramparts are stout enough to withstand a siege gun; in times past they have had to. The walls are five feet thick and there are nearly ninety rooms, none of them closed up. The old lady of the family lives

[1] Duke of Bedford, op. cit.

there alone, supported by an equally old retainer who acts as footman, armour-cleaner, dog-exerciser, occasional plain cook, and consultant on shopping. When I arrived the lady-chatelaine was giving the Skye terrier a run around the keep. The ancient walls loomed high above. She led the way along a stone passage, through the great hall, its walls glinting with a display of old musketry; through a seemingly endless series of rooms, their furnishings still intact, though unlived in. On and on round the labyrinth until at last we reached a sitting-room at the heart of the fortress, placed like the queen's cell at the centre of the beehive. On the mantelpiece were posies of everlasting flowers, postcards from friends at the seaside, a notice of a jumble sale, a fluffy doll, and a poker-work motto bearing a picture of a cottage.

Some houses still have a useful life in housing businesses and institutions. Filing cabinets now fill the old dining-room at the Grange, attended by urban-yearning secretaries. Home Office firemen exercise their drills in the grounds of the old Hall. Up at the nineteenth-century castle on the Lancashire moor, where the new cotton baron briefly dreamt his castellated dreams, approved-school boys now march sternly to their classes.

But a great number of country houses still survive and the nobility retains a substantial share of them. Nearly two-thirds of the peerage, some 600 lords, own a country house; most will also have some London address as well. The higher ranks are well represented among the country house owners. Twenty-two of the twenty-six dukes have at least one, and six have two or three; twenty-six of twenty-nine marquesses have one, and five have two; 142 of 159 earls have one country house. Among viscounts and barons the proportion is just over sixty per cent of each group, though rather more of them have a London house only. A number of these country houses are of relatively recent purchase and some are of the small 'weekend-only' variety. But the majority of the senior ranks and many of the other lords live in houses with some family ancestry.

A survey of peers with London addresses[1] shows that a decreasing number of lords now live there. Between 1935 and 1965,

[1] Preface to *Debrett's Peerage* (1965 edn).

the number dropped from 340 to 316. Only six of the dukes had London houses compared with fourteen thirty years earlier. The peers have either led or followed the fashionable drift from one postal district to another in the last few decades, but they still show a tendency to cluster together in some few areas. Thirty years ago there were 109 peers with Mayfair addresses; in 1965 this and adjoining W.1 districts had only thirty-four. Grosvenor Square, where six lords have flats, still shows one of the highest concentrations of coronets. Belgravia and Westminster had declined from 122 to eighty-three in 1965. Chelsea's quota had increased from twelve to forty-three.

Despite the decline of the stately home, it is surprising to find so many still intact and, thanks to the efforts of their owners and the National Trust, in such fine condition. Over 800 of them are now open to the public. Some of them have become museums, the owning family having departed and scattered. But a number of others are still lived in by the descendants of their nineteenth-century owners, including Alnwick Castle, Blenheim Palace, Badminton, Woburn, Chatsworth, Euston Hall, Arundel Castle, Goodwood, Albury and Syon House, Belvoir Castle, Strathfield Saye, Wilton, Castle Ashby, and Compton Wynyates. Altogether, with some of the unoccupied ones like Montacute and Hardwick Hall, they form an unrivalled collection of domestic architecture.

A number of families have had to sell paintings and other heirlooms to help to pay death duties. But at least a dozen aristocratic families have picture collections of an international notability; and at least twenty more have one or several old masters, supplemented by family portraits, landscapes, done by the fashionable minor-masters of their time. Among the finer collections are those of the Duke of Devonshire, the Duke of Buccleuch, the Duke of Westminster, Lord Pembroke, Lord Ellesmere, Lord Fitzwilliam, Lord Methuen, Lord Harewood, and Lord Radnor. These include works by Rembrandt, Titian, Raphael, and Velasquez, besides a number of important Dutch, Flemish and early Renaissance works. The Duke of Bedford, the Duke of Rutland, the Duke of Richmond and Gordon, Lord Rosebery,

Lord Bristol, Lord Exeter, and others, have valuable collections which contain works by Poussin, Canaletto, Guardi, and portraits of the English school.

With a few exceptions, these private assemblies of paintings were brought together by men who were rich collectors rather than connoisseurs. They went for the established names. They wanted to add magnificence to their houses; and they were ready to pay for the well-known and the superlative. Lord David Cecil has elucidated this point. 'Again, their taste was a little philistine,' he wrote, of the eighteenth-century Whig aristocracy.

'Aristocratic taste nearly always is. Those whose ordinary course of life is splendid and satisfying, find it hard to recognise the deeper value of the exercises of the solitary imagination; art to them is not the fulfilment of the soul, but an ornamental appendage to existence. Moreover, the English nobility were too much occupied with practical affairs to achieve the fullest intellectual life. They admired what was elegant, sumptuous and easy to understand; portraits that were good likenesses and pleasing decorations; architecture which appropriately housed a stately life.'[1]

As time moved on, and collecting came to be a more exacting matter of discrimination, aristocratic taste slipped far behind that of the artistic world; their effectiveness as patrons was hardly as great as it has sometimes been assumed to be. Nineteenth-century painters were hardly represented on their walls. Very few indeed ever caught up with the Impressionists, or even their forerunners.

The 'stately homes business', which gives the owners the income and tax relief that enables them to keep open, has found the nobility with mixed attitudes towards it. Some, like the Duke of Bedford, Lord Bath, and Lord Montagu, have discovered a career as super-showmen; other noblemen open their doors to the public, then just go away and hide. Lord Montagu claims to have topped the charts with 583,000 visitors in 1965. Beaulieu has a well-known vintage car museum, so it is known to deprecating noble rivals as The Garage. The attractions at stately homes vary. Lions at Longleat; roundabouts and animals at Woburn, and

[1] David Cecil, *The Young Melbourne*, London, 1939.

dinner with the Duke available for a consideration. At most of the others there is merely architecture, furniture, portraits, and fine surroundings.

In the last decade there has been some sign of a revival of country house life as old gentility finds the London Season overcrowded with the new business people and retreats to home pastures (though as often as not, I suspect, it is a retreat of businessmen from other businessmen: the escutcheons are not easy to read on this point). Not many can afford or find enough servants to match the size of their houses. But there are said to be at least eighty houses in Britain which muster a dozen servants apiece; and there are some six hundred butlers either in permanent service or on the agency books for temporary work. The large weekend party of twenty or more guests is said to be a regular feature at about fifty country houses every weekend. But the long, semipermanent gatherings of the past, which brought together the rich, the noble, the cultivated, the talented and, no doubt, the straightforwardly hungry, are no longer seen. A wide circle of relatives and remote cousins used to be able to batten on to a big country house for months at a time. Often, it was a discreet form of aristocratic poor-relief. This, I gather, is now generally discouraged. One Countess told me that, for uninvited guests, she makes a flat rate charge of £3 for bed and breakfast. Fair value possibly, and a sign of the times.

H

13

THE SCOTTISH NOBILITY

'Gone are the days when you approached the castle gates with fear and trembling!' said the old Scots factor who was walking me over one of the big estates. I did not know whether it was a fair statement of fact. I was still the unknowing newcomer. But the touch of drama he put into it, standing there on the hillside, a veritable Lear on his own blasted heath (he was wearing one of those Highland tweed suits which make a big man look four feet wide and twice as tall), suggested that the trembling style of approach to the citadel where the laird resided had been a commonplace of nature in his younger day. In fact, the castle was just as likely to have been seen as a place of refuge to other highlanders.

All over now, he had said. But had they, north of the border, so easily shrugged off their feudal memories? The factor did not amplify. He strode off to see about a grouse-shooting party, having put me on the road for Cawdor Castle. It was not far away, and it had seemed reasonably fundamental to begin somewhere near the world of Macbeth, in a country where dark and violent doings made a long chapter in the history of the nobility.

Across the Inverness-shire uplands in late September evening light. A timeless scene because there is little in sight to declare a history. Heather thick on the hills, stumps and remains of old birch forests, young firs in the valleys where burns run over amber stones; a flitting of quick moorland birds; a hawk hovering to the right, sliding away on an air current to find a new prospect. Over the peaty waste of Culloden Moor where the Jacobite cause was beaten into the ground . . .

The castle appeared, its turrets rising above the trees that enclosed the village. As is the fashion with the Scottish style,

Cawdor does not waste any ground. Built to defend itself on a narrow front (the oldest part of it is fourteenth century), its very height made it look formidable enough.

The Earl of Cawdor, wearing Highland dress, came out over the drawbridge to meet me. He is Lieut.-Colonel John Duncan Vaughan Campbell, sixty-seven, and runs an estate of 50,000 acres here with a couple of hundred tenant farmers. The main living room is in a plain baronial style, a spacious rectangular apartment with high beamed ceiling, big enough to dance an eightsome reel in should the need arise, but looking comfortably domesticated with the great log fire burning at the far end.

The Earl added another birch log to it. 'Yes, I suppose I *am* the Thane of Cawdor,' he said, as though the point had just occurred to him. 'It's still called the Barony and Thanage of Cawdor in old documents. We get American visitors every year saying, "Now show us where Duncan was murdered, the way it says in Macbeth." I can't oblige, I'm afraid. Duncan was killed in 1040. Our documents only go back to 1290 so it wouldn't be quite historically proper to jump the gap and claim the connection.'

One characteristic of the Scottish nobility appears to be a greater store of slightly uncertain family legend. There are other differences which mark them off from their English counterparts. For one thing, they are much more conscious of themselves as a group.

The sense of Scottishness, the geographical closeness of one estate to another, the more marked similarity of estate activities (sheep and timber) give them more in common. There have often been ties of intermarriage between one family and another from the distant past to the present. To a large extent, the Scots nobility is the 'network of cousinhood' which was once apparent among the English peerage.

This partly accounts for the keener interest they take in pedigree. This is not merely a passing interest in who is related to whom or a prideful appetite for distinction (though there are those things too) but a symptom of the more purist Scots attitude to the idea of nobility.

As the Scotsmen see it, the English titled system has something superficial about it. In their view it began to go wrong-headed in Tudor times when an artificial distinction was allowed to develop between the titled class and the landed gentry. The Scots give much more weight to lineage and the coat of arms that signifies it (the Spanish *hidalgo* figure of tradition, who retains an immense sense of dignity though behind with the rent, is one who would have an instant appeal for the Highland mind).

As one authority puts it, 'In the true sense of nobility, as understood in Scotland and on the Continent, a remote and penniless untitled cadet of Robertson of Struan (a dynastic kindred of ancient pagan descent) was theoretically far more noble than some baron created for his wealth or influence.'[1]

This is still basically true. The English tend to give primacy to the title; the Scots gentleman prefers to glide along on the ground-swell of nobility behind it. (But it should be quickly added that if the man of pedigree also has wealth and influence then so much the better for him, even in Scotland.)

There is also an extra category of nobleman north of the border. Here, what look like untitled gentry are, in fact, the Scottish feudal baronage. They are not peers with a right to attend Parliament. But most of them were originally tenants-in-chief of the Crown with an old attachment to the land from which they draw their styles. They are 'lairds' like Stirling of Keir, Cameron of Lochiel, Wemyss of Wemyss, and Stewart of Appin.

Apart from the matter of individual pedigree, there is some regard for the ties of the clan system. In early feuding times people gathered round a local chief offering fighting service in return for protection. The chiefs claimed royal descent and were given homage on that level. Recruits took the surname of the Chief as their own and formed the clan. The stranger can still quite easily draw up a map of the places of ancient clan settlement from the prevalence of a surname in a particular area, for instance the Campbells on the west coast, the Murrays to the east, the Grants and Frasers in the far north.

The clan chief may be a hereditary peer, but not necessarily so.

[1] Quoted with permission from the manuscript of *Heirs Before Scots Law* by Sir Iain Moncreiffe of that Ilk, Bt.

Ian Campbell, Duke of Argyll, is clan chief of the Campbells for example; while his near-neighbour, Colonel Cameron of Lochiel, is chief of Clan Cameron.

Since it is very much a home-distilled type of spirit, with its own subtle tang, the clan system is not an easy thing for a stranger to appraise correctly, as to flavour and proof-strength. Scotsmen differ about it, varying between scepticism and devotion. 'Bogus! Just part of the tourist trade . . .' said one Scots laird (not a chief himself) with a sidelong glance of great daring, no doubt listening for the rattle of a sword behind the arras. A few others also seemed to put it in the romantic category of after-dinner bagpipe-music.

But among the nobility there are more clan-believers than clan-doubters. One of my most forceful mentors on the subject was the Earl of Mansfield (Mungo David Malcolm Murray, sixty-seven, the 7th Earl) who is Lord Lieutenant of Perthshire. He owns 37,000 acres of land – much of which has come down through the family since 1300 – rents out to some 60 tenant-farmers, and has several herds of cattle on his home farm.

His seat is Scone Palace, a long, pale grey Gothic revival *palazzo* set in a spacious park near Perth. Its ancient traditions make an apt place to learn about these matters of principle. The Scots kings were inaugurated at Scone from early times. Even more striking to the eye is the great hillock crowned with trees which stands a few yards from Lord Mansfield's front door.

The tradition is that this is where the 'moots' of the clans were held. Clan chiefs and chieftains gathered here to do homage to the king. They are supposed to have filled their boots with earth before coming, so that they could swear fealty 'on their own soil', tipping it out before departure to their native glens. So the mound was made; and there it is, a great many cubic yards of fealty in permanent and impressive view from the palace windows.

Entering the main door of the Palace one is first confronted by a stuffed Russian bear, about nine feet high on its toes, forepaws encircling a stump of birch tree. A card informs visitors that it was shot at close quarters by the Countess's father when he was at the British embassy in Moscow. The rest of the furnishings, fine china, Chippendale, portraits, marquetry work, makes a gentler impact.

Lord Mansfield gave me the succinct, undiluted Scots view – sound malt spirit straight from the still, so to speak. 'The English really are so casual and diffident about these matters of nobility,' he said. 'Scotsmen regard it with the utmost disfavour, quite rightly, if a man doesn't take up the arms he's entitled to and he must see that the arms of the clan Chief are properly differenced on his coat. Whatever his rank, the Chief acknowledges his relationship to all the clan members quite plainly and you must do it in return to show the family solidarity. That's most important, and what is wrong with being very proud of it?'

'The English have no sense of blood, which is very remiss of them. Up here we recognise fifth and sixth cousins as relations and a lot of quite humble people are proud of their ancestry. We once had a housemaid who knew that she was seventeenth in descent from Mackintosh of Mackintosh.'

Lord Mansfield showed me out, down the corridor, through the state rooms, past the Bear. He waved me off down the long gravel drive. 'We don't want status symbols – we *are* status symbols,' he cried jovially after me.

One gets the impression that if aristocracy had not been a historical development then the Scots would have been the most adept at inventing it. They clearly enjoy it more. Dressing up appears to be less of a penance for them and, though I have no statistics to back it up, research suggests that they carry about twice as many robes and uniforms in their wardrobes as their English brethren. The apologetic phrase favoured by some London lords – 'We're just ordinary fellows really', is not at all common north of the border; or, if spoken, is *never* seriously meant.

Scotsmen seldom need encouragement to take up the insignia which is their due and – again an impression – there is a sturdy assumption that a 'gentleman (i.e. one who behaves like one, and has an affinity with other gentlemen) will inevitably and essentially possess the time-honoured tokens of the status, such as armorial bearings. Puffin's Club, for instance, a club for Scottish country gentlemen in Edinburgh, has nearly five hundred members, the great majority of them not being members of the House of Lords. But few, if any, do not possess coats of arms with some pedigree behind them.

There are few London clubs which could claim such a high proportion. Puffin's has some honorary and foreign members, a Yugoslav Prince, a Polish Count, an Albanian King, even a Red Indian chief, for example, but these will certainly be gentlemen of long pedigree too.

If this proper Scottish pride in nobility ever shows signs of ailing there is always Sir Thomas Innes of Learney, like a super physician, to keep things up to the mark. He is Lord Lyon King of Arms, in charge of all matters of heraldry and chivalry for Scotland. With an eagle-eye for detail and great erudition, he surveys the noble scene from an eyrie in the Register House in Edinburgh.

It is a small room, piled with documents, pedigrees, armorial claims, affidavits, and so on, and is reached by his own spiral staircase or 'twirrly' stairs. His salary is £1,200 a year; and those of the three Heralds and three Pursuivants who assist him are respectively £25 and £16 13s 4d a year each. The rate for the job seems to have been fixed in the seventeenth century; and no one since has apparently had the heart to break the tradition and award more.

One of the Lyon's duties is to check the pedigree of any new clan chief and, if one dies without an heir, go through the even more complex task of establishing who is the nearest blood relative.

Unlike the heraldic officers for England, Lyon has the force of statute to back him up. His Court is continuously in session and can impose fines or imprisonment for any breach of the rules governing the use of coats of arms and titles. Anyone who supposed that these matters are taken lightly would be much mistaken. The Court has been known to take a severe view of someone who designed a school blazer badge which infringed the heraldic code.

A need for the exercise of a special heraldic skill – pride and persuasion, it might be called – has sometimes arisen with the new breed of honoured men, life peers and so on, who have occasionally had the temerity not to *want* the trappings that go with honour. Some imaginary Professor Maconochie, let us say, who has achieved a modest fame in the world of embryology, may feel uneasy about becoming Lord Doomloch of Drumnadrochit, which would certainly get his identity lost in the highland mist. Then again, his branch of the Maconochies have never owned a castle (or so he reasons to himself); and he cannot quite picture himself, the modern, all-rational, scientific luminary, suddenly taking up about £150 worth of armorial bearings – with the Maconochie quartering, of course – and nailing them up on the door of his fifteenth floor Glasgow apartment.

Fundamentally, of course, these are merely symptoms of an un-Scotsmanlike delusion. The Lord Lyon is said to be especially able at restoring these misguided ones to the brighter paths of chivalry. If all goes well, Lord Doomloch leaves the consulting room with a brighter eye, a firmer tread, and a small parcel of heraldic reading matter under his arm.

The fact that the Scottish lords and gentry can feel themselves to be more of an aristocracy than their English counterparts is encouraged by the older and more conservative society they live in. Here there is a much wider social gap between the laird and most of his tenantry. Scotland has a higher proportion of tenant farmers to the acre than almost anywhere in Europe.

A big estate in the Highlands will have only a handful of full-time farming tenants but probably a couple of hundred crofters, each renting about 20 acres from the laird (at roughly £1 an acre) on which they keep a cow and a few hens, finding what daytime work they can on the estate, on the local roads, and so on. The tenants of the English lord are invariably sizeable farmers with often enough standing to meet him on fairly level terms, ride to the same pack of hounds, and so on. Crofter and laird, on the other hand, are socially poles apart.

Secondly, the sense of an aristocracy is abetted by the fact that the ordinary rural Scotsman takes much the same view of 'nobility' as the laird himself. While much of the supposed solidarity of the clan system may be no more than a bagpipe-dream, the high-lander does have enough belief in blood-ties and lineage to regard the existence of gentlemen of pedigree as one of the natural facts of life.

He is more attuned to it; so, paradoxically, while the deference is more consistently there it is less noticeable than might be the case in England. Tenants of a Scottish Duke, gamekeepers, estate workers, and so on, invariably address him as 'Your Grace'. But it is spoken with much the same tone as 'Mister' without any shuffling or uncertainty. They know their place more precisely; so they are not so uneasy about the forms that establish it.

In England, it is true that the well-landed dukes would get the same mode of the address much of the time; but the others are accorded it only if they seem to expect it (some English dukes would even be surprised).

The trick which the Scots tenantry seem to have learnt, and the English not at all so well, is to be able to distinguish the man from his title or, come to that, from his armorial bearings. The fact of pedigree is incontrovertible and is given due acknowledgment; they recognise that it says nothing about whether the holder is saintly or otherwise. It is possible that the tenantry got their grounding in this during the nineteenth century when they were put on the rack by the land enclosures. The highlander's long memory has taught him discrimination; and there is less of the English confusion which both depersonalises the titled man and credits him with some unmentionable superiority. The crofter accepts the rightfulness of the laird at the castle. But if he is a rotten landlord he does not hesitate to show it.

Cameron of Lochiel, 26th hereditary Chief of the Camerons, agreed that the highlander's long memory of past distress meant that any laird still took over his job faced with a handicap in public esteem which he had to erase. 'He has to be a very decent landlord to be popular.' But it seems that the tenantry prefers the active presence of almost any laird to the absentee landlordism prevalent further north, where syndicates have bought up big tracts for shooting.

Lochiel (as he is known) is the laird of 130,000 acres in the

H*

splendidly rugged country of west Inverness-shire. He lives at Achnacarry Castle, which is a plain, square, unfortified manor of fourteen rooms set in a deer forest. To the west, the magnificent mist-veiled hump of Ben Nevis rises above the pines. Occasionally they see a golden eagle flying by here.

The land has been handed down through the Cameron family since the fourteenth century and still occupies much the same ground as it did then. About thirteen thousand sheep run over the estate tended by fifteen shepherds. Revenue comes mostly from sheep; also from the twenty-two thousand acres of timber (which will be worth £200 an acre when it matures) and from letting out the deer stalking. There are about two hundred stags which must be killed each year.

The land itself, he estimates, is worth about £300,000 on paper. But there was a strong feeling of family trust about it, and the aim was to keep it intact even though its profit 'just ticked over' and its value would earn many times more income invested on the Stock Exchange.

Lochiel, fifty-seven, educated at Harrow and Balliol (a clan chief inevitably has a public school and Oxbridge education these days) divides his time between the estate and the wider business world. He became a chartered accountant when he left Oxford and took over the estate when his father died. He is deputy chairman of the Bank of Scotland and is frequently seen dashing off in his Jaguar to Edinburgh to various board meetings.

He thinks the clan spirit is a good thing. He was amused, though, that one of his sub-chieftains (some clans have a number of these supporters round the throne) had recently written to ask whether the Chief minded if he appointed his nephew as his heir to the dignity, despite the fact that he had much of a life-span ahead of him. 'He *is* taking it seriously,' observed the Chief. But such fore-sight no doubt saves Lord Lyon from some ultimate burden of research and decision.

They hold a clan rally every few years. About a thousand Camerons turn up, a hundred or so from overseas. There are strong branches of the clan in Canada and New Zealand and there is a fair amount of correspondence with them.

I asked whether clan loyalty was 'feudal' enough to override political feeling. Like many other lairds, the colonel is a county councillor. A laird always seems to win an election if he stands at all, though there are sometimes opposition candidates. I asked the colonel whether votes for him were automatic – just because he was the laird.

'No,' said the colonel, 'there are a good many Liberals about and I'm sure they wouldn't vote for me on a political issue. The crofters are pretty radical and they come and have some fine old arguments with me.'

The way out from Achnacarry leads through a fine avenue of poplars. They were planted in 1745 by the Lochiel of the time, just before he left to support Prince Charles on his final adventure. On the march back to the north the Prince threatened to sack Glasgow if it failed to produce supplies. The Lochiel persuaded him against it and, out of gratitude, the city elders ordered the bells of the Tolbooth to be rung for the Cameron chief on any official visit; and modern Glasgow has kept up the custom.

The decline in size of the great domains, like those of Sutherland, Buccleuch, and Atholl, has been dramatic. But there are still a number which are ranch-like in their scope, their frontiers wandering off into the blue distance, far beyond the ken of the laird himself.[1]

The hereditary pattern is still strongly entrenched. The big private landowners – apart from a few shooting syndicates – are either titled men or old-established gentry. Many, if not most, of the landowning families, descending either from very old indigenous families, or from Norman, Flemish and other gentlemen adventurers who came north after the Conquest, and were usually married to Celtic heiresses, seem to have settled on their land by the end of the fifteenth century. The really diehard purists of the Scots nobility hold the conviction that any family which had not

[1] It is not uncommon to find that owners here are unsure exactly what they own. An example: a laird's wife, driving me across a moorland estate, became agitated at seeing a small outbreak of fire on a nearby hill. The ghillie in the back seat instantly calmed her (we reported the fire later) with the dour but soothing words, 'It's no' oors' (not ours). If the English nobility are unsure about their background, the Scots sometimes have doubts about their foreground.

made its mark by the time of the Battle of Flodden in 1513 is just a shade parvenu.

Many old families, of course, have been driven off the land entirely. But the many who remain preserve, to much the same surprising degree that one finds in England, a relatively unchanged property-status to each other and with the same 'satellite' pattern visible on the map. The duke and his noble neighbours, whose ancestors rode to war together a few centuries ago, in the position of commander and supporting officers, still show roughly the same grading in the size of their estates. They go on grouse-shoots together and otherwise form a fairly close social group in a locality.

The endurance of land-holding produces some intriguing examples of the continuity of power. The big land-owning nobleman who happens to be a leading business figure – chairman of the insurance company or governor of the bank, say – holds those positions not only because of his own wealth and ability but partly perhaps because his fourteenth-century ancestor happened to be a bold exponent of clan warfare.

Despite the upheavals of the past, which drove so many Scotsmen off to the imperial outposts, and the continuing drift to the cities, the rural population remains relatively static around the hereditary estates. While the laird's ancestors may have played their part in uprooting the nineteenth-century population surplus of the Highlands it now falls to him to be the main influence holding its economic life together. As in England, he provides jobs, a feeling of continuity, possibly a sense of prestige, to some remote rural spots. By and large, the lairds are doing what they can to stop the drift by planting timber and starting other enterprises which not only make more money but give more work to a locality than sheep-farming.

In the northern highlands the clan connection is remarkably solid. In some parts of Lord Lovat's extensive estate – he is Chief of the Clan Fraser – three-quarters of the population are Frasers. For the many Americans and Canadians who come here to check their ancestry this must make it very hard to pick up the precise thread of their cousinage.

The Lovat estate, which dates in the family from before 1367, covers 160,000 acres. It is split up into tracts which stretch in a broken chain from the west coast to the east. There are 300 crofters on the land and 25 medium-large tenants.

It is in an intensely conservative place like this that the traditional or lordly leadership emerges at its strongest. A family of 'incomers' or strangers can live here for several generations, they say, and still not be regarded as 'one of us'. Here the clan feeling is also re-inforced by the fact that it is a Roman Catholic one, so that there is a vaguely religious element in the Chief's position.

Scotland has one or two peeresses who are major landowners. One of them is Nina, Countess of Seafield, who is usually tagged in press cuttings as 'the richest woman in Britain' until, right or wrong, the description becomes a matter of custom. It may well be right in this case. Lady Seafield owns 200,000 acres, an estate which includes the finest part of the Spey Valley, many square miles of woodlands (the estate plants 2½ million trees a year), wide sheep grazings, good lowland farms, and hills where you can shoot ptarmigan at 3,000 feet. Lady Seafield's son and heir, Lord Reidhaven, is organising one of the biggest forestry schemes in Britain here.

Besides the income from tenants (nearly 350, mostly on farms of about 100 acres), there is an average of £12,000 a year from the letting of nine grouse moors; £15–20,000 a year from the rod-fishing rights on the Spey; the timber revenue; and a home farm. The estate staff number about a hundred and there are twenty-four gamekeepers who look a striking company in their estate tartan, which is a uniform (and uniformly bulky) tweed suit in a shade chosen to blend with the surrounding country.

Lady Seafield herself, with an apparently unlimited supply of guests, acquaintances, and friends, divides her time between her main residence on the estate, Cullen House, which is a castle on the coast of the Moray Firth; her London house; her flat in Paris; her Inverness-shire shooting lodge; and staying with friends in the United States and elsewhere.

When I met her she was at Kinveachy, the shooting lodge (itself quite a large house), entertaining a party of friends for the grouse season. She is a small, very feminine figure, with pale blue eyes and fair hair tied with ribbon. Her attentive hospitality and charmingly un-grand manner make a stay much sought after by her friends and acquaintances. As I arrived a sports car slewed to a halt on the gravel in front of the house and a bulky young man and a pale American girl in blue jeans and sweater flopped out. I gathered they had driven non-stop from Soho to the Highlands on one of those impulses that seize everyone from time to time. The Countess's banner, three gold crowns on scarlet, continued to fly stiffly and resplendently above the lodge. Unperturbed, Lady Seafield found a dress for the girl; and everyone set off for an afternoon's salmon fishing on Speyside.

The routine of the social season in the Highlands does not look as though it has changed much in a century or so. There is more pressure for house-room than one might expect. As a guest confided to me at a big house party on the west coast, 'You hardly dare go out for a walk otherwise someone else will have come up from London and moved in to your room . . . !'

Those who avoid this self-imprisonment can have a vigorous time. A grouse-shoot, the autumn ritual sacrifice, is one of the more picturesque, if rather repetitious, performances in the whole canon of aristocratic theatre. The players, dressed with that studied negligence that indicates expensive tastes, move out on to the broad and breezy moorland stage. The lorries for the beaters, the picnic car, the truck for the spoils, the one for the guns and ammunition, make it look like a military operation; and so does the strict, sergeant-major look in the eyes of the gamekeepers.

The beaters get on the move across the broad valley, the guns crack, half-a-dozen birds just fold up and fall from the sky, and again and again they keep on coming. Strange, after all these years, that they haven't built up different reflexes.

PART FOUR

14

THE SOCIAL WHIRL

The London Season

The peculiar social marathon which became known as the London Season developed out of the round of balls, dinners, soirées, levées, routs and extravaganzas, which formed the familiar background to the life of eighteenth-century high society.

The round of festivities at the great London mansions of the Whig and Tory hostesses were a colourful supplementary to the leisurely life of the House of Commons. These glittering occasions, as well as the smaller encounters of the quality around the town, mixed the families of the politicos, the gentry, the landed nobility, and the richer merchant classes; and they were regarded as the most attractive of marriage markets.

The country aristocrats who did not have a town house were ready to spend a few thousands on renting one for a few seasons, either as a matter of course, or until their countryfied daughters had met their match, and all the negotiations that went with a betrothal had been arranged. The outlay on the season was an investment as well as a pleasure: political, matrimonial, and social. The greater nobility accepted annual running expenses of £40,000 at today's prices and were ready to spend ten times as much in raising their houses to a state of suitable magnificence.

As time went on and the greater hostesses went gradually into retirement, the Season crystallised round a few fixed events in the calendar, the most critical one being the Presentation at Court of the three hundred or so of those eighteen-year-old girls who had been privileged to be selected as the true daughters of the aristocracy. A new debutante had to be presented by a sponsor who had herself done the curtsey before the monarch; and unconnected newcomers had to avail themselves of the services of those well-bred ladies who, each year, were ready to do it for a hefty fee.

Even in the early nineteenth century there were complaints that the daughters of the *nouveau-riches* were getting in. These murmurs continued to be a normal feature of this glittering occasion.

By the nineteen-thirties most of the events – even the Oxford-Cambridge Boat Race, Henley, the Eton-Harrow match – still had their patrician following; but thirty private dances over a year then was about enough to meet the demand. By 1945, the hostesses predicted a final quietus for the Season, with higher taxation on the way and the Labour government just in. In 1958 another signal of doom went up. The Palace, moving very cautiously and slowly, decided to make its own gesture against social exclusiveness. It ended the court presentations.

But by then the unbelievably ironic was already happening. Post-war, Labour-leaning England had suddenly broken out into a rash of debutantes. Even the Labour *Daily Mirror* had made the sensational discovery (but late in the day, about half-a-century after Eliza Doolittle) that the working-class girl could look every inch as socially-stunning as the daughters of the rich. They chose their own Deb of the Year from the East End.

The impetus steadily mounted. More and more stockbrokers and businessmen plodded gamely through the Season after their bewildered deb daughters and their resolute wives. First, the inaugural of Queen Charlotte's Ball where the debs advance in waves, four abreast and curtsey in front of a giant iced cake, which stands where the monarch would have been in the good old days (Lady Howard de Walden, who presides at the occasion, is very firm on the point that the girls are not curtseying to the *cake*). And then . . . on through the Season's crowded programme . . . Royal Academy, opera, horse show, flower show, dances, parties.

Everyone agrees that the New Men, the captains of industry, have brought a new note of efficiency to the affair. No more 'muddling through'. Box at Ascot? That could be arranged. Black market tickets for the opera? They could be obtained. The only trouble was that they were competing with others, and they were equally efficient captains of industry. Ticket prices soared; boxes became scarce.

Far from the Season wilting, the dynamic surge for social recognition was making it uncomfortably overcrowded. 'Try getting to the paddock at Royal Ascot,' a columnist complained, 'and the chances are you turn up like a piece of driftwood at the Tote.' By 1967 there were at least six times more private events than there had been in the 1930s: about two hundred private dances in town and country, each with around four hundred guests, and a similar number of smaller ones; and five hundred cocktail parties. Though the number of 'official' debs had stayed about the same at four hundred, there were now reckoned to be at least 1,500 extra describing themselves as such. Competition for a mention in the gossip-columns had become fierce; public relations men were hired by some.

Reports varied about what it was like to be a deb. One columnist reported an interesting exchange of views with a deb's mother:

'What's it all for?' said the Young Man.

'To teach a girl how to cope,' said Mum. 'After a 17-year-old girl has had to walk into a dozen parties – or a hundred – filled with total strangers with whom she has nothing at all in common . . . after that a girl can cope with absolutely anything life deals out to her.'

'For the attractive girl it's not so bad. But it does a lot of harm to the half-attractive ones,' said the Young Man. 'Some girls who never suspected they were unattractive find it out as debs . . . I know one girl who spent all her time in the loo reading *War and Peace*. It was just the right length to get her through the Season . . .'

'The paperwork is hair-raising,' said the Mum. 'My daughter went to between seventy-five and a hundred dances, each preceded by a dinner, some fifty cocktail parties and thirty to forty teas. Every single one had to be accepted . . . I had writer's cramp for a year afterwards.'[1]

It was not easy to see through the smoke hanging over the social battlefield just what pattern was emerging. It was clear that the business plutocracy now provided the Season with most of its

[1] John Crosby, *The Observer*, 27 March 1966.

money, numbers, and impetus; but there seemed to be a tacit understanding that they did not claim the leadership. Peeresses and other ladies of older stock were still regarded as the superior hostesses; and, when it came to choosing a guest list, Norman blood was prized a great deal more than simple faith.

But there was still a certain partnership between the two sides, old aristocracy and new money; still some kind of algebraic equation, as there had been for centuries, which could broadly rate so much money against so much breeding, though the figures in the sum were changeable. The fact that there were exceptions – the exclusion of this or that property tycoon from the smarter inner circle, because he had obviously too *much* money – only proved the general rule.

Under the surface there were also enough doubts about the relative status of money and breeding – a dawning suspicion that a few million earned from a chain-store was not so utterly shameful as once thought – to inject new tensions and uncertainties into the upper social scene and, inevitably, offer wider opportunities for snobbery.

These social frontier lines have now become so fluid that it is not easy for any but the most hawk-eyed hostess to catch the drift. I asked a lady who is one of the most experienced observers of the social scene what she thought about it. 'Oh, the landed people and the older families count *very* much indeed still. If the Duke of Marlborough or Lord Rupert Nevill are giving parties for their daughters, or if Lady Zia Wernher is giving a dance, then you can see what a *desperate* clamour there is for invitations . . . not just because they're better parties. People get a lot of cachet in being able to talk about them afterwards . . .

'You see, people with breeding know how to do things. Their houses are always just right and they know how to do the flowers and the food. Oh, yes, *naturally* they have their own gardeners and cooks. You get some awful parties put on by people who've just got money but don't know, with tins of Beluga caviar all over the place. People who matter wouldn't dream of leaving it all to some impersonal caterer like that.

'For a deb, coming out still counts a lot. She meets new people and it broadens her outlook. I've seen a lot of Dads worried about the bills beforehand but I haven't met one who didn't admit that it had all been wonderfully worth while afterwards. The point about the gentry is that they haven't much spending money, at least not on the scale of the business people. The capital is all tied up in land or trusts. But the more social standing you have the less it can cost you to launch a daughter. A gentleman can do it for a few hundred pounds, but the others seem to think they have to spend simply thousands.

'Of course, hostesses are much more of a mixed group these days. But there are still some who are frightfully particular about who they have in their houses. Yes, I know this objection to Trade is disappearing very quickly now, but some hostesses are most particular about keeping the business people at a distance. One can never be sure they'll know what the form is.

'But most people will at least look in at a party these days whoever's running it, whether it's a banker, a Countess or a shoemaker. There's no guarantee that they'll be asked back in return, of course. People do discriminate. The other big change is that there are lots more dances out in the country. People borrow a country house if they don't own one. So many of us live in flats that it's either that, or you have to put it on in a hotel or your club.

'Yes, social climbing is still pretty fierce. Joining in the sporting interest is a very popular way of doing it, I mean owning a few good racehorses, or joining the Hunt, or trying for the Royal Yacht Squadron. And, my word, Cowes Week isn't what it was! I remember Queen Mary was always *such* a stickler for good form. If a woman walked across the club lawn not wearing gloves the Queen's eyes would simply be *drilling* through her. Now it hardly matters any more.

'Women with social ambition use the charities a lot for getting on. If she's one of these unknown, rich business people the usual form is to give a decent donation to one of the smarter charities and get on the committee. There she can meet quite a few well-connected ladies and can invite them to her house for meetings. This puts them under a little bit of obligation so she stands the chance of being asked to their places and generally being accepted.

'If she's ambitious to get known as a hostess, another trick I've noticed is to throw dinner-parties for the diplomatic people from the smaller foreign embassies – you know, the Ambassador of Ruritania and so on. No, of course, she's never heard of them before. But that's not quite the point, is it? She knows perfectly well that the French embassy people would never go and dine with someone they didn't know about. But the smaller fry do feel highly flattered. The dinner usually rates a paragraph on the social page of *The Times* next day so she's got her publicity out of it. Those of us in the know are really amazed at the nerve some of them have and aren't taken in one little bit . . .'

The inexorable tread of the events of the London season, and the close outward resemblances among the people who provide its following, might suggest that there is just one closely-intermingling social group at the top. Apart from the similarities of manner, outlook and relative prosperity among them, there is often a common background of schooling, regimental service and occupational interests. The links provided by Eton, Guards and cavalry regiments; experience in banking, the Bar, Lloyds (insurance), the Stock Exchange, or membership of the more exclusive clubs – these supply a network of connections among the majority.

There is now little sign of the High Society which Emerson estimated at 70,000 strong in 1833, which still flourished up to 1914 and, in a more subdued form, through the 1930s. It offered a recognised social leadership based upon real political power, titled rank, and substantial wealth. There was a clear dividing line between those whom the leaders found socially acceptable and the merely aspiring ones who were outside the pale.

The lavish succession of balls, galas and banquets which were mounted by the grandees testifies to their unrestrained pride in the possession and spending of large amounts of money. The fact that the present aristocracy no longer has this open-handed attitude is not entirely through lack of means. Much of their capital, it is true, is tied up in land and trusts. But a sizeable number of them could, if they saw fit, rival the newer tycoons in laying on a big social occasion, though they might well simplify the caviar display.

One reason they do not do so is because inconspicuous consumption has come to be regarded as one of the hallmarks of breeding. With no loss of face a gentleman can now spend a mere £100 or so on a cocktail party to launch his daughter down the slipway partly because newly-successful men, well known to have 'no background', are in the habit of spending extravagantly.

This is an example of the tactics of inversion which the aristocracy has increasingly and quite skilfully used over the past fifty years to try to preserve its distinctive place. The growing uncertainty of its leadership is one thing that is demonstrated by its habit of taking its cue, in this upside-down way, from the middle classes. What is fashionable used to be fairly precise, well-known, and relatively static. Now it might be defined as: what the middle-classes (and this includes the rich ones among them) are *not* doing.

The Royal Ascot race-meeting, for instance, can still claim to be one of the more fashionable events of the London season and still commands the loyalty of the upper crust. The scene has little changed; the horses run the same races. But as the event becomes a little more 'popular' and as more private boxes come to be taken by businessmen, the more elite-conscious begin to feel uneasily that their uniqueness is being challenged and they drift away. It becomes smarter to miss Ascot and go to the smaller meeting at Goodwood where it is fashionable *not* to dress up. Ladies who arrive in sweeping Ascot hats and silk dresses are regarded as a subject of lightly malicious merriment among the superior ones who invented, or know about, this latest inversion of custom. The over-dressed racegoer has demonstrated that she is not on that inner social circuit where this kind of eccentric information is passed on.

The solidarity of the social elite depends, as ever, on the insecurity of people who are not members of it by nature or upbringing. In the days of the wealthy grandees, little effort was needed from the top people to demonstrate that there was a clear dividing line between those who belonged and those who did not. The frontier was plain and obvious. New recruits to the elite could

be relied upon to reject outsiders with even more strictness than
the leading aristocrats might apply, the arrogance of the latter
being entirely natural, and not so self-conscious or defensive.

As the middle classes have grown in confidence and wealth, so
the defences of the elite have become more complex and mannered.
It is not enough, as it used to be, to swim dutifully through all the
events of the London season. It is necessary to know where a
retreat has been ordered by the invisible High Command, to be
aware that, as one socialite put it, 'simply *no one* goes to the Eton
and Harrow match these days, and one wouldn't be seen dead at
Henlah.'

The movement of the elite has thus become a sort of mysterious
flight, like an erratic migration of birds. No one quite knows, they
least of all, where the flock will settle next. Once they do, bending
all the strength of their fashionable regard upon it, they can invest
an event with enough lustre to bemuse the eye of aspiring birds –
who fly in, with a twitter of gratitude, only to find that the rules
have been subtly changed, and, as at Goodwood, that they are not
wearing the right plumage.

This somewhat casual cultivation of unease and uncertainty has
thus become a more important part of the armoury of the social
elite. It is effective as a weapon, of course, only because there are
always enough aspirants who care deeply enough about acceptance
to be vulnerable to it. One ironic side-effect of the uncertainty
about what is 'good form' is that it carries a backwash of doubt on
to the socially select group itself. The gossip columnist of the
Daily Mail recently revealed that over a hundred women of fashion, including several peeresses, were subscribing to an 'etiquette
news-letter' which prescribed which social functions in the
calendar were fashionable, and giving hints on how long to stay,
what to wear and so on – telling how it was bad form to stoop
and actually smell the flowers at Chelsea Flower Show or to wear
high-heeled shoes there, because they sink into the lawns. It trans-
pired that the authority behind the news-letter, on whom these
ladies were relying for guidance, was a retired lady's maid, living
in shabby and impoverished circumstances a long way from the
social whirl.

What used to be High Society is now an elevated plateau accommodating separate groups and leaderships, bearing only vague background connections with each other, the main thing they have in common being that they are not middle-class (in the worst sense of the word). There are the various 'county' sets in the country, largely centred on the local Hunt, mixing gentry and business newcomers. Through their attachment to the horse and all that it stands for in England, (the most symbol-burdened animal in the world since the cats of Pharaoic Egypt, the bulls of Mithras and of Spain), they often have a close attachment to the sharp, hard-edged, wealthy, racing elite. The mothers and the deb daughters whom they are steering through the Season have only slight connection with any other group for the moment since their heads are too intently bent on the collusions and rivalries which are essential to the ritual. Ex-debs and their circles, who mostly seem to recall the tedium of coming out, may or may not keep up with the swim.

It thus becomes hard to find any specific group which sets standards and decides what is fashionable as the old guard did so effortlessly fifty years ago. It is all about as vague as a wind through the trees. All the modern purveyors of the idea of gentility, like the London clubs, the deb-list, the various Hunts, keep up the general outline of a traditional dominant class. At the same time, there appears to be a group which, while connected to all these, preserves some concentrated essence of behaviour which is valuable to the tribe as a whole, rather like a Queen Bee.

The Smart Set

Observers who have ventured up to the centre of the English social plateau do, in fact, report what might be called a Smart Set. It seems to be about two or three hundred strong at its maximum though no explorer has seen them all at once. It contains a number of titled people, a Duchess or so; some sophisticated landed gentry, baronets and so on; a sprinkling of people connected with ballet, the theatre, or the aesthetic side of the financial scene such as Lloyds and merchant banking; and a surprising number of men-about-town, non-men-about-town, and various socially-alert women who are not necessarily well off and whose main claim to membership is that they fit in with the manners of the Set.

What exactly the Set stands for is not easy to grasp since there is nothing particularly positive that they seem to do in unison, except to be their group-selves. All it appears to amount to is that they have especially sensitive antennae for detecting the absence of 'smartness'; and they are able to decide, well before the rest of the upper classes, that the traditional cachet attaching to the Royal Henley Regatta, for instance, with its slender view of wood propelled along water, often these days by efficient-looking and *unamusing* foreigners, no longer deserves their presence.

In this sense, the members of the Smart Set are the arch-preservers of the 'aristocratic' social manner against the persistent inroads of the aspiring middle-classes. Unlike those Lords whose keenest expressed desire is to be accepted for their own sakes, as ordinary working citizens, the Smart Set has by no means given up the struggle.

There is something disdainfully gallant about it; and I was reminded of a story which one peer (Common Man or downwards-aspiring variety) had told me about his Oxford days. He was trying to illustrate the relatively humble and dutiful demeanour of the English peerage compared with its continental counterpart. It seems that the young Balkan aristocrat with whom he shared a tutorial marched in on the professor one day and announced that he had just volunteered to drive a lorry through the workers' picket lines in the General Strike (of 1926). Was that wise, asked the professor, with his Finals just coming up? 'Sir,' declared the aristocrat, 'wherever I am, and wherever they may be, my duty is always to fight against the people.'

Likewise, the Smart Set is still intensely engaged in fighting the Cavaliers and those damned, bourgeois Roundheads. Looking down from their battlements they see a people eternally occupied with the dull machinery of living, surrounded by their insurance policies, their cosy homes, their toilets, doileys, fish-knives, serviettes, and pastry-forks – all the impedimenta of timid security-seeking and pretensions to refinement.

Up on the heights – according to reports that trickle down – they scorn such timidities. Up there they breathe a finer air, untainted by any ignoble fear of the neighbours. I wondered how this Cavalier style managed to maintain itself now against all the challenges. I asked several people who are acquainted with the customs of the *beau monde* for their impressions; and I think I can most conveniently set these down as a composite monologue. If a certain dash of malice is detectable in their reports, this need not mean that they have not had an enjoyable time among the Set. As will be seen, the tone can be partly ascribed to their house-training.

It begins with an impression of weekend house-parties at some of the smarter country houses. 'Once you get beyond the gates you're in a different world, absolutely cut off. They like to keep it like that, too. No one reads the papers, though someone might borrow the butler's *Daily Express* just for the racing. Don't get caught listening to the radio news either, even if the Middle East is going up in smoke, otherwise they'll think you're frightfully earnest and don't really belong there.

'The service you get at some of these places is still pretty grand, or it might be if it was organised properly. I stayed at a place up in Scotland the other day, and they've got thirty bedrooms, a butler and three footmen. And there's a valet who seizes all your clothes and has them pressed and washed whether you like it or not. But a lot of these places are crazily disorganised behind the scenes. Once the last footman's gone off duty you've had it. Some of the hostesses just don't know their way around their own kitchens, I mean simple things like knowing where the bread's kept.

'One of the good things about them is that they don't have many of these petty little middle-class intolerances. So long as a guest doesn't behave in that awfully nervous little middle-class way they'll accept pretty well anybody, not bothering much about what school you went to or background. I think that's why they take to queers so well: they make themselves at home just anywhere. I mean, have you ever seen a queer who was socially awkward? But I must say they never seem very curious about anyone else. Except, now and again, someone drops in from a slightly different background – so long as it's not just middle-class – and then they're curious in a wistful sort of way, as though they'd just met someone who'd been to the South Pole.

'They're astonishingly tolerant with their staff too. They'll take lots of eccentricities the middle classes would just get stuffy about. At this place I was telling you about, his Lordship told the butler to have a talk with the three footmen and come back with a list of economies, the house was costing such an awful lot to run. It just didn't occur to him that three footmen was going it a bit. When the butler came back the first thing he had on his list was, "No cooked breakfast". He really meant it.

'One odd thing is that they don't regard the servants as middle-class. It's assumed they've been sort of dusted with aristocratic attitudes. That's often true enough, the way the butler is absolutely unshockable whatever he stumbles on, and that kind of thing.

'I know they always say they're the only ones who aren't snobs but that's ridiculous. They just can't get away from these jumped-up people just below them. This Mrs X, who's terribly smart, she went along to hear some new-rich Mums discuss a debby dance and she was absolutely wicked describing it, you know, all those airs they were putting on. Really had everybody rocking. They're astonishingly outspoken about each other too, tongues like scalpels and they just adore malice. The women especially will tell you the most amazingly intimate details at first meeting, not a second's hesitation. If you ask them, "Who's that across the room?" they don't whisper – that would be awfully middle-class – they just say in the loudest voice they can, "Oh, that's the Brazilian tart who married Lord X."

'They make it look so absolutely spontaneous, too. I once heard one saying to another, "My son's just gone to Istanbul. I don't know whether he'll avoid the vice. But he's staying with a middle-class family . . ." Then the other says, "Oh, that's *far* worse !"

'Another way the anti-middle-class thing shows up is that they just can't stand the happy medium because that's too dead safe and bourgeois. At a house party you find some of the smartest women wearing the cheapest chain-store dresses and others are all in their

Dior and Givenchy. Then when Lady X comes to London we either go and dine at the Ritz, or else it's some ten-bob Chinese restaurant down the Bayswater Road. Anywhere else she would meet the middle classes throwing their money about and she wouldn't feel different.

'What worries them is a situation where they can't take their superiority for granted. It makes them feel unsafe in a funny sort of way. What they're really guarding against is letting anyone into the group who's going to cause embarrassment – that's a middle-class feeling so they shun it like the plague. No, I don't mean "embarrassment" like someone's skirt accidentally falling off in the drawing-room. *That's* no trouble. What bothers them is someone who hasn't got the same assumptions about life they have, someone who's too deadly earnest, someone who's going to jar a bit by asking the wrong questions.

'This taking everything for granted is one of the basic things about them. If you go and stay at one of these top-class stately homes for a house party it's regarded as a little bit boring if you wander off and look at the architecture or the pictures. Even if the host's got a new Rubens hanging up in the dining-room, I mean you're being a bit heavy if you go and stare at it too long. You give them this dreary National Gallery feeling. It's all right just to *notice* it. The drill is, "Nice Rubens you've got there . . . [informant turns head away in glancing motion] . . . and, by the way, how's Veronica getting on with her riding?"

'Another thing quite a lot of them keep up – even outside the Smart Set – is the idea that anyone who does services for you at whatever level can't really be brought in as an equal. I don't know whether it's snob or just because it might be boring. So, people like the family doctor, the solicitor or the clergyman are the least socially acceptable of all. A chum of mine once took a friend, who was a doctor's son, home from Cambridge for a weekend. His mother, who was a marquess's daughter, took a poor view of this and said, "Twenty years ago we wouldn't even have had a doctor in the house for *dinner*." When my friend asked why on earth not, she said, "Well, a doctor might get called away in an emergency and it would *ruin* the evening."

'It's sometimes a bit puzzling who's going to be acceptable. They're very unsure about vaguely classless intellectuals unless they know them well. You're absolutely no use really unless you can join in the gossip and it's the most trivial and detailed shop-talk you could ever imagine. But foreigners are generally all right because somehow they don't count, they're not a threat. Americans often make a lot of social headway because of that, and they seem to find the gossip pretty impressive.

'But house-parties are an overrated pastime. There are party games that only the stately home people seem to play any more. There's a sort of charade thing called The Game with people acting the letters of a word, and it goes on until everyone is bored rigid. The other mad game is just doing a floating independent ballet round the room until the gramophone stops. Of course, they cheat like anything.

'Up at this castle place the only thing to do apart from bed, booze, and these games was going on shopping expeditions to this one-horse town down the road. You'd get all these smart women going off to the local Woolworths to buy cheap costume jewellery and all sorts of bits and pieces. They seemed to find it enormously off-beat and exciting.

'Funny the way they've suddenly worked up this passion for chain stores, things the middle classes have taken for granted for ages. Old Lady B., who's frightfully smart, told the others about how terrific the dress department was at her local Marks and Spencers. So suddenly they're all trekking out there to do their shopping, though most of them have got exactly the same sort of branch in the next street. Amazing, really.'

Clubland

While the socially ambitious Mum can nowadays steer her deb daughter through a London season on the strength of money alone, the male preserves of London's clubland still manage to keep up their look of exclusiveness – at least enough to indicate that there remains a quite sharp distinction between the Gentlemen and the Rest.

Behind the eighteenth-century façades there is a rather more defensive and uncertain air these days. Memberships have been slipping, some clubs have closed, and the old mysogyny which excluded women has had to be relaxed. The gentlemanly classes have become more home-based. They no longer feel that London is the hub of their kind of social life, a place where their superior ethos will count as it used to. They are ruefully nervous about the squad of non-gentlemen which might be disposed around them in the best theatre seats, what free-spending bounders will be dominating the best restaurants. The gentleman is mortally allergic to competition of this kind. He supposes his attitude to be based on breeding and this may be largely true. There is also a grain of fear beneath it. The gentleman dislikes the idea of fighting in a more competitive world because he cannot too easily bear the risk of being defeated on something which he considers really important – not being rejected by a club, for instance, or not being bested by someone socially inferior or foreign (which is much the same thing). The burdensome English philosophy of 'the good loser' simply camouflages the fact that there are some areas of competition which the gentleman refuses to join.

So the gentry who come less to town leave some yawning spaces in some clubs of an evening. But club atmosphere still has to be based on the unspoken assumption that every outsider – well, everyone who matters a damn – would like to join if he could. A club's self-confidence, like that of any elite institution, depends very much on the feeling that there is always a group of aspirants struggling to get in, and that some of them will be rejected.

It is true that a number of the smarter clubs have long waiting lists – five years, ten years even, so that unless a candidate has had his name down for Whites, or Pratts, or the Beefsteak, while he is still a callow youth he stands the risk of losing a lot of socialising when he grows up. Endless waiting lists are also used as a tactful way of indefinitely delaying the election of an undesirable member; it is probably more humane than the old 'black-balling' method.

There are about sixty clubs which count as having some social standing. They vary a good deal in size and character. Some are animated and noisy; in others, during the drowsy afternoon hush, you can catch the sound of *The Times* being dropped from some limp and sleeping hand. Some discourage conversation between members unless they have been introduced, as at the Athenaeum (bishops, professors, senior Establishment figures). In others, like the Beefsteak, the informal talk is almost obligatory.

Money is not directly a criterion for getting into a good club. Too-glaring evidence of recent riches can be a positive bar (possibly, one dare say, out of sheer jealousy on the part of the selection committee). The annual subscription in most places is around thirty guineas. But there are a good many tycoons, able to afford this fifty or a hundred times over, who know they are unlikely to get into a club that matters and take care not to apply. Money does talk obliquely of course: it is important to have the air of having been gracefully acquainted with a certain amount of it.

Each club develops a collective picture of what it supposes itself to be like. Whites, which opened as a Chocolate House in 1698, is the oldest and usually regarded as the smartest to belong to. Swift described it as the 'common rendezvous of infamous sharpers and noble sullies'. Lords and heirs to estates frittered away large slices of their fortunes here. It is still attached to gambling and seems to think of itself as somewhat rakish and raffish, hard-edged High Tory. Not every member quite lives up to the description: but it is the effort that counts.

Bucks Club was started after the 1914–18 war to keep up the camaraderie of the trenches among ex-officers. Its membership now includes a big contingent of young officers from the smarter Guards and Cavalry Regiments.

One can almost measure the gentlemanly status of a club by the number of generations its members are ready to see roll by before they redecorate the place. The decor at Bucks – at least when I last saw it – features old chintzy furniture, old hunting prints, old ochre-coloured and varnished walls, and doors whose paintwork has been mortified by time. The small dining room, with its ancient cruets and time-worn cutlery, might have been left over from some forgotten private house of the last century. A cavalry-man from the Crimea could drop in and not feel totally estranged. The talk among the young subalterns at the bar (whose speciality is a champagne and orange juice mixture, good for hangovers) is bang up to the minute, of course.

It was once said of Brooks's Club that it was 'like a duke's house with the duke dead upstairs'. This would be even more true of the Turf Club except that the Duke, however non-committally, is very much alive. The Turf has the strongest aristocratic con-nections. No less than sixteen of the thirty-one dukes belong. This is a rare example of the idea that the grading of a title does, in fact, mean something to the holder (one would not have supposed that there was a right or a wrong club for a man to join, simply because he is a duke).

The Turf membership is made up of several distinct groups, mostly with a landed and titled background. There are members of the old, ennobled, English Roman Catholic families like the Howards, Stourtons, Fitzherberts, Dormers, and Scropes, who are much intermarried and related. There are Scots lords who are also well-acquainted and generally closely-related. There are peers from the older Irish Protestant families. In addition there are members of the senior racing families, officials from the royal palaces, officers from the Household Brigade, and Masters of Fox-hounds from the shires.

Since so many of the members come from a distance, clubs like this can be deserted until well on into the evening. When I visited it there was only one member, an Admiral, there. He was chal-lenging himself to a game called Slosh in the downstairs billiards room. 'What we aim at here,' said the nobleman who was obligingly showing me around, 'is a place where the visiting country gentleman can get the same amenities and atmosphere he would have at home. At the Turf we just like to amble on a bit. If we had a power cut you'd find a few peers lolloping around looking for matches. Over at Whites, where they like to be on the ball, you'd get a pair of secretaries instantly appearing with lanterns.'

What's the test for joining? 'Well, clubs ought to be fun.

I

I don't like that nasty exclusiveness game that happens in some places. But a chap's got to be known to a few members or he wouldn't be proposed at all. Some of us would have a pretty good idea about him from school or a regimental mess and we'd know if he was inclined to behave badly, was a bit of a cad or a bounder. If we hear someone runs the risk of not being taken on we gently say to his proposer, "Is your chap really keen on joining? Might be a bit embarrassing." Well he gets the message and comes back and says, "No, my chap isn't keen on joining after all." But I've known committees let in pretty doubtful cases just out of good manners. One doesn't want to let in chaps who are going to be a bore . . .'

A vital code word. What is a *bore*? The arch-enemy of the gentleman, yes; but it is clearly something more subtle than an ability to tell four-hour golf stories. My guide, an extremely patient man, and incidentally of some brilliance as a lawyer, knitted his brows and groped for elementals of meaning. In the pause came a faint clicking from below as the Admiral no doubt lined up a difficult one for his cunning *alter ego*.

Gamely shrugging off the stifling boredom of the question itself, my companion came up with the answer. 'I'll give you an example. For instance, we get quite a few politicians in. But if you as, shall we say, an *uninstrrructed* member' – eyes narrow shrewdly – 'went over to one of them and said, "Now, Sir, I don't like your Common Market policy" or something like that, he would naturally turn round and say, "Oh, really, don't be a bore old fellow . . ." '

Pratt's probably has the most interesting membership and the most memorable, nay unforgettable, decor. It is in a cellar off St James's, originally used by an eighteenth-century duke to change and have a drink in after fox-hunting around the area. Though it has 750 members its premises are tiny; its communal dining table seats barely a dozen.

Half the club space, meticulously old-fashioned, is a sort of kitchen which is used as an idling-room and bar. Its fireplace is a fine, cast-iron kitchen range of the kind which the more house-proud working classes were discarding thirty years ago. On a winter's evening the coke glows splendidly, illuminating the faces of the comfortable-looking peers, landed gentlemen, courtiers, politicians, civil servants and others (no more than a handful at any one time) who sit with a negligent air at the two or three kitchen tables which are disposed irregularly about.

A Pickwickian steward at a hatchway takes orders for drinks, which are generous in size. The decor displays the plain, homely taste of about a century ago, hallowed by non-interference into something divinely, ineffably gentlemanly. There is a dresser in the corner with an assortment of oldish, but not valuable, china. The walls are festooned to the ceiling and up the stairs with odd, old pictures which no one looks at any more and probably never did; and with glass cases containing dead things acquired, whether proudly or reluctantly, over the patient years.

The eye lights haphazardly upon a pair of stuffed avocets, a stuffed salmon presented by the Prince of Wales of fifty years ago, a pike and a couple of middling trout given by someone else; a spread of antlers, a phlegmatic rhinoceros head, a duck-billed platypus in an alcove.

Conversation among the few who filter in for supper covers a fascinating range of experience between courses.

'So we managed to land the plane on the glacier. You see, we had to work out how dangerous it was so the insurance rate could be fixed properly for the others . . .'

'And then Jamie – that's the gardener up at the castle – had this dream about one of his ancestors who fought at Flodden, and he had all the arms and uniform absolutely dead right though he'd never read a thing about it before. Strange how dreams must run through families . . .'

'She really was the first lady I knew – I'm speaking of about forty years ago now – who was ready to do it in a restaurant. Pretended to look for a napkin. Quite extraordinary how you can carry off anything if you operate the face muscles properly. Odd how unobservant people are . . .'

'You know, deer never behave as they should, not even in Austria. We were out in the forest imitating the mating call with an old windpipe-horn. But the beggars just didn't come . . .'

The County Set

The County Set, or sets, is one of the most dreadnought of English institutions and, I think, one of the more difficult to explain satisfactorily to a foreigner. Indeed, the mystery of how a fashionable society could sustain itself out in the sodden shires, centred very largely on the totem of the Horse, has not yet been entirely solved by the English.

But it is one of the more distinct of the elite varieties. The adjective 'county' as in 'She's not quite *county*' would be untranslatable into a foreign tongue but, for those who use it, it has a fairly precise meaning. It implies a certain high-tempered breeding which is rather harder in tone than even the urban society-word 'smart' (used of total behaviour, not simply of fashion), which itself is tougher than the French 'chic'.

Most English counties have a set, that is a social group connected by their affinity for field sports, racing, decently moneyed status, good military-officer background, and so on. The Sets have usually been strongest in counties at some distance from London, where the farming may be prosperous and the hunting most active, or where the idea of a social hierarchy, as in the north, is more widely accepted.

Counties like Yorkshire, Cheshire, and Leicestershire, for example, have the elements that a strong county set seems to need. There are just enough of the old nobility and gentry to act as planets in the system; enough landed people with horse-loving daughters, and members of the retired-officer class, to consolidate the group; several Hunts; and, more subtly, the stimulating fringe contrast of the big industrial conurbations, from which the new-rich social aspirants occasionally emerge, struggling to shed their accents like alien refugees.

As with other upper social groups, its strength has partly depended on two things: the existence of outsiders who want to join it, thus acting as a mirror to the group's sense of solidarity and importance; and the existence of a strict enough frontier, so that it is quite clear who has a passport and who has not.

These lines have now become rather more blurred with the

increasing exodus of business people towards country retreats and
the fox-hunting life; and one has to look back to find a period
when the Set was more sure of itself and at a greater level of self-
awareness. I suspect that the nineteen-twenties and 'thirties were
an especially 'county' period, when there was still a good deal of
rural Big House entertaining, and gossip columns had their
tweed-and-deerstalker clad reporters out in the field as much as
in town.

In back-numbers of the *Tatler* magazine of the period – it was
the arch-chronicler of the doings of the Set – one finds a scene
that has been frozen in time. There is a hint of caricature about
the looks and manners; but caricature has a way of being true of
its time. Even the way they stand has its differences. One or two
of the fellows affect a stance, almost Chaplinesque, in which
right leg is nonchalantly crossed in front of left, right foot
pointing to the ground at the side. It conveys an air of somewhat
caddish relaxation.

The photographs of the race meeting, the point-to-point, the
Hunt Ball, give a distinct sense of leisure seen as a full-time and
quite earnest occupation. Faces are set, hardly mobile, as though
supported by invisible book-ends. Expressions carry a hint of
indefinite but decent wealth, stoically borne like an incurable
disease of the blood. They are faces whose absence of scepticism,
whose disbelief in anything cataclysmic happening outside the
confines of the hunting field is so intense that only a conviction
of immortality could have justified it.

Were they still there? I made a sortie to one of the northern
counties to look at the hunting scene. It was November and the
Hunt, the smartest in the county, was rallying for the first meet
of the season. The hounds, tails quivering, circled the pink-coated
Master; the horses' breath came out in little steamy puffs in the
sharp winter air.

Though it was a mid-week engagement there were about sixty
mounted followers, at least a third of them women. This seemed
to confirm the estimate of the British Field Sports Society that
there are even more people hunting now than before the war.
They calculate that fifty thousand people in Britain ride to hounds

each week, attached to 195 separate packs, and there must be at least as many regular unmounted followers turning out.

The faces on view, compared with those immortalised in the *Tatler*, had not greatly changed, though they may have loosened up a little. On duty, though, with a group identity to express, the style, the gestures, the distinctly self-conscious sense of theatre, are just as they always have been.

The manner, more especially of the women, is distinctly 'county'. Two ladies of a certain age, in veils, riding side-saddle, teeter their horses across to each other. 'What, Angela not here yet! What the devil's she up to?' The style is gruff and tough, the hallmark of feminine good breeding in at least one sector of the Set. Ladies should not, above all, be effeminate. One of these Amazons had recently shown true manly mettle, a hunt-follower told us.

She was addressed by a stable hand as she cantered back at the end of a day in the field. 'Old horse is sweating all right, ma'am!' he observed. 'By God, Jenkins,' the huntress forcefully replied, 'you'd be sweating if y'd been between m'legs for seven hours!'

Some of the mounted hunters are gentlemen of a cavalry-officer cast. Others are young farmers with time off and a feeling for style, ones who still know how to doff a topper gracefully. Behind them come some demure young ladies who still seem to prefer the riding to the theatrical aspect. And finally the ruddy yeoman-farmer types who wear odd hunting rig-outs and provide the hearty Merrie England framework in which the hard-core County displays itself.

Though it outwardly looks much as it must have done fifty years ago, the County has changed a good deal and become a strangely hybrid affair, especially in those areas where the well-moneyed business people have moved in, often buying up the houses of the declining gentry. Half-a-century ago, the affluent Manchester raincoat-manufacturer or the broad Bradford wool-man would hardly have been accepted by the Set himself; though it often happened that their sons and daughters married into the county gentry, and the family's industrial earnings would thus become 'disinfected' for the next generation.

The big change now is that the businessmen and their wives, instead of being supplicants begging to join some mystique-surrounded group, are more commonly running the show. Unlike grandfather, who still worked in his braces after he had made the first quarter-million, the newcomers have social confidence as well as money; and, against this combination, what was known as 'breeding' has been shown to present a very weak frontier line.

The relationship between the traditional County and the New Men is a complementary but a shifting one. The minor gentry who used to make the rules and do most of the social entertaining are now quite grateful to tag along behind, lending the group (they rather hope) what tone they can. Though some are resentful of having apparently slipped a social place and are envious of the newcomers' free-spending social life, most of them recognise that without the new arrivals' money, the exorbitant cost of running a hunt could not be met.

Hunting is the main pastime of the neo-County people. The wives may turn out twice or three times a week. Husbands give varying allegiance to business hours, depending on their seniority, but are usually in the saddle on Saturdays. One affluent executive in the north has used a combination of private helicopter and Rolls Royce to get him from office desk to hunting scene. It is also the younger businessmen who find they can spare the £4,000 a year needed to play polo.

The older gentry and the new-moneyed people meet frequently at social occasions in the county. They dress similarly – headscarves and good tweeds for the women, or riding kit around the house. The executives' wives even tend to acquire the strongly 'county' manners and voice of the locally-rooted. But the two groups never quite coalesce. Money both draws the groups together and forms a barrier to any close involvement. The minor gentry cannot quite keep up the pace of the confident new-rich ones. The country houses of the latter usually have expensive furnishing, featuring heavy brocade, Regency stripes, bits of new silver, and new oil-portraits of the family. Confronted with this, some gentry hint at their superiority, in that charmingly inverted English way, by maintaining studiously neglected households with heavy, misplaced furniture, outhouses in a state of arrogant neglect, staircases that have a profoundly satisfying creak as you ascend past the ancestral portraits, up and away from the crowd.

The Rich

Another group discernible up on the plateau, one which now represents the true centre of the elite, can simply be described as The Rich (meaning very rich). Through part of their membership, which moves in a slightly wider social field, they have connections with other groups such as the peerage, both the landowning and business sectors, the Smart Set, even with some of the more affluent leaders of the County Sets. But, generally speaking, they circulate within their own planetary orbit.

The number of those who count as belonging to The Rich is perhaps somewhere between one and two thousand, certainly not more. The group comes together in an area of the plateau where the worlds of the influential business plutocracy, of inner Tory politics, and the wealthier members of the old aristocracy, meet and find that they have something in common.

All they do have in common, fundamentally, is the size of their bank balances. It is at first sight a little odd to find this fact acting as their social cement or lowest common denominator since, according to reports, The Rich do not discuss money (except in very large and serious amounts) half as much as the merely moderately-rich members of the nobility, the group which is supposed to be an arbiter of taste on these matters.

The connecting link between the membership is, of course, the set of common assumptions that goes with money on this scale. All can be reckoned to be influential in some degree. There is also an element of safety-seeking in their collusion, a means of security from embarrassment by outsiders. Conversational exchanges about holidays in the Bahamas or the Caribbean, the fittings of private yachts, the purchase of racehorses or expensive jewellery or a property block, can take place without some non-member jarring sensitivities by making the wrong comment or finding these things remarkable.

As a group, The Rich have really taken over the primacy of social place which was held more exclusively by the greater landed nobility about a century ago. At that time, this upper crust of the elite would probably have drawn perhaps two-thirds of its strength from the hereditary landed families or those closely related to them.

Nowadays perhaps no more than two hundred members of the nobility (say, twenty per cent) circulate at all regularly among The Rich; and a good many of these are not from the older families but are titles of recent vintage, men who have become top-dogs in this or that business combine. Where a hereditary nobleman qualifies by reason of wealth, family prestige, or political sense, or all three like the Duke of Devonshire (three country houses, one town house; great estates; former Tory junior minister) then he is regarded as one of the natural leaders of the group.

Apart from the well-landed class, the group represents a wide range of moneyed interests: industry of all kinds, property groups, newspaper ownership, television, publishing, the bigger names of the Stock Exchange, merchant banking, Lloyds and the other more prestigious insurance companies. They still carry more than a superficial dusting of the old 'aristocratic' or gentlemanly taboos in the sense that being several times a millionaire does not at all guarantee admission to the circle. A certain maturity about the bank balance is still required, even if it is only the ripeness of an early summer. The Rich are those whose families have been well-bolstered for long enough for the moneyed look to have been absorbed comfortably under the first layer of skin, so that faces do not betray too much of that fixed look of self-congratulation radiated, for instance, by some of the more recent property and television tycoons.

In background, too, they are often strongly homogeneous as a group, with Eton, the Guards and cavalry regiments figuring largely in their pedigrees, however brief these may be. The Rich are ready to recruit interesting outsiders for their weekend house parties from time to time (though not with the same catholic taste as the Smart Set): the brighter politicians who think they know what is going on (even a handful of Labour men of the smoother cut), the occasional celebrities from theatre, television or the arts. There are also a few foreign visitors.

It goes without saying that these visitors are expected to pay their way with entertainment or information. The Rich insist on a high level of gossip at the dinner table. If a political scandal is about to break they would rather hope to know the obscurest details before the Prime Minister; and, more than once in recent years, they have. There are also a few foreign honorary members, like the Greek multi-millionaire shipowners, who recruited themselves into the group long ago, evidently fascinated by that secret English process which knows how to absorb mere prosaic money into the bloodstream like a vitamin, with all its complex and elevating effect on the total personality.

The manners of The Rich, in the broadest sense of the word, are a good deal less complex than in some other sectors of the elite. The security of really big money seems to lend a certain unworried directness to the social attitude. Unlike the Smart Set, for instance, who seem to spend a great deal of their time in a state of acidly-amused recoil from the quaint behaviour of the bourgeoisie – that is, most of the rest of the population – The Rich require no such defence works. They have a simpler security system. They ignore the existence of the middle classes completely.

Up on these heights, manners retain a relatively pristine simplicity. Unlike some of the older nobility and the various 'sets', The Rich have not been rich for so long that they have needed to acquire the more studied intricacies of the gentlemanly code. There is no particular shame attached to saying 'lunch' for luncheon, 'mirror' for looking-glass, or any special need to follow the devious by-ways of U-speech.

The vocabulary of the women usually runs to the extremes – 'heavenly' or 'disaster' – to describe the whole range of human experience that lies between buying a new scarf and hiring a nanny, with not much time to spare for the middle register. But there is much less use of cipher-words and the foreigner would not be as mystified as he might elsewhere on the plateau.

Above all, The Rich are characterised by a high degree of

straightforwardness about the facts of wealthy life. They do not have the outlook of old Lord X, say, who, though he owns £2 millions worth of land, is just a shade too anxious to demonstrate his relative penury – compared with the family position in 1850, or thereabouts – by driving himself around in a last year's Ford Zephyr, or the estate car with an assembly of garden tools in the back. The cars of The Rich will be the uncomplicated, chauffeur-driven Bentley or Rolls, or the self-driven Ferrari and suchlike.

The women's dress shows little or none of that playful and esoteric mixture favoured by the females of the Smart Set, who find it stimulating to have chain-store off-the-peg and the very best French models at the same party. Again The Rich opt for candour . . . Dior, Chanel, St Laurent, and no nonsense about half-measures.

Though the merely rich now clearly and numerically predominate over the noble and rich, it is much the same marriage of convenience between the two which has existed since Tudor times and before; and there is every reason to suppose that this happy matrimonial state will continue.

15

MONEY AND MANNERS

The Wealth Psychology

Writing in 1755, a French-Swiss who had lived in England made a brief and lucid assessment of the class system. 'The Englishman,' he wrote, 'always has in his hands an accurate pair of scales in which he scrupulously weighs up the birth, rank, and above all, the wealth of the people he meets, in order to adjust his behaviour towards them accordingly.' New variations are always creeping into the pattern, but the same outline is still clearly enough there.

Weighing up the simply rich man is hardly any problem, even in England: he is rich, and the head-waiter or other assessor can adjust his approach according to scale. With the aristocracy and the upper gentlemanly class that surrounds them the process becomes infinitely more difficult. Studying the typical figure, the weigher-up can hazard a guess that the hard reality of money is the whale-boned foundation garment; but this one simple fact is decently, but obscurely, veiled by the diaphanous layers of outer clothing – of 'breeding', manners in the widest sense, the assumptions which the aristocracy have about themselves, and which others have about them. It is, needless to say, not made any easier by the fact that all these elements that go to make 'position' – both of individuals and the elite as a whole – are all woven together into a one-coloured cloth. But, moving a little closer, one can begin to make out a few of the main threads.

Money, for example. I was talking to one of the landed earls about his estate in the drawing-room of his country house. He was complaining mildly about the burdens of ownership, of the drawbacks of owning too many country cottages, of the constant need

254

for capital and how, at the end of it all, his agent's calculation was that they were making only one-half per cent profit. I did not disbelieve his figures. Still, what puzzled me a little – having heard similar stories elsewhere – was that he seemed to be taking a needlessly uncheerful view of his financial standing. It is true that there were no Rembrandts among his small and pleasant family collection of portraits and landscapes. The hock he had served at lunch was nothing grander than the palatable ten-bob South African also drunk by the middle classes.

Though his way of life was not showy, it seemed to have much to offer in classical English comfort. So I asked who he would regard as the truly prosperous landed families in the county. He sat back reflectively. He was still thinking when his wife, the Countess, answered for him. 'Oh, there's Willy Loamshire down the road. He's pretty well off...' Considering that the distinguished lord she had named was in the territorial magnate class, owned one of the country's finest houses and an outstanding art collection, this seemed an understatement. I was surprised that the Countess evidently did not include her own family in the 'pretty well off' class, though their estate ran to something over seven thousand acres of good arable and grazing, and they lived in a thirty-roomed mansion with no obvious shortages.

I knew that ordinary income earners got most of their sense of social placing by comparisons with those above and below them. Seeing the aristocracy from below as an amorphous but consistently 'rich' group, it hadn't occurred to me that much the same system of self-grading might operate. Even up on the high plateau everything is relative.

When I mentioned this experience to a friend, one with a much longer acquaintance with the titled classes, he recalled hearing a certain Lady So-and-So complaining to a visitor about her financial burdens. 'Come now, Minnie,' the friend replied, as the hostess reclined among her *objets d'art*, 'how would you like to have to raise four children on £12 a week like your game-keeper's wife?' The hostess rose nobly to the challenge. 'Ah, but *she* doesn't have to find the money to pay three servants like I have.'

In other words, a way of life which is 'normal' does not neces- sarily count as being 'rich'. And if one considers the *personal* characteristics which have traditionally separated the elite class from those below then one usually finds that what might be called a 'wealth psychology' is fundamental to them. It is also what distinguishes the elite from those who merely have a great deal of money; the latter have the cash, but only the rudiments of the psychology. *'Gentilitie is naught but ancient riches,'* said Lord Burleigh some centuries ago; and the definition is as good as ever.

In its intricate and various modes of expression, this psychology is possibly the most elaborate art-form so far devised by the English. One of the curiosities about it, and an indication of its strength on native soil, is that the psychology can to some extent be exercised without the wealth (or could be until the war: it is harder now). In the nineteen-twenties and 'thirties there was a distinct class of impoverished gentlemen whose social status was not questioned – because of their general look and manner – though they were often on their beam ends. But it is not something that travels well. Once divorced from the English class structure and placed in front of a disbelieving foreign audience – a Brook- lyn cab-driver, say – its effect wilts quickly; or else the personage concerned is simply regarded as just another rich man, which is not at all the same thing.

The psychology or outlook obviously developed with the system of inherited property; but it is hard to say just how far back into the past the roots of the modern version lead. It was a tree already sprouting in Tudor times when the gentry were eagerly looking about for way of colouring their possessions with the fine lustre of arms and honour. They studied such Renaissance handbooks as Castiglione's *The Courtier* which advised the gentle- man to 'conceal all artificiality and appear to do everything without design and as it were absent-mindedly'. (Note 'conceal' and 'appear to': it was meant to be an actor's performance.)

In the period of the Whig aristocracy, 1770–1830, the gentle- manly idea was cultivated to its highest point, and there was 'a distilled civility never surpassed or equalled. There was natural- ness, self-assurance, frankness, an ability to hold one's liquor, and to be cultivated without being a dandy . . . though their [the aristocracy's] social conscience was remarkably primitive.'[1] In the nineteenth century the ideal became rather stiffer in manner and the cultivation thinner; the glint of money could sometimes be seen reasserting itself through the psychology. A parallel development to the main stem at this time, and one which Castiglione and the Whigs would have regarded as a pale shadow of the courtly ideal, grew out of Dr Arnold's Rugby and those academies modelled on it. It was the public-school gentleman, trained to play games heartily, to be a good loser, to be a leader of men, and then sent out with this conflicting philosophy to hold together an Empire.

In the modern version of the gentleman most of these elements are probably mingled. Some would argue that there is no need to rummage through history to find his progenitors: six years at Eton will do the trick just as well. True, to some extent. Yet it is among the estate-owning dynasties that one still finds the mystique of 'ancient riches' in its most confident form. The celebrated Scott Fitzgerald–Hemingway dialogue ('The very rich are different from you and me' – 'Yes, they have more money . . .') is an analysis that will serve for the United States but not for the English landed classes. In England, wealth became associated with a complex of assumptions and attitudes – social and political leadership, effortless superiority, gentlemanly obligation, prejudices against 'trade' and other taboos, a special code of manners and vocabulary.

Some foreign visitors found it attractive. 'They [the aristocracy] have the sense of superiority, the absence of all ambitious effort which disgusts in the aspiring classes,' wrote Ralph Waldo Emerson. Others found a seamier side in it. Edmund Wilson saw the English upper class as representing 'the passion for social privilege, the rapacious appetite for property, the egoism that damns one's neighbour, the dependence on inherited advantage, and the almost equally deep-fibred instinct to make all these appear forms of virtue . . . We [i.e. the Americans] find money exhilarating, but we also find it exhilarating to spend it. Money

[1] Harold Nicolson, *Good Behaviour*, London, 1955.

for us is a medium, a condition of life, like air. But with the English it means always property.'[1] The difference is true enough, and so are some of the strictures. The American system does have its exhilarating side. Jay Gatsby, the archetypal hero, is cheered on as he makes his climb to the top; people are glad for him. It is when he gets near the summit that the great objective begins to peter out into a misty uncertainty. There is, ultimately, nowhere to go: only that elusive green light to go on pursuing.

Few of the dollar fortunes ever took root; even the wealthy New England families, though they had 'breeding' and much of the wealth-psychology, did not have that close association with a particular community which was a fundamental of the English model. The frontier beginnings, the geography, the temperament of the people, never encouraged wealth to become static and thus to transform itself into a psychology. The dollar millionaires and heiresses have typically been the dissatisfied nomads that, given another chapter, Jay Gatsby would have become. The English wealthy class, on the other hand, entrenched themselves with a local habitation and a name. They gave money a home to go to. They became the solid keystone supporting a class system of often outrageous unfairness and a political system which was, for long periods, mulishly unprogressive. But they did also find a way in which money brought responsibility, so that they and their possessions remained attached to life and not unhappy wanderers like much of the American plutocracy and some of the European aristocracy.

The psychology lingers on even in cases where the family fortune is not what it was. Modern lords who do not have expense accounts resent the fact that they are expected to tip waiters more lavishly than commoners who may be far richer. But, of course, they have only their history to blame. The intuition of waiters and hall porters is right in sensing that the confident 'natural' manner, all the Castiglione-complex of the typical gentleman *ought* to indicate a well-moneyed background. It is also an extraordinary fact of English life that inherited wealth still carries more esteem than a fortune that has been made by a man's

[1] Edmund Wilson, *Europe Without Baedeker*, London, 1948.

own efforts. This inversion of the normal order of things is peculiar considering that ninety-nine per cent of people in Britain start more or less from scratch. One of the younger lords, volunteering me an explanation, thought it had to do with the fact that ordinary people would feel envious or suspicious of their neighbour, old Fred, who suddenly made a million out of selling television sets. He was too close to them. But to find a young lord inheriting a few millions' worth of land was more respectable and interesting simply because it hadn't been earned. It reinforced some deep-seated English faith in the magic of chance, he thought. I wondered about this.

The present-day aristocrat's attitude to his wealth is made rather more complex by the defensive note that accompanies their 'inconspicuous consumption'. This more especially applies to the landed classes. Some psychological reason is needed, I think, to explain why an Earl owning £2 millions worth of land prefers to see his possessions in terms of difficulty rather than as a cause for moderate celebration. Part of the explanation is that the older members of the aristocracy can only see their status as a decline from something surer and grander. One also forgets what attacks it has had to weather in the past. The *Queen* magazine, the society journal, became almost feverish in its defence of the aristocracy in Edwardian times. In one issue it said:

'The bitter abuse of the upper classes is cruel and unjust and bids fair to become a danger to the nation... The English aristocrat has a just sense of his responsibilities and has always been ready to give service in return for privilege. Let the Socialists rail as they will, our upper classes are the finest body of thinkers and livers in the world.'[1]

The wealth-psychology is much the greater part of what is known as 'breeding'. The point is worth making since people who speak of 'breeding' often make the implication that it has a great deal to do with length of lineage or pedigree, as though the aristocracy were so many blue-blooded racehorses whose performance could be judged from the Form Book. This would be more convincing if there were any *consistent* difference between

[1] Quoted by Quentin Crewe, *Frontiers of Privilege*, London, 1961.

the Etonian of Norman blood and, say, the similarly-educated lord whose family was scarcely heard of until it made its pile in nineteenth-century insurance. True, one can find occasional instances to support the theory of pedigree-length being important. One peer I was visiting – a nineteenth-century creation, in fact – mentioned an example. I thought he was reasonably well-equipped himself with the easy-going gentlemanly manner. But he said, 'Now take Eddie So-and-So' (mentioning an untitled landed-gentry neighbour – family there since seventeenth century – whom I had just visited) '. . . now he really has something special – so natural, such a *gentleman*.' I got the impression that this peer was just a little afraid of 'Eddie's' extra ration of wealth-psychology. I could see what he meant to some extent; but it would take very deep research to discover whether his neighbour's manner owed itself simply to two centuries' longer attachment to the land.

Except among the Scottish nobility and the older English noblemen, length of pedigree hardly counts for much as a measure of status. Unless the lord concerned has a lineage stretching back to the Conquest period he is inclined not to lay any great emphasis on it himself; and the possession of a reasonably detailed knowledge of how the family rose to fame and fortune is less common than I had expected. 'I'm pretty sure it was either Henry VII or Henry VIII who gave us that bit of the estate,' says the peer, uncertainly scanning his background. 'Anyway, my secretary knows more about us than I do . . . you might give her a ring.' Or another says, 'We got the barony in the eighteenth century . . . one of those political manoeuvres to pack the House of Lords and get a Bill through . . . no, afraid I forget what on earth the Bill was about.' (As one very pedigree-conscious Scots nobleman said to me – though pitching it a trifle high – 'Some of those English lords don't care who their own *grandmothers* were.')

The other difficulty about accepting 'breeding' as meaning simply length of lineage is that most of the older families have ancestors who were extremely varied in character and who, as a group, put rather a strain on the drawing-room version of what a lord ought to be like. So the interesting point arises, how much consciousness of family history should the well-bred aristocrat allow himself? To be aware of the leading Tudor statesman, the dashing Cavalier general, no doubt gives a heart-warming sense of naturally belonging to the heights. But does breeding allow uncensored memory of the tough rack-renter, the eighteenth-century political fixer, the Restoration rake who nearly lost the lot, the hopeless landlords in the family?

The answer is, of course, yes. Scandal in the archives causes no personal embarrassment whatever to the aristocracy. They would hardly count themselves as gentlemen if it did. The rogues of the past are seen as rather amusing, in their way; and they know that the other people in the company, or the audience at the charity fête will do all the censorship necessary and project on to them the sort of well-bred and clean-living history that suits the definition of 'gentleman' at any one moment. Middle-class admirers of aristocracy inevitably see the aristocracy within their own definition of 'gentleman', i.e. what a proud mother would expect of her favourite son. The aristocratic meaning of the word is rather wider in scope.

The first function of wealth-psychology, whether deliberate or incidental, was to remove the hard and avaricious edge from the ownership of great possessions. The link between the aggressive-ness (in the broadest, business-sense of the word) which acquired the wealth, and the subsequent code of manners which liked to suggest that it had arrived like innocent rain from heaven is an obvious one. Meeting the easy, decent, modest-seeming figures who run some of the biggest estates one is constantly wondering what happened to the tough ambition and self-seeking that must have been needed to build up these great acres. The aristocratic code of manners aimed to transmute money into some semblance of a personal quality; also to demonstrate that there is so much of it in the vaults that, paradoxically, its existence is of not the slightest consequence. Until recent times, talk of money in a noble household was taboo, because it would break that fine network of assumptions on which the whole aristocratic structure was based. It was simply there, like the air available for breathing. It was also presumably a way used by the elite to distinguish themselves from the rich parvenus of commerce, who were imagined to spend every waking moment discussing the day's takings.

The gentleman's attitude to his possessions is still, or should be, essentially casual. If, like the earl mentioned above, he lives in a thirty-roomed mansion and the estate is not making striking profits, he is inclined to describe it rather humbly as 'a way of life'. By definition, all his expenditure is on *essentials* ('luxuries' is possibly the most bourgeois word there is: never on any account used in upper-class circles). He sees himself as not at all extravagant, rather economical in fact, and by his own reckoning he certainly is. But among the essentials he would naturally regard upkeep of the mansion, and such items as an Eton education for his sons, and a private allowance to see them through a spell in the Guards or the Cavalry.

He is also more flexible and relaxed about his possessions. My definition of a *gentleman's* house, having now seen and admired a good many of them, is that it is a place which contains a large number of things which the middle classes could not possibly afford; and a number of other things which the middle-class housewife would instantly throw out. In the houses of the gentry (I naturally except the grander stately homes) one finds good silver, and so on, sharing equal place with furniture that is held together only by the patina of age. No one is bothered about it, and it is bad form to bother. The gentleman does not niggle his environment with questions, searching glances, doubts about what is missing, what needs to be done, how it could all be improved, as the middle classes (from the lower to upper) tend to do. To do so would, again, be fatal to the sense of assumption.

This custom of not noticing surroundings can take a quite piquant form. I was visiting the house of one lord of old family in the north and he began to show me the house, where the family had lived for several hundred years. Half-way round, he let slip the fact that he had spent the previous afternoon studying his own stately-home guide-book so that he could answer any of my questions about who had painted this or built that. The sacrifice involved in getting to grips with these details at last was, I thought, an example of *noblesse oblige* at its finest.

Mr Randolph Churchill has mentioned another telling instance in his biography of the late Lord Derby. He tells how, in the 1920s, the Earl of Crawford and Balcarres, a good judge of works of art, was visiting the old peer at Knowsley. 'Noting the general ugliness of the furniture, Lord Crawford felt moved to say to Derby, "That's a very fine set of Charles II dining-room chairs". Derby made no comment but after his guest had left he snorted and said, "Damn cheek, that fellow noticing my chairs!" Neither he nor any of his ancestors had noticed them before. Evidently he thought it an impertinence and even rather common that a guest should draw attention to something which all his life he had taken for granted.'[1]

These assumptions, that is the habit of 'not noticing', are the major part of wealth-psychology. For the outsider they are the vague but important smoke-signals which relay, from the plateau, the news of the existence of an identifiable tribe. The real significance of the smoke-puffs takes time to learn. What looks quite trivial can mean much; and vice versa. I was visiting one of the much-landed lords in the far north. Summing up his talk to me, he turned to the views from the windows and said, 'Yes, it's a fine place for a boy to grow up in.' It was not until a week later (this was in the early stages of my inquiry) that it suddenly registered with me that what he had meant by the remark was not simply the dozen acres of lawns, gardens and shrubbery around the house, which was my own constrained idea of the maximum amount of space any one person could either use or hold in his mind as an image of a private world. No, he was not seeing it my way. The whole estate had long ago gone through the conversion process, from thing into assumption.

In his own mental terms of reference, I am quite sure that by 'place' he meant the whole rambling expanse of the domain, whether in sight or not: those autumnal woodlands, the dark barrier of conifers to the north, the long stretch of sheep-grazing before them, which any old cavalryman's eye would have picked out for a battlefield, the miles of rough moorland beyond them which rolled on until they reached the sea. The idea of this space,

[1] R. Churchill, op. cit.

and the ownership of it, was as much a part of his mind as the twice-times table.

The important thing to note is that none of the throw-away lines – as they seem at the time – are affectations. Only the aspiring classes are 'affected', by definition. The gentleman is essentially 'natural'; but exactly how far he can be natural has inevitably shown some variation over the years. It must have been difficult, for example, in some of the grander and more compli-cated households, even in the present century. If one of the dukes, let us say, insists on using a pair of limousines and eight men to move one guest's weekend luggage (as they did at Woburn) then he is quite obviously not within the Castiglione ideal of doing everything 'without design and as it were absent-mindedly . . .' (Or, on surprising second thoughts, perhaps he *is*.)

The utterly relaxed view of (or total ignoring of) the environ-ment can refer to both big and small things. It can mean that a whole great estate is contained, without any pretension, in a quiet verbal aside. It can apparently mean an acceptance of domestic surroundings so total, and of such an unconscious degree, that a great house has become merely a notional space in the lord's mind; and an afternoon with his own guide-book is necessary to restore it to proper mental detail. This naturalness may also simply mean lack of effort on some quite minor point. For example, I was visiting one of the richest of the landed dukes at his country house – a relatively small but comfortable one – in one of the northern counties. He set about the task of pouring a drink. He rummaged in the cupboard, looking for the soda; and eventually produced, not a siphon, certainly not a siphon in silver-filigree container (which would be normal for a well-off household) but a screw-top bottle of ancient appearance with a torn label. This is one of the things that the true middle-class household could not have tolerated within its orbit for a moment, with its accusing hint of cheapness and insecurity. The duke, of course, was not a bit bothered or apologetic about it. One reason why he was not bothered about it was that there was a Velasquez hanging in the hall outside.

This casualness about possessions which marks the wealthy-gentleman class often makes it difficult for the outsider to place its members in a scale of affluence. The wage and salary-earning classes normally spend to the top of their capacity, the underlying maxim being, 'You can't take it with you . . .' The notion of continuity and inheritance, the lack of any need to impress (at least openly), as well as their current belief in 'inconspicuous consumption' makes it a matter of some indifference to the wealthy gentleman whether the car he is driving is a year out of date. In fact, the sense of thrift will induce a greater sense of comfort and quiet superiority in him.

Bragging about possessions – that is, pointing out what *ought* to be assumed and allowing a temporary crack-up in the habit of restraint – is permissible within the class so long as it is done discreetly enough. It is, for instance, entertaining to hear two landed lords ostensibly discussing the cost of maintaining certain estate buildings when what one is trying to get across to the other – and finally comes out with it ('We've damn well got *six* to look after!') – is that he has twice as many lodge entrances to his Park as the other. The throw-away grand manner can also, used with proper timing, make a point. There is a story of a former Duke and Duchess of Devonshire paying a visit to a former Duke and Duchess of Portland. To impress, the Portlands had laid the family collection of gold plate at dinner, and the visitors commented on it in a suitably flattering manner. When the visit was returned some time later the Duchess of Devonshire, not to be outdone, had the staff lay out every last piece of her own magnificent collection, down to the ultimate gold gravy boat and salt cellar. Taking her place at dinner, the Duchess of Portland sweetly remarked, '*What* a pretty set dear. You really must let us see the rest of it some time.'

The very casualness of the gentleman-elite, its emphasis on so-called natural behaviour, might deceive the total stranger into thinking that it has no rules, no cohesion, no defensive barriers, and that it is completely open to all comers. This would be a grave error. Like all other social groups – working-class social clubs, gangs of Mods and Rockers, middle-class golf clubs – the upper class is alertly sensitive to any attempt at intrusion by the outsider who does not 'belong'. In the nineteenth century it was reckoned to take between two and three generations, and the right education and background-development, before a family of outsiders was accepted. Now the period of probation is much shorter. The Eton-educated son of the self-made businessman would find most doors open. But for the first-generation social climber the going will be harder. Rejection may well be discreet enough. There he is, holding the rapt attention of some fashionable dinner-table company with an account of his war experiences in Thessalonia . . . only to find that they have silently hoisted up the drawbridge, leaving him on the far bank.

He may find it quite impossible to see where he has gone wrong. He has taken care not to be too sharply-dressed; he has avoided talking about the price of things, except in the most languidly off-hand way; he was able to refer to his old commanding-officer, General Sir Manningham-Anstruthers, as 'Bobo', without any affectation; he expressed High Tory principles at several points, when the table had fallen silent; he used words like 'table napkin' and 'chimney-piece' with consummate ease; he pointedly avoided staring at the new Titian across the room. So why such drab and heart-breaking failure?

Possibly the first mistake was to presume the existence of a book of rules, simply because everyone else seemed in some vague way to be conforming to a code of behaviour. But there are no rules, only a few main strategic principles on which the defensive outerworks are established. They have changed remarkably little. Each century has merely added its own small flourishes to the main outline. The system's most resilient point is its deceptive ambiguity – the fact that it is based on the unspoken assumptions which create an aristocracy; and these can hardly be learned in a short course at a school of deportment.

Another strength is the instinctive ability to change the signals system – slightly but decisively – as soon as it has been learnt too well by too many aspirants. The old cipher-books are ditched, and new ones devised, just as the enemy has acquired enough confidence to make a mass bid for the plateau. 'The third generation of an aristocracy, observing that the manners . . . and

even the shibboleths of their grandfathers have been acquired by
the bourgeoisie, invent new formulas, which when their own
grandchildren come of age, will in their turn have been absorbed
by the community.'[1]

Sometimes the technique is a simple inversion. As soon as the
middle classes adopt more of the social formalities and begin to
dress expensively the gentleman-class becomes more pointedly
nonchalant about observances and clothes. It becomes familiar to
hear a lord (or a by no means dowdy peeress even) say that they
have a suit or costume in the wardrobe which is fifteen years old
or more. There is a certain pride among some in being slightly
out of step with fashion, since the mode is often set by another
class of people. Mr Harold Macmillan, recently pictured in the
papers wearing patched trousers, clearly won a *prix d'élégance*
according to this scale of values. When the other classes are
spending freely and showing off their possessions, it is the aristocracy which affects poverty and extols the trouser-patched virtues
of thrift.

Then again, any tribal observance can be broken with impunity
– so long as it is done with a proper sense of easy style, and by the
right person. For instance, the visiting Martian notes that there is
a gentlemanly ritual attached to the drink called port, which is
always passed around in a clockwise direction. After studying
this observance for a month or so he suddenly finds the host
shoving the decanter straight across the table to someone whose
glass happens to be empty. The Martian joins the group, tries the
same variation, and is immediately ostracised for being too
socially ambitious.

Miss Nancy Mitford notes in *Noblesse Oblige* that one of the
prime characteristics of the aristocracy is that they are all 'impervious to a sense of shame – shame is a bourgeois notion'.
While this is generally true, I think it needs amplifying. 'Aristocrats are impervious . . .' might take it as far as accuracy allows
since what is shameful varies according to class. The aristocrat,
the utterly natural man, has always been proud of his freedom
from bourgeois guilt – a unilateral declaration of independence

[1] H. Nicolson, op. cit.

from it, without any help from Freud. As testimony to this there is an old-standing custom in stately homes that butlers don't knock before entering. The implication is that the lord will either not be doing anything shameful; or, if he is in fact in a compromising position with the second parlour-maid, he will be able to carry off the situation with the style becoming a gentleman. The aristocracy is possibly rather less impervious as a group than as individuals. This was much the case up to Edwardian times. Then – unlike the eighteenth century, when sexual escapades were carried off with some bravado – the aristocracy began to feel highly embarrassed about the figure they were cutting as a group, under the adventurous leadership of Edward VII and other mistress-chasing public figures. They were not worried about the opinion of other gentlemen: they knew they could take it. They were only concerned to keep the news away from the lower orders. Nowadays there is only a very slight 'group morality' in that sense. Some of the older peers feel that the side has been let down if some lord figures too prominently in a court case, but that is about as far as it goes.

U-Dialect and Folk-lore

Another thing that links the class together, and which acts to some degree as a first line of barbed-wire entanglement, is language. Before the development of the public-school system in the nineteenth century produced a standard upper-class accent many of the Tory squires spoke with the earthy accents of their county. The late Lord Derby never spoke anything but sound, hot-pot Lancashire. The growth of 'posh' speech seems to have roughly kept pace with the increasing competition and pretensions of the new commercial rich.

But some forms of special verbalising were common before this. One nineteenth-century writer recalled meeting an old lady reared in Queen Charlotte's court who used to say goold for gold; yaller for yellow; laylock for lilac; balconey for balcony; 'ooman for woman; cowcumber for cucumber; 'potticary' for doctor; and used the phrase 'much obleeged'. He says these variants were fairly common among admirers of the archaic in the early part of the century, and an 'aristocratic drawl' was often affected.

Accents have now become so standardised at the top that there is little difference between the accents of the English, Scots, Welsh, and Irish peers and gentry; and the gap between this style and professional-class speech is a narrow one. Still, a short search of clubland by a Professor Higgins would still produce a varied enough pattern – Punjab-military, cavalry-mess languid, House of Lords drawl – to remind us of greater days. A distinctive accent and vocabulary persists more among the younger set of both sexes, guardees, debs, and suchlike; among the aspiring set and those who are fearful of slipping back into it; and among the womenfolk of the aristocracy generally. A number of the latter still prefer the side-saddle manner, in which 'gels' is preferred to 'girls'; ' 'ospital' (or ' 'orspital') and 'otel are common for hospital and hotel; and so are 'cun-stable' and 'Cum-pton' for constable and Compton. The dropping of the final 'g' in huntin' and suchlike has become dated, even among aspirants.

The subtlety of upper-class English is that it is absolutely un-learnable by the enemy, even if they are lucky enough to seize such cipher-books as Miss Mitford's. It is both casual and pedantic; follows the mother-tongue in several perfectly obvious ways; then drifts away into an area where one gentleman communicates with another by empathy and strength of common assumptions. In this unlearnability, it contrasts with some other elite languages which, like Mandarin Chinese or Court Malay, have elaborate prefixes and suffixes or glottal variations to distinguish them from the speech of ordinary people, and which can be written down and learnt.

As Professor Alan Ross points out in *Noblesse Oblige*, aristo-cratic speech likes economy of effort, and he instances the stressed first syllable in 'temporarily' ('temp'rly'), 'interesting', and 'for-midable'. One might add that a certain panache is added to one's claims to be a U-speaker if a mumbling tone is adopted (indicates relaxed manner again) with only the first syllable of almost any word enunciated. The total effect should ideally sound like water

gently simmering in a saucepan with, at intervals, a bubble of
meaning breaking surface. The whole point of the style is that the
U-listener is able to fill in the gaps between bubbles to form a
complete message.

A number of pedantries peculiar to the class are slipped in from
time to time, like boulders in a stream. These words are usually the
original, long-winded version of an abbreviation in common use.
Their significance is partly, I imagine, to demonstrate that the
speaker has all the time in the world to spell things out. Perversely,
though – and it should be apparent that the whole subject is full of
perversities – the speaker will insist on clipping every other word
in his message down to the barest shorthand. The result is that the
speech-rate of the U-speaker, despite all the indications of leisure,
in the end covers the ground faster, I would estimate, than that of
any social group.[1] If it were a case of speaking a message, then
rushing for a cab, the U-speaker would always get there first.

Some of the pedantries mentioned in *Noblesse Oblige* are in
fairly common use among the class: like 'luncheon' (the meal the
gentleman does *not* have soup with, according to a former Lord
Curzon) and 'telephone' (not 'phone' or, worse, 'ring up'). This
shows a valiant attempt to avoid vulgarisms now so old that they
have long ago crept into the dictionaries.

Another group of words seems to represent the aggressive
Englishness of the upper-class against foreign importations. The
anglicising of the pronunciation of Beauchamp and Belvoir into
'Beecham' and 'Beaver' has the same no-nonsense look about it as
Churchill's preference for 'Narrzi' Germany over 'Natzi'. But
there is no logic or consequence to it. Miss Mitford sees 'mirror' as
non-U, preferring 'looking glass'. But the non-U version was
evidently good enough for the (no doubt non-U) writer of *Snow
White* ('*Mirror, mirror, on the wall etc.*'); and for Chaucer ('*Thus gan
he make a myrrour of his mynde . . .*'). To be logical, the elite should
find robust Anglo-Saxon equivalents for such Norman-French
vulgarisms as beef, mutton, and *le porc*. They like to give a word
time to mature.

[1] An average platform speaker talks at about 140 words a minute. Club-gentlemen in
conversation will touch speeds ranging between 160–300 words a minute. I do not count
the moments of silence, when information is also passing between them.

Another small group might be called illusion-words. *Noblesse Oblige* insists on 'chimney-piece' rather than 'mantelpiece', presumably because the latter is the shelf, bearing two symmetrically-placed vases, supposedly only found in middle-class homes. But a chimney-piece is essentially stately-home equipment, often of heavy stone or marble construction, below which it is possible to incinerate a young oak. So those many unfortunate lords who now live in flats and have to warm themselves by the electric logs are risking the grandiose if they do not call the thing a mantelpiece.

In conversation, it is generally preferred to keep the talk in an area where the unspoken assumptions will take a good share of the communicating. As Professor Brogan, among other intellectual diners-out, has noted[1] it is considered bad form to ask for specific information on any subject – or, one might add, to reveal oneself to be too much of an expert on anything.

The partiality for inversion is seen again in the U-habit of turning the expected upside-down so that the trivial is charged with passion and grave events are treated lightly. A heavy battle is 'a bit of a show' or 'quite a party'; while genuine war-terms or reactions are reserved for minor social upsets (cf. Miss Mitford's 'horror' at being introduced socially by Christian name and surname only).

A sense of relaxation in speaking is one of the objectives and, despite the high rate of verbalising mentioned above, is outwardly achieved. Miss Mitford again goes further on this and makes the interesting point that, 'Any sign of undue haste is apt to be non-U; and I go so far as preferring, except for business letters, not to use air-mail.' The only snag I see in this is that the Post Office, theoretically geared to the age of speed, moves ninety per cent of the mail to and from the Continent by air, whether people like it or not. The aspirant to the leisured class will just have to try harder to retard his letters.

With language, the really odd thing about it is the U-belief that the class is speaking only one identifiable private language, instead of several contradictory ones. At one moment the elite sees itself as tough, direct, candid, unsentimental, ready to avoid such

[1] D. W. Brogan, *The English People*, London, 1943.

timorous middle-class euphemisms as 'home' for house, 'mental' for mad, 'dentures' and 'toilet'. Next they emerge as guardians of linguistic purity (luncheon, telephone). Next all the meanings are going wild in ways that are *ghastly, frightful, horrid, monstrous, beastly, livid,* all referring to very quiet happenings. Next it is shooting off into a fantasy in which we live in a world of chimney-pieces. It avoids minor euphemism; but all the time forgets that aristocracy itself is a grand-scale euphemism built around money, a metaphor of continuity which strives to give the illusion of permanence.

EPILOGUE

During the war the Germans kept a special group of prisoners under secure guard in a castle at Colditz, in central Germany. There was nothing specially dangerous about them. All that they had in common was that they were British officers who happened to have close connections with the aristocracy. They included the Earl of Harewood, Earl Haig, the Earl of Hopetoun, the Master of Elphinstone (the Queen Mother's nephew) and others. Hitler's purpose was to hold them as hostages – regarding them as personages of supposedly special importance to Britain – in case any high-level bargains had to be made. The aristocrats were the first to perceive the ironic wrong-headedness of the German conception of their importance. Similarly, when Rudolf Hess made his abortive solo peace flight to Britain, the first person he sought out as a presumed man of influence was a remote Scottish nobleman.

They are good examples of the way in which the nature of the British aristocracy induces puzzlement. If it is hard enough for the natives to comprehend it entirely, it is apparently fiendishly difficult for outsiders to get it right. It is unthinkable that the lives of the Colditz aristocrats would have weighed more in the minds of the British government than they would if they had been a group of private soldiers. Where did the German estimate go wrong? During the nineteen-thirties the Germans received a stream of reports from their diplomats and foreign correspondents describing the nature of English society. Several of the latter (Karl Silex, von Stutterheim, Abshagen, and others) wrote books containing a medley of interesting and quite true-to-life detail, though the emphasis was occasionally wrong. They noted the 'extraordinary leisure' at the disposal of the gentlemanly class; they noted the servility of servants, the great regard for wealth and rank, the anti-intellectual outlook of the upper class, the 'medieval' strength of titles and class distinctions, the fact (or so they observed) that ordinary people displayed more snobbery then the aristocrats themselves. Abshagen, a very influential correspondent, noted a degree of 'serfdom in rural areas' and was struck by the rigidity of the 'feudal class divisions'. He, like his colleagues, noting the gulf between the aristocracy and the lower classes seems to have concluded that the former must be people of consequent power and political influence.

By the date they were writing the power of the aristocracy was largely a social one which did not go very far into the inner sanctums of government, though the great house-parties at Cliveden and elsewhere may have given that impression. Most of the details they observed were true enough. The mistake they made – I think this is the important one – was in taking aristocracy to be entirely a flesh-and-blood animal instead of (to return to the metaphor with which I began) a creature more like a unicorn. Certainly, as I have tried to show, there are real lords with a real and important place as landowners, businessmen, professional workers, social leaders, politicians, and so on. But their role as aristocrats is a more fugitive thing that does not care to stand up to a showdown nor, probably, is it meant to. Aristocracy is an amalgam of a number of things which means different things to different people. It can mean a dislike for modernity, a respect for tradition, or the continuing regard for prestige, wealth, and rank, which give the illusion of having sprung magically out of the past. It gives an aura of naturalness and propriety to the class structure and reassures people about the need to preserve it.

A proper balance-sheet of the benefits and drawbacks of having an aristocracy would be a very complicated one. It undoubtedly helps to give Britain a fustian, backward-looking attitude to a number of things. Social change moves by inches. But one would not get republican attitudes simply by removing the monarchy tomorrow; nor would one necessarily get a more open, fairer, more self-confident society simply by dispensing with titles, though I would personally agree that it is a move that ought to be made. Aristocratic attitudes have done much to devalue the industrial side of life, to cast an absurdly arbitrary scale of esteem on the different ways in which people earn their living. It may have given stability; it has also, in its time, thrown its weight on the brake against worthwhile progress. It has exercised a great deal of self-interest under the guise of altruism. On the other hand, looking around one can see no other aristocracy which has done quite so well in useful administration and honest leadership of particular communities, and some of this still survives. The fact that Britain is still a snob-ridden country cannot more than partially be laid at the door of the aristocracy. In the good and the bad it has struck a pretty fair balance in its time. E. M. Forster once awarded Democracy two cheers. On that scale, I fancy that one-and-a-half rousing ones for aristocracy would be quite in order.

K

INDEX

Clubs, London, 240–5
  Beefsteak, 241
  Brooks', 243
  Bucks, 242–3
  Pratts, 241, 244–5
  Turf, 243
  Whites, 241, 242, 243
Clumber Park, Notts, 64
Cobbett, William, 178
Cobbold, Lord, 105
Cobham, Viscount, 152
Colditz, 273
Collections and Recollections, G. W. E.
  Russell's, 83
Colville, Viscount, 119
Complete Peerage, 133
Compton Place, 201
Compton Wynyates, 209
Conservative Party,
  battle for leadership (1963), 96
  battle for leadership (1965), 125, 127
  Central Office of, 126
  dilemma over merit v. class status of,
    126–8, 143
Conservative Party in History, The,
  Christopher Hollis's, 187
Cooper, Duff, 36
Cooper, Lady Diana, 36
County Set, the, 246–50
  business men and their wives in, 249
  hunting in, 247–8, 249
  polo in, 249
Courtenays, the, 166–7
Courtier, The, Castiglione's, 256
Cowdray, Viscount, 152
Cozens-Hardy, Lord, 138
Craster, Northumberland, 195
Craster of Craster (Sir John Craster),
  38, 152, 195–6
Crathorne, Baron, 152
Craufurd of Craufurdland (Mr J. P.
  Hewison-Craufurd), 38
Crawford and Balcarres, Earl of, 263
Crosby, John, 229
Crown and the Establishment, The,
  Kingsley Martin's, 6
Cullen House, 223
Curcun, Richard de, 29, 32

Curzon, George Nathaniel, Lord
  (Viceroy of India), 32
Curzon, Sir John, 31
Curzon, Sir Nathaniel, 32
Curzon, Sir Richard Nathaniel, Bt. See
  Scarsdale, Viscount
Curzons, the, 27–33

Daily Express, 237
Daily Mail, 234
Daily Mirror, 228
Dalhousie, Lord, 155
Darlington, Prof. C. D., 86, 87
Davis, Alexander, 162
Death duties, 156, 174
Debrett's Peerage, 19, 208
Debutantes, 228, 229, 230–31
Deene Park, Northants, 165
Defoe, Daniel, 130, 131
Demography of the British Peerage, T. H.
  Hollingsworth's, 86
Derby, 17th Earl of, 125, 186, 263, 268
  political influence of, 187
Derby, 18th Earl of, 152, 190
Devon, Earl of, 152
Devonshire, Dowager Duchess of, 106
Devonshire, Duke of, 152, 190
  estates of, 163, 164, 209, 251
Devonshire House, 201
Devonshire, the nineteenth-century
  Dukes of, 24
Devonshires, the, 265
Disraeli, Benjamin, 6, 16, 159–60
Dormers, the, 243
Douglas of Kirtleside, Lord, 80
Douglas-Home, Lady, 69
Douglas-Home, Sir Alec, 45, 71, 96,
  127, 155
Dukes, 16, 162
  as territorial magnates, 163–4
  contemporary, 73
  grandness of in nineteenth century,
    14–15
Dulverton, Lord, 138
Dunsford, Devon, 39
Dundee, Earl of, 121
Durham, Earl of, 152
Dymokes, the, 182